Praise for
Ambition Redefined

"Moms' family schedules don't always meld with a 9-to-5, in-office, 5-day-a-week job, which is why the advice here is critical, so mothers can keep caring for their children and gain financial stability."

—Meredith Bodgas, Editor-in-Chief of
Working Mother magazine

"As Sollmann wisely advises, when it comes to work it's not about leaning in or out but leaning in the direction of financial security. Combine this with myriad other suggestions for how you can redefine how you work and how much you earn and you'll find yourself on a path that leads to a fulfilling and stable future on your terms. It's a great read for women of all ages and career stages."

—Lois P. Frankel, Ph.D., author of *Nice Girls Don't Get the Corner Office, Nice Girls Don't Get Rich,* and *Nice Girls Just Don't Get It*

"Balance is bunk! But creating greater harmony among the different domains of life is possible. Sollmann's *Ambition Redefined*, which offers a clear path to realizing how you can make flexwork a real and enriching part of your life, is an essential guide for getting there."

—Stew Friedman, founder of the Wharton Work/Life Integration Project and author of *Total Leadership*

"Women, especially those acting as caregivers, don't need to view their careers in terms of two stark choices: either opt out entirely or aim for the C-suite. Opportunities are growing every year for women to engage in the workforce in a flexible way. Flexible and remote work options help women stay professionally active and financially on-track before, during, and after those caregiving years. In my experience in the flexible job market over more than a decade, I've seen first-hand exactly what Kathryn Sollmann is recommending. Professional, high-quality flexible jobs do exist for every age and stage, and this book shares fantastic information and advice for women to find them."

—Sara Sutton Fell, CEO, FlexJobs

"Kathryn Sollmann doesn't pull punches in her provocative new book. *Ambition Redefined* is a must-read for women of all ages, as they navigate their careers and make crucial choices about what kind of work fits their life stage. Earning a paycheck is your power. Never give that up. This smart guide is a wake-up call that underscores the fact that being in control of your financial life is non-negotiable."

—Kerry Hannon, *New York Times* columnist, career and personal finance expert and author of *Money Confidence: Really Smart Financial Moves for Newly Single Women* and *Great Jobs for Everyone 50+*

"Finally! A smart book for women who want to balance meaningful work and caretaking obligations—without sacrificing their long-term financial security. Chock full of practical advice, tested strategies and vetted resources, *Ambition Redefined* is a must-read that will guide your work-life choices at pivotal moments throughout your career."

—Nancy Collamer, Founder of MyLifestyleCareer.com and author of *Second-Act Careers*

"The literary love child between Betty Friedan's *The Feminine Mystique* & Leslie Bennett's (spot on and surprisingly controversial) *The Feminine Mistake*. In *Ambition Redefined* Kathryn Sollmann says the unsayable: it's not mere power that we need to help women achieve at work, it's the power to engage in consistent workplace participation. So forget trying to figure out whether to "lean in" or "lean out." Instead read *Ambition Redefined* and learn how to sway, how to flex your career, so you can blend money and meaning together in the proportions that create the life you really want to live."

—Manisha Thakor, CFA, CFP(R), Founder of MoneyZen.com and author of *On My Own Two Feet: A Modern Girl's Guide to Personal Finance*

"Kathryn has a way of sharing the facts about the deep financial need for women to keep a foot in the workplace, but also giving "been there, done that" advice on how to make it work when managing a family. *Ambition Redefined* is the playbook for how to get flexibility in your career. I can't think of a mom who wouldn't benefit from having this smart book on her bookshelf."

—Molly Beck, author of *Reach Out* and founder of MessyBun.com

"In *Ambition Redefined*, Kathryn shares her extensive knowledge and incredible hands-on experience as a woman entrepreneur and flex activist! Her goal is to boost women's confidence to choose paths that combine work and other life activities in positive ways. If you want to understand, explore, and pursue new models of working, this book is a must for you!"

—Sophie Wade, Workforce Innovation Specialist, Flexcel Network, Speaker, and author, *Embracing Progress*

"The most valuable career advice for women is not to lean in, but to stay in. In *Ambition Redefined* Sollmann explains how women who stay in the workforce, even in part-time positions with lower pay, make big contributions to the long-term financial security of their families. She discusses different ways women can find flexwork to pursue their own versions of success, pursuing fulfilling work that better fits their lives. This is an important topic and I applaud Sollmann for having the courage to advocate for a new type of feminism."

—Beth Cabrera, PhD, author of *Beyond Happy: Women, Work, and Well-Being*

"*Ambition Redefined* is a great resource—a comprehensive book that provides essential, must know information for women of all ages who want straightforward answers about different flexwork options, the repercussions of gap years, financial issues surrounding elder and childcare roles, and how to plan long-term for future financial challenges. Sollmann's approach helps women ask the right questions and find their own unique answers and solutions."

—M. Cindy Hounsell, President, Women's Institute for a Secure Retirement (WISER)

"In *Ambition Redefined*, Kathryn Sollmann makes a compelling case for women to remain in the workforce despite their variable seasons of caregiving. It's a reminder that the first purpose of employment is to provide a livelihood and secure our financial future and that it's difficult to change the world when our personal corner of it is fraught with financial uncertainty. Sollmann advocates that we 'lean in' to what she aptly labels one's own personal measure of success, rather than a monolithic vision of the ideal career, an effort which assuredly does not require that every woman aspires to the C suite, or even to uninterrupted full-time employment."

—Whitney Johnson, *Thinkers50* Management Thinkers and critically-acclaimed author, *Build an A Team* and *Disrupt Yourself*

"Life is more complex than the usual arguments about women and work make it out to be. *Ambition Redefined* challenges assumptions: both that it's impossible to do challenging work while raising a family and that if you're not gunning for the C-suite, you're letting down the sisterhood. Sollmann is reassuring that work need not be all or nothing, but she's also advancing this radical notion that will change women's lives: earning money is part of caring for a family. We serve our families by fitting some sort of paid work into our lives, every step of the way."

—Laura Vanderkam, author of *I Know How She Does It* and
Off the Clock: Feel Less Busy While Getting More Done

Ambition Redefined

Why the Corner Office Doesn't Work for Every
Woman & What to Do Instead

KATHRYN SOLLMANN

nb

NICHOLAS BREALEY
PUBLISHING

BOSTON • LONDON

First published in 2018 by Nicholas Brealey Publishing
An imprint of John Murray Press

An Hachette UK company

23 22 21 20 19 18   1 2 3 4 5 6 7 8 9 10

A CIP catalogue record for this title is available from the British Library

Library of Congress Control Number: 2018938209

ISBN 978-1-47367-909-2
US eBook ISBN 978-1-47367-911-5
UK eBook ISBN 978-1-47367-910-8

Printed and bound in the United States of America.

John Murray Press policy is to use papers that are natural, renewable and recyclable products and made from wood grown in sustainable forests. The logging and manufacturing processes are expected to conform to the environmental regulations of the country of origin.

John Murray Press Ltd
Carmelite House
50 Victoria Embankment
London EC4Y 0DZ
Tel: 020 3122 6000

Nicholas Brealey Publishing
Hachette Book Group
Market Place Center, 53 State Street
Boston, MA 02109, USA
Tel: (617) 263 1834

www.nbuspublishing.com

CONTENTS

APPENDIX

AUTHOR'S NOTE

This book encourages women to consider if they personally have rock-solid, long-term financial security—and to make decisions about life and work in the best interest of their families now and many years down the road. Throughout the text, you will see comments gathered from the "Motherhood and Career Ambition Survey" taken by a sampling of my *9 Lives for Women* blog readers—insights from nearly 600 college-educated women nationwide (60 percent with advanced degrees) in their mid-30s to mid-60s who shared their views on the financial and family impact of work and life decisions.

Beyond my own survey, I provide top-line information relative to the many sudden—and often unexpected—situations that can put lifetime financial security at risk. Although data about complex topics like Social Security, Medicare, retirement savings, and eldercare costs varies widely among experts, and each topic could be a book of its own, here you will find just enough information from respected sources to get you thinking and motivated to continue researching and asking the right questions.

As with all decisions in life, there are no "one size fits all" answers. You need to consider your own financial picture and personal circumstances and seek the counsel of professional advisers. Consider *Ambition Redefined* a valuable starting point for frank discussions with your family—and yourself—about how to find work that accommodates caregiving roles and generates a secure, fulfilling, and productive life.

INTRODUCTION

Up Is Not the Only Way to Move Women Forward!

Did Hillary Rodham Clinton's near win of the presidency inspire scores of women to turbocharge their professional roles? Are most women energized by Sheryl Sandberg's call to "lean in"? Is the typical woman caring for children and aging parents looking to achieve the highest positions on the career ladder? Is the answer to blending life and work really just a matter of letting go of household perfection and getting partners to pitch in with the kids?

In answer to all these questions, I make what many will perceive as a counter-feminist statement: under any circumstances, relatively few smart, capable women have the desire or family bandwidth to break the glass ceiling. It's time to acknowledge that most women want and need less life-consuming *flexible* work to accommodate the roles of caring for children and aging parents—and that women who choose to pursue professional fulfillment and financial security in less lofty, highly-visible ways are not weak, lacking in ambition, or letting down the sisterhood.

For nearly two decades I've coached thousands of impressive, accomplished women who feel the push-pull of family and work. They represent two demographics: young women in more-than-full-time jobs who are wrestling with the idea of a family hiatus, and middle-aged women who left the workforce and are either waffling about or desperate for a return. Both cohorts of women are educated—often at the schools that confer the most prestigious BAs, MBAs, and JDs. Their tax brackets are middle to upper class. They begin careers with great gusto—determined to capitalize on educations and progress in responsibility and earnings. They want to make their mark and make a difference…until wedding bells ring and their first or second child is on the way. Then the professional determination loses steam as two heavyweight forces compete for their hearts and minds: a growing family and a job that often seems to need the same constant care.

Younger women who feel they can get by without working rely on the financial support their partners provide *today* and leave the workforce. They rarely think in a long-term way about how this departure will affect their retirement savings or their ability to weather unpredictable financial challenges. In many cases, the loss of the woman's paycheck also makes current household finances tenuous and very tight. Regardless, women often weigh financial issues against what they feel is "the right thing to do," and then they choose to invest *all* of their time in being home with the children rather than finding more flexible ways to contribute money to the till.

If caregiving is not the issue that drives women out of the workforce, then childcare math is next. Women often conclude it's not worth it to work—and sacrifice time with their children—for the money they will be left with after paying for childcare, as well as commuting and (if it's an option) more help for household chores. Many women—and often very traditional partners—say that only a high salary warrants leaving the house. That's when I know they are basing their decisions on truly shortsighted thinking, because even small after-tax savings make a big difference if you consider the power of compounding over time.

Women step out of the workforce with the justification they can always return. Some think they'll leave for only a few years and pick up professional work where they left off. Others think they can safely put any idea of working on a high shelf until their kids are off to college. In either case, time slips away, volunteer work replaces professional work, and many years later women suddenly realize that because of one or more of life's financial challenges, such as mounting household expenses, multiple college tuitions, or scant retirement savings, they can no longer afford *not* to work. After so much time out of the workforce, though, the return can be quite difficult. Women who used to be at the mid to senior level often have to put egos aside and ramp back up to their former professional selves. Even those who are not concerned with title or prestige frequently generate—at least initially—paychecks that are not too far beyond the entry-level wage.

Then comes the irony: just when many women feel that their children have reached an age that eases their motherhood role, one or more aging parents suddenly need their direct or oversight care. Women often forget that they have *not one but two caregiving roles* and that there is no perfect time to work.

Without question, resumé gaps represent expensive time away. A hiatus is often an emotional decision—fueled by motherhood guilt or an aging parent's illness—rather than by a pragmatic analysis of the funds needed to lock in financial security for life. The reality is that *a woman forfeits up to four times her salary each year she is out of the workforce.*[1] In what I've seen as the average 12-year hiatus just to care for children, there are 144 monthly paychecks that are not invested and saved.

That's why I advise women to never leave the workforce—and if they've left, to get back in.

Women interrupt their earnings and put themselves into precarious financial situations because they still define "work" in one narrow, traditional way. Too many women throw in the towel and completely exit the workforce without fully exploring alternatives to the more-than-full-time corporate grind. The exodus is not surprising: flexwork opportunities often seem under the radar, and media coverage of progressive employers is few and far between. It's difficult to know where there is a true culture of flexibility; we often hear more about big household-name companies requiring crazy hours in the office and forcing women out in droves.

Women leave because their SOS signals largely go unanswered, and they have limited resources to find ways to blend work and life. Corporations spend more than $30 billion on leadership training overall,[2] but, in my experience, they spend only a small percentage of that money on helping women deal with real-life family issues that impact productive

and sustainable work. Only half of employers even have training specifically directed to women.[4] Funding for internal corporate women's
networking groups (often a forum for work and life discussions) is not
a priority budget item. The internet lists endless career resources pre-
dominately for traditional full-time work. Countless books, articles, and
women's professional associations extol the virtues of the high-flying
career. Relatively few women can afford to hire a career coach to guide
them away from inflexible corporate jobs.

Though the most logical first step is to try to get flexibility in a current job, standing up to the corporate hierarchy is no easy task. Women
who believe they are showing weakness by asking for a softer schedule
tend to lob only tentative requests—say, to work from home on Fridays—
rather than make a comprehensive, professional pitch for the flexibility
they really need.

To be fair, among many larger companies, flexibility remains an
employee benefit in an awkward-adolescent stage, and only 37 percent
of employee handbooks contain a formal, written flexibility policy. Most
employers struggle to institutionalize work structures that have little uni-
formity. Confusion reigns when 67 percent of managers offer flexibility
at their own discretion[4]—creating inequities among departments and
teams, inconsistencies in what is deemed possible or prudent, and insecurity when reporting structures change. Flexibility is also inconsistent
across industries. It is widely granted at technology companies, for example, but it is still hard to penetrate in investment banking and financial
services as a whole. Some job functions bend easily to fewer hours and
work at home, while others require more face time than many women are
willing to give. There's still a lot of uncharted territory, and most women
are forced to advocate for and find flexible jobs on their own.

Women are aware that the majority of corporations have yet to institutionalize flexwork across a large workforce, but many don't realize
that less traditional work structures are much more common at small
to midsize companies in every industry. Changes in required healthcare coverage (benefits that are likely to be in flux for many years) have
forced smaller employers to rethink their hiring strategies, leading to

fewer full-time hires, a contingent workforce that ebbs and flows, and part-time employees who focus more productively on very specific niche roles. With smart and strategic networking, it is indeed possible for women who prefer not to be chained to an employer's office desk to find a wide range of quality employers who are open to part-time hours, flextime, telecommuting, job shares, compressed workweeks, and other workforce solutions.

Though working women are often portrayed as stretched-to-the-limit overachievers running breathless through bipolar work-versus-family lives, the fact is that many *do* find *work that fits—and enhances— their lives. Blending work and family is a smart choice* because no woman can logically bank on the fact that a partner's job and earning power have lifetime guarantees. Women live longer than men, invest for fewer years in employer-sponsored savings plans, and typically have smaller benefits from Social Security. For these reasons, caregiving should be put in practical perspective: It's not just about loving, nurturing, and tending to daily needs. It's also about working toward long-term financial security—for ourselves and our families. Women who, for example, devote every minute of their lives to young children now may in fact burden those same children by running out of money later in life.

As I say in my *9 Lives for Women* blog tagline, just as few families view life or homeowner's insurance as foolish investments, it is equally wise for women to always "find the work that fits your life." The ability to generate an income is as important as insuring your life against illness or your home against fire. Flexwork makes it possible for women to earn money whether they have one child or 10.

Ambition Redefined puts to rest persistent, highly charged "can women have it all?" debates, and it underscores the real issue: the link between work and long-term financial security. Under normal circumstances, work should not be perceived as a selfish pursuit of money, status, or power that does not *benefit* family. When women view work as a means to a very necessary end, the debate, the moral judgments, the angst, the guilt—and the choice—disappear. You work if you don't have all your long-term financial bases covered—and the fact is that few women do. Most women have to find a way to "do it all," and the easiest way to do so is to carve out some kind of flexwork that fits the caregiving in their lives.

If women run the numbers and face the facts head on, few can dismiss the wisdom of flexible, lifelong work. Indeed, most have experienced life challenges themselves and see other friends and family members who have struggled as well. There's no promise that a breadwinning partner who gets laid off will find comparable work. It's not possible to predict if illness will strike your family, causing unreimbursed medical bills or triggering a breadwinner's long-term disability. Many marriages end (often the couples you'd least expect), and divorced women can be at a great economic disadvantage. One or more elderly parents can outlive their savings and need the financial support of their adult children. Even just one of these calamities combined with the typical expenses of maintaining a home, buying cars, sending children to camp, paying for tutors, financing college, and more can push saving for your own retirement to the last priority on your monthly budget list.

If nothing else, retirement should be the reason women always stay in the workforce. By any measure, few Americans—even those in affluent communities—have enough money saved to fund a retirement that could last 30 years or more. In most households, this means that more than one income is needed to reach even modest retirement savings goals—and insure against life's less favorable twists and turns. We've all been advised to "save for a rainy day," but in this book, that's the cart before the horse. It's hard to save money until earnings exceed expenses. Many women need to contribute some money to the household income to generate the surplus that can be invested and saved.

Through my entrepreneurial ventures focused on women and work, I've coached too many women in wholly unexpected financial distress who wish they never took any absences from work. A large part of the problem is the disconnect between seemingly universal expectations about the kind of positions ambitious professional women *should* want to achieve, and the reality that most women who have one or two big caregiving roles don't have the singular focus or energy to claw their way to the top.

Contrary to the fixation on breaking the glass ceiling, the most burning issue is not how high women should rise in the corporate ranks. The more critical and widespread workplace issue for women is participation, not power. The female labor force participation rate in the US has been stagnating since 2000 (peaking in 1999 at 60 percent and since declining to 57 percent). This decline is likely attributed to the difficulty in balancing work and family. When women stay in the workforce there is not only a personal benefit, there is a widespread workforce benefit, too: every 10% increase in women's share of total employment is associated with real wage increases of nearly 8 percent for all other women—and men.[5]

Flexibility makes it possible for more women to participate *consistently* in the workforce—alongside two major caregiving roles—and *fulfill their own measures* of ambition and success. Huge compensation from top corporate roles is not the only path to financial security: when women become better educated about saving and investing steadily at all ages—and they stay in the workforce in some way at all times—they will build more-than-adequate nest eggs, too.

Let's focus then on the masses of smart, talented women who want and need jobs that provide greater flexibility—not just the much smaller percentage of women who are actually vying for the corner office. When we redefine ambition, we acknowledge that challenging, lucrative, interesting work can be found in many flexible ways—and in ways that favor personal satisfaction over public applause. We send the message that all professional work is *worthwhile* work, we put caregiving on par with resumé building, and we pave the way for more sustainable earnings at every age and life stage.

Work flexibility is in fact leading to a new feminism: a different work equality for women that encourages many respected paths to professional stature. Women who want to populate the highest echelons of business and government should absolutely have a path to do so, but that is not a path that all women should feel pressured to follow. *Ambitious* women now have many professional options and many ways to develop their own brand of success. The best career advice is not "get to the top;"

it is "stay at it." Always find work that fits *your* life. Plan for life's surprises. Make sure you earn, save, and invest toward a long and comfortable retirement. Explore the ever-widening world of flexwork—and you'll find many interesting and exciting ways to tuck all generations of your family into a future that is financially secure and safe.

—Kathryn Sollmann
Wilton, Connecticut

PART 1

Why You Should Always Work (in a Flexible Way)

Chapter 1

Pursue Your Own Definition of Professional Ambition (There's No Law to Lean In)

M ANY WELL-EDUCATED MEN GRADUATE FROM college, start an entry-level job, work steadily with professional tunnel vision to advance their careers (even after marrying and becoming fathers), and rise progressively in title and compensation.

Conversely, many well-educated women graduate from college, start an entry-level job, reach middle management, marry, have children, and work for less than 10 years. Feeling the pull of family, many leave the workforce for what they intend to be "a couple of years" to focus on their children, but they end up staying out for an average of 12 years. They begin to think about returning to work just as their aging parents start to need help. Consequently, women often have big earnings gaps, save less over their lifetimes, and have careers that stop, start, and sputter because it's hard to set their lives in the traditional corporate mold.

66 *When I left the workforce, my expectation was to be out four to six years. In truth, it was eight."*
—Woman in her 40s, North Carolina, master's degree

Since 2002, I've coached women as they move in and out of the

3

workforce, wrestling with decisions about what they *should* do to be a "true feminist" (that is, pushing the professional envelope for greater women's equality at the highest professional levels) versus what they *want* to do in their hearts. I've helped women who initially chose to stay on the sidelines but then needed to find work after they were hit by one of life's big curveballs, and I've watched just about every mother I know return to some kind of paid work (even the "Marge in Charge" diehards who make motherhood an extreme sport). In all the years I've worked with women, I've never met one who said she hated working. I have met thousands who have told me, mistakenly, that based on their often long-ago experience, there is no possible way to make work fit life.

These are ill-informed and outdated views; the workplace women experienced in the 1980s, the 1990s, and even the early 2000s is simply not the same. In these earlier eras, more women than ever were joining the professional ranks, striving to raise the stature of women, buying into the idea (at least initially) that career success meant aiming for the executive suite, and working the same hard-driving hours as men. Now women at the start of their careers are asking for and expecting flexibility, and women of all ages are continually finding ways to be valued contributors without sacrificing their personal lives. Companies realize that less traditional work structures are powerful recruiting tools to attract—and keep—the best talent. It was once the case that employers *expected* women to leave the workforce, viewing their tenure as limited to the years before marriage and children. Today, though there are varying degrees of effort, resources, and creative thinking about work structures that blend work and life, it's safe to say that the vast majority of employers now view women as a *long-term asset*, and these employers are searching for solutions that make work fit life.

> ❝ *At first, I was working to get to the top of my field . . . but then when I got close to it, I realized it's not what I wanted. I had been striving for the top because it was what was expected of me.*"
> —Woman in her 40s, New York, bachelor's degree

    " *My ideal is a flexible full-time job in a mission-*
    centered place where I can still be available for
    the important things like taking my kids to school,
    being at their games/performances, etc."
                    —Woman in her 40s, Illinois, master's degree

Indeed, there has never been a better time for women to

- assert their personal ambitions;
- let themselves off the hook if they're not striving to break the glass ceiling;
- achieve financial security; and
- rethink how to capitalize on their educations and expertise.

Today, women can experience a full "9 Lives" career with continual renewal and reinvention at every age and life stage.

My 109 Professional Lives

When I created my blog, *9 Lives for Women,* one of my friends joked, "For you it should be 109, not 9." Though I may have had more jobs over my lifetime than many women have had, I think my story shows that with creative thinking it's possible to find all kinds of meaningful, resumé-worthy work that generates respect, money, and fulfillment. With a more expansive mindset about the kind of work that's possible— well beyond the traditional, more-than-full-time corporate job—there's great freedom and comfort in knowing you can always find ways to support yourself and your family.

I credit my attitudes toward work to Mary Tyler Moore, the first career woman to hit 1970s TV. As a preteen, I was an avid "Mary Richards" fan: I loved her job, apartment, clothes, ambition, and purposeful independence, and I was determined to grow up to be her twin. Mary seemed to lead a full and interesting life as a news producer (both as a single woman and later as a mother), and to my recollection she revealed no burning desire to be the TV station's top dog.

In my eyes Mary Richards had, as her theme song proclaimed, "made it after all." As I schemed my way toward replicating her life (landing, for example, the job as editor of my school's *Inky Press*), I role-played the office life with my half-hearted younger sister. My sister wanted to play dolls, not "office," but I often prevailed, sending "memos" that were filed between the staircase banister slats.

Professional pursuits were in my genes: my paternal grandmother finished just two years of high school, got married and had children before age 20, became a single mother at a time when divorce was rare— and was unstoppable in her drive to provide for her family. In the 1940s when most women were happy homemakers, she was a seamstress in a dressmaking factory. A formidable and outspoken woman, she was the factory's union representative, ensuring the right working conditions for the coworkers who cheered her on.

As time moved on, my grandmother's sights were even bigger. In the 1950s, she became her own boss by establishing a large factory of women who sewed for the very tony Anne Fogarty dress label. This entrepreneurial venture brought her to the New York City Garment District, where she was often the only woman haggling for the best prices on high-quality fabrics from around the world.

Key to my grandmother's story is the fact that she always found ways to blend work and life. When her children were young, she could not afford full-time babysitters, and daycare facilities were not yet in plentiful supply. Rather than letting the not-so-minor detail of two children who needed oversight get in her way, she brought my father and his sister along to all meetings, expecting they would catch the sparks from her entrepreneurial fire.

At a time when opportunities for women were scarce, my grandmother saw every professional obstacle as a problem that could be solved. Long before the term *reinvention* was in vogue, she consistently found new and flexible ways to earn an income. After selling her dressmaking factory, she needed another path to a weekly paycheck. Never afraid to dive in and learn, she spent the last years of her professional life in banking, changing to an industry she knew nothing about and working her way quickly to the head teller spot.

Like my grandmother, there was rarely a time I wasn't thinking up ways to make money, and I never thought I was unqualified to try something completely new. Before I was of age to be on an employer's payroll, I shunned the typical babysitting route and instead created business after business that kept my wallet full. There were the drawstring pouches (made with scraps of my grandmother's fabric) I sold at the Youth Adult Council store. The quilted ironing board covers I sewed for a quirky local retailer. In college, I launched "The Kitchen Libbers," a catering business, and corralled friends to tend bar, make hors d'oeuvres, pass trays, and catch a flurry of $20 bills, which alcohol-fueled hosts threw our way. Using my writing, editing, and typing skills I finagled a long string of personal assistant jobs, including one that involved a personal memoir of 90-year-old Elizabeth Knowlton—one of the first women to make a 20,000-foot ascent in the Himalayas. Over and over again I proved that with creativity and tenacity there was always a way to provide a service and make a buck—on my own schedule and on my own terms.

Entrepreneurial ventures later gave way to full-fledged and (as often as possible) flexible employment: temp jobs answering phones and typing for every kind of business under the sun, a summer job in the circulation department of a local newspaper, another at a small marketing agency writing copy for Pepsi. I pursued fellowships in my college career-planning, annual fund, and career services offices, and I gave miles and miles of tours for the admissions office. A free day to me was always a potential day to make money.

It Sounded Like Gloria Steinem Told *Me*: "*You* Can Have It All"

By the time I was a senior at Wheaton College in Massachusetts (an all-women's college at the time), I had a resumé filled with many resourceful years of pre-professional work. It was 1980, and women's empowerment was in full swing. Gloria Steinem spoke on campus, encouraging us to pursue careers with gusto and giving us the impression we could "have it all": both careers and family. (Now, decades later, Steinem says that women can't have it all unless there is great equality between men and women and more sharing of family and home responsibilities.) No one needed to convince me. From a young age I was bound and determined to pursue a robust career—always thinking a husband and family would be relatively easy add-ons down the road. I don't remember Steinem specifying that having a career meant only a top corporate job. As I sat in her audience scheming my post-college life, I assumed there was more than one path to fulfilling, respected, and successful work.

Though Steinem's words were a rallying cry toward a major commitment to professional work, I soon learned that being young, single, and childless allows women to view the business world through very different eyes than their married-with-children peers. As I was editing, writing, and presenting training programs in my first post-college job at Peat Marwick Mitchell (now KPMG), I was also noting that few women with families were among the ranks of employees burning the midnight oil. I saw a fair number of female partners, but they were all childless and wedded to their careers.

> **❝** *I had ambition and assumed I'd do well, but when I was unmarried and working full time, I didn't realize how all-consuming family responsibilities can be."*
> —Woman in her 40s, Minnesota, master's degree

The fact that women had difficulty blending work and life was still very evident when I joined Institutional Investor, a company filled with smart, high-achieving women. As I then created and led business conferences, I watched many go-getter women lose steam as they married and had children. They left the workforce because at the time there were no part-time jobs. Like at most other companies, the unspoken formula to get ahead was to work the more-than-full-time schedule— or opt out. When I announced my engagement to the senior team of middle-aged successful women—all divorced with grown

> " *I expected to strive to reach the top, but I had to change my goals once I had children.*"
> —Woman in her 60s, Connecticut, master's degree

children—they looked at me with amusement. Knowing my capabilities and how much I loved to work, they suggested that my fiancé would make a good "first husband" until (they predicted) round-the-clock work would cause a split.

At first, after I changed my status from single to married, I was fine to continue the rigorous and demanding work schedule. I got several promotions, I was making a competitive salary, and there was the thrill of meeting people in the headlines: prominent thought leaders in Washington and academia and on Wall Street. I didn't intend to have children right away, but the stories I was hearing from the motherhood front begged the question of whether I would still be able to keep up the travel and fast professional pace when I did. Determined never to relinquish my career and follow the same path home as so many of my peers, I decided the easiest way to blend work and family would be to take the employer out of the equation and be my own boss.

Though I was in no rush to be a mother, I believed in planning ahead. I dusted off my entrepreneurial hat, left Institutional Investor, and began my own marketing strategy and communications firm. Capitalizing on many high-profile relationships established through my former employer—and maximizing a very robust network of alumni employees—I generated a steady stream of consulting assignments that I fit neatly around my personal life. I developed an array of conferences for top investment firms who wanted to educate and entertain clients; created large-scale events on women's health and personal finance for Saul Poliak, the trade show pioneer; created the conference division for Morningstar when founder Joe Mansueto was a young entrepreneur; and established a long list of clients who didn't care if I was working down the hall or in a different state. With each project and each invoice, I had more and more confidence I would always be able to do interesting, meaningful, lucrative work; meet fascinating people; and never sacrifice a full personal life.

A few years into my marketing communications consulting venture, our first daughter was born. With the help of babysitters and nearby grandparents, I eventually juggled with success (and a modicum of stress) my business, that same husband, one daughter, one dog, and a busy household. The ability to set my own hours, work all night if need be while my daughter was sleeping, and duck out to school events kept me professionally and personally sane.

When you're lucky enough to build a base of loyal clients and work on your own terms, there is great reluctance to return to the regimented life of the traditional employee. However, despite my reservations about giving up my independence, an Institutional Investor founder convinced me to take a hiatus from my own consulting firm. Together we launched a startup that published custom books, newsletters, and conferences sponsored by Wall Street firms. As the senior vice president and managing editor of the firm, I had oversight responsibility for many employees. Most of the time I worked at the company office, but some strategic negotiating gave me the flexibility to work at home as well. The experience taught me that with trust, clear communication, and a culture of "give and take," it is possible to give *all* employees some leeway on the inflexible "9 to 5."

After a lot of exciting work—especially with personal finance guru Ted Benna, known as "the father of the 401(k) plan"—I found that the management of a complex and growing startup and a seven-day workweek (including calls from the company owners at all hours of the night) was increasingly at odds with my health and our growing family. At the time, I was pregnant with our second daughter. I decided to leave and return to my own consulting firm, where I had the greatest flexibility and time to breathe. But, after the events of September 11, 2001, many of my investment firm clients stopped using outside consultants. My phone wasn't ringing, and I was home feeling underemployed for one of the first times in my life. I had a babysitter, a 2-year-old, a child in elementary school, and a lot of time to ponder my next professional move.

This difficult business environment called for a pivot from my consulting work. With a business partner, I explored the idea of career programming for a forgotten audience: women who were contemplating a return to work after a long absence. It seemed like it wouldn't be hard to fill a room: Everywhere I went, I met women who would say, "Oh, it's so great that you work. I've been thinking of returning to work, but I've been out so long I don't know what I could do or who would want me." After listening to hundreds of polished, well-educated women tell me some version of this story, I realized there was a curious lack of confidence in epidemic proportions. It was especially perplexing because, more times than not, these women had MBAs from Ivy League schools and once held high-ranking positions at major corporations or Wall Street firms.

In 2002, when the media noticed that many stay-at-home mothers with professional pedigrees were feeling restless and unfulfilled (often portraying them as desperate souls who could hope for nothing more than a job at Starbucks), my business partner and I launched the Women@Work Network, spending a decade helping women transition back to the world of work. Part of what women needed was the realization that they were not alone, and through our membership of 10,000 nationwide, they found solace in the fact that lots of former professional women felt paralyzed by insecurity, too. We held "Opportunity Knocks" seminars to discuss all the financial, logistical, professional, and psychological aspects of returning to work. We offered a job board, recruiting and career-coaching services, job search strategy boot camps, high-level job fairs, workshops on resumé writing and interview skills—and the reminder that these women had continued to develop business skills in myriad volunteer roles.

After the 2008 economic crisis, the contingency recruiting business (our greatest source of revenue) became an uphill battle, and after a few years I decided to leave Women@Work. I wasn't quite sure what my next entrepreneurial gig would be, but I knew I'd continue to focus on women and work. The biggest takeaway from my Women@Work years was the misconception that women are either working or not working. I knew it wasn't so black-and-white: working women often have one foot on the exit ramp. Stay-at-home mothers are often tired of giving away volunteer time. There are times when women pull back from a heavy work schedule because of an elderly parent who needs help, and there are times when they need to rev their professional engines, facing, for example, an unexpected divorce or a partner's unemployment. Before too long, I knew my next mission was to help women navigate moves in and out of the workforce, explore nontraditional ways to care for their families while building financial security, and pursuing flexible work that always fits their lives.

My strategy for delivering on this mission was to start small, turn off my Type A personality for a while, and let things meander and evolve. One thing I knew from the outset was that writing would be at the core. Though I've held many job titles over a long, uninterrupted career, I've always considered myself first and foremost a writer. In 2012, the blog world was exploding, and I wanted to try my hand at this relatively new genre, too. Recognizing there would be no "one size fits all" blog on the topic of women and work, I landed on the name *9 Lives for Women*— encompassing nine stages (listed with specific advice for each stage on page 19) women often experience between college and retirement. My blog acknowledges that few women have linear careers; most stop and start and move sideways, forward, and back. The work that fits now is not always the work women did at age 25, and it may also deviate completely from degrees they've earned. I've never met a woman who wants to return to a law firm job. I've met very few who want to return to finance. The big, traditional, often inflexible corporations are no longer the average woman's cup of tea. I've encountered very few women who tell me they have the stamina or family bandwidth to

> 66 *My ideal is a full-time position, but I don't want all that comes with being on the fast track to the C-Suite.*"
> —Woman in her 40s, New York, bachelor's degree

sustain sixty- or seventy-hour workweeks and global travel for more than a few years. Very few have told me they're aiming to be CEO, but I've met thousands who want to capitalize on their degrees, do interesting work, make significant money, and advance careers—all in a way that enhances, not overwhelms, their lives.

My Own Near-CEO Experience

Though I've always worked, it was never my specific aspiration to climb the ladder rung by rung to reach the title of CEO. It was not a lack of confidence, an inability to find mentors or sponsors, or any feeling, ever, that men were holding me back. With strategy and tenacity, I think I would have had as much of an opportunity as any other woman who set and reached that goal. I just never wanted the all-encompassing, uber-executive responsibility from which there appears to be no escape.

That's why it was such a curveball when in 2014 a CEO job landed on my lap.

A prominent woman I had known professionally told me about an opportunity to invest in a company that intersected with my work. Discussions about the investment opportunity led to a meeting with the company owner and more discussions about a senior position at the company. Quite unexpectedly, I was offered the CEO role. It was hugely flattering, energizing, and daunting all at the same time. On the plus side, I'd be doing the work I love to do—on a bigger stage. I'd have the chance to work alongside high-profile professionals who have stellar business careers. And I'd have a title I never yearned for, but was exciting just the same.

At first, I informally took the job. Then after waking up at 3:00 a.m. in a panic six nights in a row, I thought, *"Can I really do this?"* Putting the positives aside, I turned to the many negatives. I'd report to the company owner, who works seven days a week. I'd be commuting more than three hours each day and managing a team of people delivering a huge array of products and services. I'd at some point need to travel domestically and internationally. Days would bleed into nights, with many evening events scheduled every month. On the family side of the equation, my daughter was just starting high school, and I wanted to be focused on her as she made the big transition. My father-in-law's health was declining rapidly, and my mother-in-law needed more of our help, too.

> 66 *I started my career with ambitions to get to the top. But after a few years, I despised the stress and competitiveness. I still want to make good money, but I'm doing it to have a good life with my family, not for the sake of a great career. Being a CMO or CEO sounds like hell to me."*
> —Woman in her 30s, New York, master's degree

The more I thought about it, the more luster rubbed off the shiny title of CEO. On the one hand, I knew I was facing an opportunity that could possibly be a high-profile capstone of my many professional years. On the other hand, this opportunity could completely upend my life. I felt the "push" toward the job from the general expectations that women should strive for the top—and I felt the "pull" back to my family and an independent professional life where only I would call the shots. Before too long, I reversed my decision and backed out. For many months, though, I felt the sting of giving it up. Despite all I've accomplished in my career, I questioned if I really was a "serious" and "ambitious" professional.

Any lingering "coulda, woulda, shouldas" I had about declining the big job fell away when I recalled several conversations I had during my Near-CEO Experience. These conversations shed light on four frequent judgments in the upper-echelon business world that very narrowly define ambition and success:

1. Three minutes into our very first conversation, the company owner, a woman, told me emphatically, "I am very, very ambitious." At the time I thought, "OK, so am I." But the more conversations we had, the more I realized that her comment aligned with the objectives of the highest-level professionals—those

aiming for top jobs or huge entrepreneurial ventures; overseeing the largest, most visible initiatives; and driving exponential product, service, or company growth. *I realized that I have a different brand of ambition—pursuing important work in a more low-key, life and family-friendly way.*

2. During conversations with my references, the company owner asked, "Why hasn't she had a big hit?" In other words, why hadn't one of my accomplishments or business ventures led to a multimillion-dollar sale or front-page news? Clearly, many of the highest level professionals believe that "big hit," big impact, big compensation work is the only work that is truly ambitious. *I realized that I don't need headlines to validate what I perceive as my own personal success.*

3. When the prominent woman who introduced me to the company owner (who could possibly have profited financially if I took the job) found out that things weren't playing out as she hoped, she said vehemently, "You're a nobody, and you had the chance to be a somebody." Top professionals often marginalize accomplishments unless you are the "somebody" at the top of a big-name organization—and success can be measured shortsightedly only in terms of title and visibility. *I realized that it was never my burning desire to be celebrated on the cover of a magazine—just to always have a strong professional persona and do challenging, interesting work.*

4. Many months after I declined the job, the company owner and I met to see if there were other ways we could collaborate. The CEO slot was still open and she first asked if perhaps I had changed my mind and I was ready to "go back to work." I was confused until I realized she was suggesting my independent coaching, speaking, consulting, and writing lacked a level of intensity or complexity found in *real work*—at the helm of companies very visible to the public eye. *I realized that what had always made my work "real" is my ability to consistently earn, save, and invest toward long-term financial security.*

I thought long and hard about these judgments and expectations imposed on me and masses of smart, capable women trying to find ways to fit work into their everyday lives. I asked myself these questions and formed these conclusions:

1. Could anyone who turned down a CEO job be really, truly ambitious? *Yes.*
2. Was work that I found fulfilling (and that was called "life-changing" by the individual women I coached) actually significantly less important—or less ambitious—because it was never front-page news? *No.*
3. Do you have to be a household name—or at least a widely recognized name in your field—to be "somebody" and achieve true career success? *No.*

At that point, all my work with women came full circle. I realized that judgments about what constitutes ambition or "real work" make women who aren't seeking top jobs think that returning to the workforce is for naught. These judgments also cause current professional women to fear that if they choose to B-Sane in middle management instead of "leaning in" to the life-encompassing C-Suite quest, they will be letting down the power sisterhood.

❝ *My ideal is earning a good income in a flexible job, working with bright people, and having the chance to do something interesting. I've never been shooting for the top job . . . just more and more responsibility that's closer to strategic core importance. I've never needed to run the company."*
—Woman in her 60s, California, MBA,
The Wharton School

Ironically, women are holding other women to these outdated standards of ambition and success. Many women's organizations pride themselves in their programs designed to hoist more women to the top. Few of these organizations give women substantial guidance on anything other than the traditional corporate path—or help women find the flexwork they really need to stay in the workforce. There are few senior-level women who are visible role models for alternative choices— showing women who want to forego the responsibilities of top corporate jobs that there are other more personal, and less lofty, measures of success. Interesting, too, is the fact that more than a few women who take senior-level jobs have partners who have reversed roles and stayed home with children (more evidence for the fact that two traditional, demanding, very senior-level jobs and families are a difficult mix).

> 66 *I'm still striving to accomplish a lot in my career, but what 'success' looks like has changed. Success is on my terms, not determined by those pushing to break the glass ceiling."*
> —Woman in her 30s, Connecticut, law degree

For both men and women, the fact is that ambition and success can play out in many different ways, and there's no financial wisdom in either spouse staying out of the workforce. Huge salaries or huge profits from the sale of entrepreneurial ventures aren't the only numbers that make working "worth it." Consistent smaller earnings that are invested and saved can make vital contributions to retirement nest eggs and soften the blow of many of life's negative surprises. You can be a successful small business owner with revenues that don't come close to $1 million; a moderate hourly rate freelancer in hot demand; the industry expert who gets plum consulting assignments; or the respected 30-hour-a-week worker who contributes to a team's success, enjoys a competitive salary, receives good benefits, and has more time at home. Indeed, there are not masses of women clamoring for the executive suite, there is no universally sanctioned career trajectory, and we must give women the leeway to set their own definitions of ambition and success. The fact is that any professional path to financial security can be a good, worthy, and fulfilling journey.

Find Happiness & Financial Security in Your Own "9 Lives"

Every life has its ups and downs—times when all cylinders are firing and times when you just don't feel you're hitting your stride. My life has been no exception, but my work has always been a source of great pleasure and a grounding force that provides purpose and fills many interesting hours in every day. In my personal life and in my coaching practice, however, I've met many women who feel something is missing from their very full lives. Those who are working often lament that work leaves no time for life. Those who aren't working often say they want to work but they don't want to give up their lives. Everyone is searching for what they too quickly assume is the impossible: the lucrative, fulfilling, interesting work that fits life.

> 66 *Since I started a family, my professional ambition has changed, not waned. I'm okay if I don't make it to the top, as I don't want to put my job before my family. However, I work hard to find the right opportunities that challenge me and grow my expertise—but also provide the right work and life blend based on my family situation."*
>
> —Woman in her 30s, Texas, master's degree

The dissatisfaction many women feel both in and out of the workforce often coincides with the average age many people reach their lowest point of happiness: sometime in their 40s or early 50s.[1] This is a time when many women feel lost at sea. Women who have left the workforce often have children entering middle school (or generally becoming more independent), and they start to realize that college tuitions and retirement plans are not so far away. Women on hiatus often deliberate for years about whether it's the right time to return to work, whether it's "worth it" to go back for a moderate salary, and whether there's anything they're still qualified to do. Full-time workers in this age range often feel dissatisfaction, too. Women worry that they're missing time with their kids; wonder how much longer they can keep up the relentless, more-than-full-time pace; and struggle to identify what kind of flexwork would pay well or keep their careers on track.

Though both groups of women struggle, they're not facing block-ades. I've watched—and helped—many women repurpose careers they long left behind or rebuild titles and compensation down entirely new and compelling paths. I've shown corporate women many more flexible ways to make a big impact and garner recognition among high-flying former peers. The common links between these two groups are a need for purpose

> ❝ *I want and have always wanted a balance of work and motherhood. I've chosen flexwork over the 'top.'* ❞
> —Woman in her 30s, Maine, bachelor's degree

(beyond family) and financial security (beyond what a partner can provide).

To get this personal and financial satisfaction, women who are currently working and women who are returning to work need to

- think ahead;
- be open to unfamiliar territory;
- redirect previous career paths; or
- have the courage to reinvent.

In the context of my *9 Lives for Women* blog, I offer this life and work stage-by-stage advice:

1. For young women *choosing and launching careers,* aim for a life that maintains true happiness long beyond your 40s and 50s. Fun, meaningful, and mind-broadening work is an enriching part of life, and often the happiest women are those who always "have something for themselves" and find a way to work (even just a few hours a week). Choose a career that will give you the flexibility to work as your family life gets more and more complex.

2. For women deep in the throes of *building a career,* assess if the work you've chosen can be sustained at every life stage. Consider the long-term needs of your family (not just children, but also elderly parents). Decide if a career change would be wise so you don't eventually feel stretched in too many directions or unable to fit work into the ebbs and flows of family needs.

3. For women *looking for new opportunities*—especially if you're nearing or in the "middle-age" years—don't believe anyone who tells you it's impossible to find a job past a certain age. It's simply not true: work possibilities don't disappear at age 40, 50, or even 60. Job seekers are not unsuccessful because of their age; they most often fail because they make too many assumptions about what is and is not possible and go about their search in a haphazard way.

4. For stressed-out working women who are *feeling the pull of family and are thinking about leaving the workforce,* don't make that leap unless you think carefully about the financial and career cost of a work hiatus. There's a way to make employment *work* at your current company, at another company, or through an entrepreneurial venture. The vast majority of stay-at-home mothers I've coached regret that they entirely gave up work (for any period of time) and the security and independence it provides.

5. For women disillusioned about spending endless hours *volunteering and wondering where it all will lead,* become more strategic about how you donate your time. I've yet to meet a mega-volunteer who doesn't eventually want a paycheck, and the fastest way back to the workforce is to choose business-oriented projects. All your volunteer hours count when you can show potential employers you continued to develop business skills in your time out of the workforce.

6. For women *waffling about returning to work* (and feeling unhappy with their indecision), make sure you're focused on the long-term. Those who have the luxury of waffling about work usually feel financially secure *today.* Know that financial

security can turn on a dime: if a partner loses a job, if there's an unexpected divorce, if aging parents suddenly need financial support. With few exceptions, most women should always generate some kind of income as insurance for life's changes.

7. For women *itching to return to work* after a long hiatus, don't ever think your ship has sailed. Returning professional women often embark on new careers that last much longer and are more substantial than the careers they launched after graduation day. When you package yourself as a *returning professional*, resumé gaps are diminished, and you have a long runway because work no longer ends at age 65.

8. For women who are feeling stuck in a rut but are *daunted by reinvention,* hark back to your younger self. Remember all the times you threw caution to the wind and forged boldly ahead. You're the same person who went off to Europe by yourself, found a job in a strange city, paid the rent with three odd jobs, raised a child with no user's manual, and more. You've still got that mojo; you're the only one standing in your way.

9. For women *facing retirement* and feeling "end of an era" blues, know that there are endless ways to stay productive and earn money in the years to come. There's more opportunity than ever for seasoned experts to lend their skills and knowledge to companies, nonprofits, and startups of every kind. Retirement signals one door closing and multiple doors still very much waiting to be opened.

Give Yourself Permission to Hop Off the Career Ladder

If you're a mother who has chosen to leave the workforce, you'll find like-minded women who have decided, at least for some period of time, that any sort of ambition is okay to put on hold. Stay-at-home mothers can be very vocal among themselves. In contrast, current professionals tend to keep a stiff upper lip about their work and life choices. Many are afraid to admit that the traditional climb up the corporate ladder is actually not their ideal.

66 *I considered motherhood a very serious full-time job and worked on my career as well—but I didn't aim to be the president of a company."*
        —Woman in her 50s, Georgia, bachelor's degree

In fact, professional women often have conflicted feelings about leaning away from fast-track and life-consuming jobs. Most do not want to be perceived as anything less than highly competent, career-focused, and ambitious. Yet as I've mentioned earlier, ambition, a prickly topic, can be defined in many ways. What kind of job constitutes real ambition? Consider the fictitious cases of Jane and Mary.

Jane is a graduate of a top business school, and she's on track to be one of the few women who are heading the healthcare division of a top consumer products company. She earns a mid-six-figure salary and has been named a high-potential "woman to watch" by a prominent women's marketing association. She travels at least 50 percent of the time to global locations, works long hours, takes calls and answers emails all day and night, and spends time with her two young children primarily on the weekends. She loves the attention and recognition her job generates, but she feels disconnected from home, pulled in many directions, and stressed out most of the time.

Mary is also a graduate of a top business school. She left her position as a senior brand manager at a big consumer products company when she had her second child. Several of her former colleagues have progressed rapidly to higher titles, but Mary is happy with her decision to launch her own marketing consulting firm for a greater work and life blend. As an independent consultant, she has several steady consumer product clients within driving distance of her home, works about 30 hours a week, and contributes at least $75,000 per year to her household income. This year, one of her marketing campaigns was the runner-up for a prestigious industry award. Her work schedule is flexible, and she is able to volunteer at her children's schools, exercise regularly, and keep stress to a dull roar.

Who is more ambitious: Jane or Mary? Who is more successful: Jane or Mary?

Recently I shared these examples during a flexwork presentation to a group of professional women. Some said (with obvious trepidation) that Mary is as ambitious and as successful as Jane. A pregnant woman with a midlevel advertising job confessed that she feared backlash from her peers if she admitted she was not interested in the promotion to a bigger job and a bigger commitment to frequent international travel. A woman in management consulting (an MBA and a mother of two) then wondered aloud if her hard-driving, former business-school classmates would consider her a lightweight if she veered off the fast track to an entrepreneurial venture that focused on tutoring kids. One by one, women revealed closely held secrets about the work they wanted to do, along with what they thought would be negatively perceived as less ambitious paths.

In so many cases women have to *give themselves* permission to create their own brand of ambition and success. When we buy into the idea that success is attached only to the rich and famous, we diminish the opportunity to pursue many interesting professional paths that may not put you on the cover of a magazine, but will give you *personal* fulfillment, and consistent, life-friendly ways to earn money toward long-term financial security. The primary dictionary definition of success is "a favorable or desired outcome": you can desire and achieve a flexible work life and get to the professional place you truly want to be.

Break Free from the Power Sisterhood

Ambition is a personal thing. Women in the power sisterhood know they will only die happy if they achieve the highest levels of professional and financial success. To reach their goals they play a complex chess game, strategizing each move toward their ascent and leaning in with gusto. Most other working women view life and work with a little more fluidity—capitalizing on their educations, contributing their skills in a meaningful way, earning a living, and having ample time to enjoy their families while they enjoy their work—without having a be-all, end-all goal or feeling a burning desire to be at the top of any organization. One group of women is not more talented or ambitious than the other; it's just a matter of lifestyle and personal choice.

> 66 *When I first graduated, it was important for me to strive for the highest levels of my profession. Then I worked part time for five years to spend more time with my kids. I now work full time with a flexible schedule. With all my work arrangements, I've been able to progress in my career."*
>
> —Woman in her 40s, New York, master's degree

After former State Department official Anne-Marie Slaughter wrote her wildly famous *Atlantic* article, "Why Women Still Can't Have It All,"[2] she perhaps inadvertently became a hero to women who packed it in and left the workforce. While the title of her article seems only to proclaim that work and family are oil and water, it's necessary to dig deeper into Slaughter's personal story. When her son was going through a difficult teenage phase, she left her demanding full-time job working for Hillary Rodham Clinton at the State Department to return to a relatively less demanding, full-time academic job at Princeton. *She did not leave the workforce entirely.* Instead, she did two things all other women can do: she opted for a full-time job closer to home, and one with more predictable hours.

Most women believe that the doors to greater flexibility are slammed tightly shut. In fact, this is far more perception than reality. In my recruiting days, one of my favorite success stories was helping a woman on the partner track at a prestigious and intense New York City law firm move to a general counsel position at a small private equity firm closer to her suburban home. She traded one demanding job for another—but the new one required a more reasonable output of time and didn't involve selling her soul. Yes, she gave up some green dollars, but she made a bundle of what I call "psychic dollars" (what you earn in personal fulfill-ment). In the process, she brought her stress down to a low boil.

Every professional career does not have to be a race to the top—especially if you'd rather not live on airplanes or see your children only for a few minutes as they get out of or into bed. If you're not interested in the executive suite, the partner track, or any other "grab for the brass ring" role, it's possible—and more than socially acceptable—to always get your professional fulfillment from less high-profile and demanding jobs. Indeed, as this book's introduction explains, for smart women at every age and stage, up is not the only professional way forward. We all have the freedom to define our own brand of professional success and ambition, and chart our own paths to long-term financial security. There's no shame in the everyday sisterhood.

> 66 *Working and being a success in my field (not necessarily the TOP but high enough while having a family) was and is important to me.*
> —Woman in her 40s, California, master's degree

Chapter 2

Ride the Roller Coaster with Wide-Open Eyes (Be Ready When Life Turns You Upside Down)

A S I WAS WRITING THIS book, a conversation I had with a 37-year-old, first-time mother convinced me that young women need as much education about the flexwork route to financial security as their mothers do. She had not had the energy to put herself forward for a promotion while on maternity leave, she struggled to blend work and life after the birth of her daughter, and her desire for an all-encompassing, high-powered corporate job had waned. In fact, she was only one of a few women in her circles who had returned to work after starting a family.

> ❝ *My professional ambition didn't fizzle when I had*
> *children, but I put my ambition aside to be around more*
> *for the kids and allow my husband (the real breadwinner)*
> *to work without worrying about the home front.*"
> —Woman in her 40s, Massachusetts, master's degree

This new mother told me her friends are leaving the workforce in droves because (a) their employers aren't set up for parents to succeed, and

(b) they rely heavily on the incomes of partners, whom they believe will support them financially (and sustainably) in the future. One of her married friends was pregnant when she got her master's degree at an Ivy League school; that woman has never worked since. Another one of her friends, at age 27, completely stopped working when she moved in with her fiancé, who is a successful hedge fund manager. I see the same general storyline over and over again in my own personal and professional circles.

6 6 *Because of my spouse's demanding profession, I was unable to continue my career because of the demands of raising a family."*
—Woman in her 50s, New Jersey, master's degree

In other words, very little has changed. Young, well-educated women still drop out of the workforce to care for children because they think the only way to work is within the traditional, inflexible structure. And they are still buying into the 1950s idea that they can achieve long-term financial security solely through the income of a spouse. A 2015 study of women who graduated from Harvard Business School (arguably women who invested great time and money to gain a strong and prestigious foundation for careers) bears this out: more than one-third of millennial alumnae interrupted their careers at least once to care for children (typically for a six-year period).[1]

I've seen higher opt-out numbers in my own work with women and in my *9 Lives for Women* "Motherhood and Career Ambition Survey." Only 35 percent of the nearly 600 mothers I surveyed agreed to this statement: "I've been working and focused on getting to the top of my career since I finished my education." This response is evenly distributed across the mid-30s to mid-50s age demographic, and the women aren't only well educated; they are *highly educated.* The majority (60 percent) also earned advanced degrees. Though 25 percent of the women surveyed agreed with the statement that their primary reason for pursuing higher education was "to become a well-rounded, educated woman," it's safe to say that most women in graduate programs are hoping, at least initially, to reach a higher career level—not just amass more intellectual knowledge.

Don't Focus More on Today than Tomorrow

No one argues that the traditional, inflexible, more-than-full-time corporate job is exceedingly difficult as women care for families, but the alarming issue is that few women have fought for or searched relentlessly for the flexwork that can fit *alongside* their family roles. Women are clear about what constitutes "ideal" work for mothers: 72 percent of women I surveyed put in these options in the preferred work category:

- A professional position that may slowly advance my career via part-time or flexible hours
- A part-time position that generates some income and work fulfillment, but is not necessarily the same level, income, or challenge I once pursued
- A business of my own

But most believe their ideal is just too hard to find. Through my own coaching practice, at women's events, and in the many emails I receive from women every day, I see more hope than action in finding work that fits their lives.

This inaction is largely because many women who *can* move in and out of the workforce or leave entirely for decades without crippling financial discomfort simply *do*. This may be due to a deeply ingrained belief that motherhood is the only job that must be consistent, and it may be that too many women still feel they don't have responsibility for their own financial security. It's telling that only 31 percent of the women I surveyed say they pursued their education so that "I would always have the foundation to support myself financially."

Perhaps it's human nature that women feel comfortable focusing more heavily on the day-to-day life they're mired in today and not

66 *My ideal is a fulfilling full-time or part-time job that is flexible enough to allow me to care for my family."*
—Woman in her 30s, California, master's degree

worrying about what could happen tomorrow. But time and time again I've seen the bubble burst—and evidence that total reliance on a partner is reckless is evident in two more of my survey data points:

> 66 *I felt a bit less ambitious after having children, but a major factor was that my husband was no longer supportive of my working outside our home."*
> —Woman in her 50s, New Jersey, MBA from Kellogg
> School of Management, Northwestern University

- Sixty-five percent of women have experienced a partner's job loss and subsequent inconsistent or absent income.
- Twenty percent have abruptly lost major financial support through divorce or a partner's early death or long-term disability.

I know this scenario all too well.

The affluent Connecticut town of Westport where I grew up is located in Fairfield County, ranked in the top 10 richest counties in America. It is a prestigious address for some and a stark contrast to the experience of many families living below the poverty line in the county's economically depressed cities.

In the 1960s and 1970s, women in my hometown of Westport weren't thinking about life's sudden detours. The traditional suburban life was in full swing, and few women thought they had any part in ensuring their own financial security. Men rode the train to New York City, and women were in charge of households and children. Since the early 1990s, my

> 66 *My ideal is a position that lets me advance professionally and also offers me the flexibility required to be a parent."*
> —Woman in her 40s, New York,
> bachelor's degree

children have attended school in Westport, and today there is little sign that things have changed dramatically. In this school community, a large percentage of mothers don't pursue professional work.

The success of professional men has always been very evident in Westport, but in my era, there was a particular brand of fame and fortune. In high school, my best friends had access to Bloomingdale's charge cards (and I watched them buy whatever clothes they might want), the town fell quiet during Spring Break as families flew off for tropical tans, the houses were big, the cars were sleek, and general glitz and glamour were in the air. For a while we studied alongside childhood movie star Linda Blair (of *The Exorcist* fame)—and there was great lunchroom buzz about the fact that a classmate's father was defending one of the Beatles in a court case on national TV. At the local Army & Navy store, I bought jeans next to Paul Newman, and I exchanged hellos with Robert Redford as we passed each other bicycling at the beach. It was anything but an "average" childhood experience.

Life was a little less glossy, however, in my own home, where my father had lost his big New York City corporate job. Like many men today, his career never fully recovered after this layoff—and my family struggled financially for many years. As a young person, it seemed to me like every other family was living high on the hog, but that was an immature and distorted view that came into focus decades later as I was taking a walk at the town's beach.

Look Closely: There Are Rags Among the Riches

On this morning, I noticed a very well-dressed woman in heels and pearls arranging many grocery bags in the back seat of her car. My initial thought was that she seemed out of place among all the morning walkers in their exercise togs. As I got closer, I saw that her grocery bags were filled with clothing, and I was shocked to see that the trunk of her car was arranged like a bureau drawer with compartments for sweaters, pants, shoes, and more.

At that moment, I realized this woman was living out of her car, driving with all her belongings neatly packed inside. From my own childhood experience, I certainly knew that a person's financial situation could suddenly decline, but the frequency of this story wasn't clear until I met LouAnn Bloomer of TBICO, a woman in the business of helping other women identify skills and find jobs after their comfortable financial situation takes a deep and scary dive.

❝ *As soon as I started a family, the demanding responsibilities made it impossible to put the extra effort into my professional growth."*
—Woman in her 50s, Georgia, master's degree
in computer science

TBICO is an acronym for "The Bridge to Independence and Career Opportunities." Though it is based in the low-income area of Danbury, it doesn't draw women only from areas that have more blue collars than white. When Bloomer founded TBICO in 1993, it was primarily a "welfare-to-work" program focused on women who had always been in the lower economic strata. But now Bloomer says her nonprofit serves GEDs to PhDs: economic and job market downturns have brought many once-higher-income women to TBICO's door.

About half the women who attend the organization's free six-week business training course are from middle- to upper-class backgrounds gone awry. Most often, economic situations have taken a drastic plunge after a partner's job loss or a divorce. Because of assets like a house or a car, these women aren't eligible for state assistance—but from a cash perspective, they can hover close to the poverty line. These are also women who never believed their comfortable lives would ever change. When I told Bloomer about the woman I saw living out of her car, she was not surprised. Many of the once-affluent women who come to TBICO travel with all their possessions. One woman arrived for class each day in her "home,"—a Jaguar—and another shared her car "residence" with a cat and dog.

Coming to TBICO is a humbling experience and, as Bloomer points out, "the great equalizer." Suddenly women who always had life's ducks in a row sit alongside much-less-educated women who have the same challenges of finding affordable housing, childcare, and a job that can pay the bills. Women who have bachelor's degrees from the best colleges and universities—as well as law degrees and MBAs—need the same job training and confidence building as women who have never risen beyond the clerical or entry levels. The need for this basic training among once affluent women is the result of many years out of the workforce—and often a lack of computer skills for the current business setting.

Though many of the well-educated women who now need TBICO's services held long-ago jobs at the management or senior levels, their resumé gaps often make it hard for them to land administrative or midlevel jobs. As Bloomer notes, wherever women fall on the economic spectrum, they often have trouble creating Excel spreadsheets and PowerPoint presentations or doing complex scheduling on Outlook—all skills required for many of today's administrative jobs. The comprehensive TBICO training covers the full Microsoft Office suite as well as communication skills, conflict resolution, resumé development, networking, and job-search strategy.

66 *When I became a mother, the ambition and energy I devoted to working adjusted to accommodate the needs/responsibilities of a growing family. I still consider myself professionally ambitious, but not at all costs or as a detriment to my family."*

—Woman in her 40s, Florida, MBA from
Columbia Business School

As a recruiter for 10 years—focused largely on returning professional women—I coached many who had the same resumé gaps and training needs. They had left the workforce voluntarily for long periods and waffled about returning to work for several years. Many felt the push-pull of family and work: not feeling "right" leaving children in the care of others, but also not feeling fulfilled through the life of the mega-volunteer. Women who never expected to work again would come to me saying they suddenly had to find a job quickly to alleviate a current financial crisis.

Work at Every Age and Life Stage to Manage Life's Surprises

In my experience, women who leave the workforce entirely for a long period without pursuing high-level, resumé-worthy volunteer jobs have a difficult time immediately returning to significant salaries. One newly divorced mother, whose resumé was limited to work as a flight attendant in her 20s, was perceived as unqualified for a receptionist position; potential employers believed she wouldn't be able to handle the technology of multiline phones.

Many women rush impetuously to retail jobs when a return to more professional roles seems daunting and out of reach. A job is a job when a paycheck is critical, but these same women come to me for career coaching when they realize they cannot cover monthly bills with salaries that hover around the minimum wage. One former marketing executive was quickly promoted at her retail sales job—with an hourly raise of just 50 cents.

There's no getting around the fact that life has many unplanned twists and turns. In my "Motherhood and Career Ambition Survey," *73 percent of women report that they have already experienced at least one life event that has had major financial consequences.*

A brief from the PEW Charitable Trust, "How Do Families Cope with Financial Shocks?" gives more detail on the overall vulnerability of American households—even those with higher incomes:

- Sixty percent of households surveyed had experienced a financial shock in the past 12 months. One-third of these respondents experienced two or more types of financial setbacks.[2]
- More than 50 percent of the financial setbacks are related to divorce, death of a spouse, illness, or a change in compensation.[3]
- For many households, financial hardship is only one unexpected expense away.[4]
- Households experiencing financial shocks are much more likely to tap into retirement accounts, jeopardizing future financial security.[5]

Since caregiving for children and aging parents is so consuming, women out of the workforce often put blinders on as they tend to daily responsibilities—not taking steps to return to work and insure against the ramifications of what I've coined as the "Life Surprise Index":

What's Your Life Surprise Index?

Check all that are possible:

✓ Personal or partner job loss

✓ Inconsistent personal or partner income

✓ Financial support for one or more elderly parents

✓ Long-term financial support for adult children

✓ Major illness in immediate family and unreimbursed medical expenses

✓ Disability of household's major breadwinner

✓ Divorce

✓ Insufficient Social Security credits for benefits eligibility

✓ Inadequate retirement savings

If you checked one or more of these possible life surprises, the answer to long-term financial stability is flexwork that always fits your life!

Happily Married Until (Surprise!) You're Not

66 *I thought I was happily married for 30 years... until my husband told me I wasn't."*
—Woman in her 50s, Connecticut, bachelor's degree

Many women who suddenly find themselves in job-seeking mode are blindsided by divorce. Though the often-cited fact that 50 percent of marriages end in divorce may not be precise, any number in that vicinity means many women who depend largely or solely on the financial support of partners will see the end of their marriage well before "death do us part."

Lori Price, CFP, head of the wealth management firm Price Financial Group, says that among her clients, women in the 38–50 age bracket often initiate divorces because of a partner's affair. In the age-50-and-over set, she says marriages may end as life evolves and couples want different paths for their future. When children are out of the house, husbands and wives live alone together for the first time since they were newly married. The whirlwind activity of raising children may have masked the fact that some partners grew separately instead of together.[6]

External factors can also cause irreparable damage to marriages. In divorce attorney Louise McGlynn's practice, she sees marriages dissolve due to the stress of raising children with special needs or sustained periods in which a partner is unemployed.[7] Whatever the reason for the split, divorce strikes hard and often.

Though Price says wealthy clients can often divide assets and live comfortably apart, it's the couples in the middle—neither rich nor poor—that fare the worst. The house (possibly their biggest asset) goes on the market, often one or both partners end up in rental homes, and money to raise and send children to college is tight. According to McGlynn, couples with household incomes in the $150,000 to $200,000 range often have barely enough to support two households when the divorce papers are signed.

At least half the time, McGlynn and Price work with women who have been out of the workforce for many years. Often the first sentence these women say is, "I never thought I'd be here." Once they realize that divorce is inevitable, fear sets in—and they face the reality that they need to return to work. Then fear turns to confusion and a severe lack of self-confidence.

According to McGlynn, women who have MBAs and JDs from leading schools frequently have no idea what kind of work they can do after a long break from the workforce. They assume their only option is retail sales, but as mentioned before this lower-paying job is not necessarily a resume-builder or a no-brainer for those who have not kept up with technology. As McGlynn points out, "You need to be computer literate to work the cash register at the Gap."

One returning professional I coached saw the handwriting on the wall when her marriage began to falter. She immediately signed up for classes at a local continuing education program to get her computer skills up to speed. This turned out to be a good move when reduced alimony propelled her toward any job she could find. She felt forced into a retail job at a women's clothing chain and found the cash register system as complicated as spaceship controls. She told me about well-educated friends who had been out of the workforce for many years, noting that many were puzzled by the editing term "cut and paste." Educated women in that position can lack the technology skills for even low-paying jobs.

Price notes that recently divorced women (and those in the process of getting divorced) often need higher-paying jobs when they return to the workforce because unexpected circumstances have left them in a drastically lower financial state than they enjoyed during their marriages. There are many incidences of men hiding money in secret accounts, directing income through "business partner" girlfriends, and cancelling credit cards and insurance coverage while long divorce proceedings are underway. The financial and emotional cost of divorce also causes many women to "just want it to be over;" Price says that too often women take a less-than-optimal settlement so they can get on with their lives. Few want to take their case to court, which can involve attorney fees ranging from $150 to $1,000 an hour. As a result, women often succumb to the other extreme: not arming themselves with comprehensive information or hiring the best divorce attorneys who ensure that, for example, there are built-in cost-of-living increases for alimony and child support.

Once the divorce is over, alimony (which can be up to 40 percent of a spouse's earned income) can provide at least current-day financial security. But when ex-husbands lose jobs or see their compensation plummet, alimony payments dwindle in size, too. Though there's often a financial need to generate an income post-divorce, many women must keep their earnings below a certain ceiling to avoid reducing—or losing—their alimony payments. According to Price, many divorce settlements don't safe harbor a woman's income. This puts divorced women between a rock and a hard place: the alimony is not enough to live on, yet their earning potential is capped.

The combination of compensation restrictions and resumé gaps forces many women into jobs that don't resemble the careers they pursued in their 20s and 30s. Price has seen women take on nonprofessional cash jobs like dog walking or babysitting until the children go off to college and the alimony and child support decline.

After a divorce, some women get on their feet faster than others—especially when they take a strategic and professional approach to finding part-time or full-time work. The universal lament, Price notes, is, "I should have kept a hand in my career…maybe I shouldn't have completely stopped working."

No Job Comes with a Lifetime Guarantee

Today few corporations hand out gold watches for many decades of service. The average job tenure is now about four years[8]—which means that by choice or by need most workers are frequently in job search mode and continually taking employment risks with new employers.

One of my career-coaching clients told me she once assumed her husband had a job for life. He had more than three decades into a Fortune 100 company and a position near the top rung. My client's thrifty mother-in-law would say, "You two need to stop spending so much money…you never know what could happen to that big job."

"Nothing is going to happen to his job," my client would think. *"We're safe."*

Like many other women, my client was foolish to think her husband's big executive job was indeed eternally safe. One day, seemingly out of the blue, a new CEO regime reshuffled the executive ranks, and he joined many age-50-and-over professional men who held the less lofty title, "unemployed." Though he was fortunate to join another company,

I've heard of many other husbands (or alimony-paying ex-husbands) who take a long time to recover from a job loss—or never recover at all.

> **❝** *I had to return to work because my husband lost his job and didn't go back to work for three years."*
> —Woman in her 40s, California, MBA from University of Virginia Darden School of Business

For the more highly compensated, it's simply a matter of supply and demand. The number of jobs narrows at the top of the corporate pyramid. Whatever the income level, many sole breadwinners become one of the "long-term unemployed"—out of work for six months or more (a demographic that included 1.7 million Americans in 2017 or 25 percent of the total unemployed).[9] The longer these job seekers are out of work, the less attractive they become to employers. Age discrimination can also play a role, since less-seasoned candidates demand lower salaries, have fewer medical and disability claims, and offer a longer career runway.

A six-month-or-more period of unemployment can take a huge toll on a one-income household. Just 31 percent of Americans have saved six months of expenses in an emergency fund[10]—due largely to the fact that expenses grow faster than many can save during home-buying and family-raising years. Though severance pay softens the blow of a job loss, it's not a legal requirement, and it is offered by only about 60 percent of employers. At the executive level, a severance benefit is usually six to 12 months of regular compensation (not bonuses). At the nonexecutive level, the cushion is far less soft—generally two weeks' pay for every year of service up to a maximum of 26 weeks. In both cases, continued health insurance coverage for a limited period of time may or may not be part of the severance package.[11]

With all the volatility in the business world, no one can gamble that a job will endure the ups and downs of the economy, industry and company-specific fluctuations, and the whims of power-wielding individuals. Even when women have a smaller part-time income, it still means some money is coming in while a partner looks for a new job.

Paying the Bills in Sickness and in Health

Next in the category of negative life surprises is a situation when a bread-winner partner with a good, stable job could develop a serious illness or disability that interrupts earning, saving, and investing in a one-income household. Despite our society's obsession with good health, one in four of today's 20-year-olds will become disabled before they retire. This fact and the statistics that follow in this section are from a website I venture to guess few healthy people visit: The Council for Disability Awareness at disabilitycanhappen.org.[12]

> ❝ *When my husband was diagnosed with leukemia, I was lucky I always worked, but I needed to work in a more flexible way. I switched from full-time to independent consulting and from marketing to healthcare. Healthcare is a booming area that needs good business skills and analytical thinking—and even on a flexible basis my MBA can really add needed value.*"
> —Woman in her 60s, California, MBA from
> The Wharton School

It's pretty much a roll of the dice. We can make positive lifestyle choices to ward off illness, but many less obvious biological factors come into play. Households that rely only on a male breadwinner have a 21 percent chance that disability will strike for three months or longer during his career in an office job. These are statistics for a 35-year-old male who is in good shape: 5 feet, 10 inches; 170 pounds; a nonsmoker who exercises moderately and leads a generally healthy lifestyle. That same man has a 38 percent chance of a disability that would last five years or longer—with an average disability lasting a full 82 months.[13]

Though women generally live longer than men, they have a slightly higher risk of disability. A typical 35-year-old female has a 24 percent chance of becoming disabled during her working career for at least three months.[14]

The factors that cause disability statistics to increase are common problems afflicting men and women in every age and economic demographic: excess body weight, tobacco use, diabetes, high blood pressure, back pain, anxiety or depression, alcohol consumption, and substance abuse. Despite these widespread problems, most workers believe they are at very low risk: 64 percent say they have a 2 percent or less chance of being disabled for three months or more during their career.[15]

Once an illness or injury of any kind causes employees to miss three to six months of work, they're put on long-term disability leave. At that point, their regular income stops and any disability insurance kicks in. Not all employers offer disability insurance, though: for 69 percent of private-sector workers, this benefit does not exist. Only five states (California, Hawaii, New Jersey, New York, and Rhode Island) require employers to provide partial wage replacement insurance coverage for non-work-related sickness or injury.[16]

Even when employees can rely on disability insurance, it's often a fraction of their regular salary. Many people mistakenly assume that Social Security or worker's compensation will *replace* their salary during disability leave. The first reality is that the average approval rate for disability claims is 36 percent. If a claim is approved, then long-term disability insurance pays a percentage of the employee's salary—usually 50 to 60 percent.[17] The average annual benefit paid by Social Security Disability Insurance is $14,160,[18] and if this were the only income it would be below the poverty level for a four-person household ($25,100).[19]

Without a doubt, disability causes severe financial hardship for many families. The average disability period of more than seven years is a long interruption to a regular income stream. Fewer than half of all workers have discussed disability planning—and when injury or illness occurs and employment income is lost, 65 percent of working Americans say they cannot cover normal living expenses for even one year. Routine bills are not the only problem: catastrophic medical benefits do not cover all costs, and medical problems contribute to 62 percent of all personal bankruptcies and half of home foreclosure filings.

Recently, during a family trip to Europe, the potential for debilitating illness or injury came very close to home. I fell over a low concrete sidewalk barrier, broke my wrist, and ended up in a Berlin emergency room. One minute I was making plans for lunch, and the next minute I was talking to foreign doctors about surgery. In the scheme of life, a broken wrist is more a nuisance than a tragedy. But I've thought many times that my accident could have been much worse. If my wrist hadn't broken my fall, in a split second I could have had a severe injury to my head or neck, with many medical ramifications and the possibility of a long period when I'd be unable to work. I wasn't skydiving, skiing, or riding a motorcycle without a helmet. I was simply walking slowly on a city sidewalk, testimony to the fact that we could all be disabled for a long or short time—in the blink of an eye.

Till Death Do Us Part

Most women who say the "till death do us part" phrase in their marriage vows think they won't have to face this life change until they are well into their retirement years. In reality, one-third of women who become widowed are younger than age 60, and half are widowed by age 65.[20] Since an early death of a spouse is not something you anticipate, it can be especially hard for women to pick up the financial pieces and move on. If a spouse dies well before age 65, it's likely a retirement nest egg is only a work in progress. Like divorce, early widowhood forces many women back into the workforce.

In the New York Life "Loss of a Spouse" study,[21] 55 percent of widows reported challenges adjusting to a change in income level, 38 percent needed to cut discretionary spending, and 21 percent said they were no longer saving adequately for retirement. Many wish they had saved more

(42 percent) and had discussed what might happen financially when one spouse passed away (30 percent).

> **❝ ❞** *I never expected to work my whole life, but my husband died at age 42—leaving me to raise and support our four young children."*
>
> —Woman in her 60s, Massachusetts, master's degree from Georgetown

A survey of recent widows[22] offers additional insights from women age 70 and younger who lost spouses within the past five years and had financial assets of $50,000 to $1 million. Three in 10 widows reported that they did not have an emergency fund and that they had not been primarily responsible for financial planning and investment decisions. In all cases where financial issues arose after the death of a spouse, the situation would have been less precarious if the woman had kept her skills current and generated an income while her husband was living.

Though the "bag lady" fear may seem extreme, it's not ridiculous for women to have concerns about running out of money in old age. Women live an average of 20 years as a widow, and they often do so in perilous financial situations. The average annual Social Security benefit for women is less than $20,000, and almost 50 percent of elderly unmarried females rely on this money as 90 percent or more of their income.[23]

Elderly Parents Might Need Your Time and Wallet, Too

In the realm of financial security, many couples need to worry not only about their own longevity (and ability to support themselves throughout a long retirement), but also about the health and financial well-being of several elderly parents as well. This is often a surprise, however, because many elderly parents guard closely or discuss only superficially their own financial information. Seventy percent of elderly parents surveyed by Fidelity Investments believe they have had detailed conversations with adult children about their net worth or how to pay for long-term eldercare. In reality, more than half their children claim this isn't true. Most importantly, adult children underestimate the value of their parents' estate by an average of $278,000.[24]

As a result, many adult children don't prepare for the fact that at some point they may need to provide financial assistance to parents or in-laws. This financial burden affects adult children at an early age: 19 percent of millennials already provide an average of $18,250 to parents (most often a single mother) each year—a huge chunk of money since the average millennial salary is $35,592. Three-quarters of the financial support provided by adult children of all ages is for one or more parent's general living expenses, and another quarter of the support is for medical bills. At least half of adult children are surprised by the fact that their parents need financial support for daily living.[25]

While financial support for elderly parents affects both a husband and wife, women provide the majority of informal care to parents and in-laws.[26] Though many assume that only hands-on care is burdensome, the fact is that more part-time, arm's-length roles—such as care manager and surrogate decision maker—are enormously time-consuming and emotionally taxing. Generally being "on call" as needs arise means many interruptions to daily work and life.

It's often overlooked that women will be drawn into at least oversight care for aging parents and in-laws regardless of the amount of non-family help an aging parent can afford. The adult children who live the farthest away from aging parents also do not necessarily get a pass. I know one woman in a senior-level job in New York City who frequently flies back and forth to Ohio to "do her part"—joining her siblings in selling the family home, buying and furnishing a smaller retirement home for their mother, and handling mountains of other eldercare details while, at the same time, trying to manage the investments of her high-net-worth clientele.

In my 50s, I've had three elderly parents in my life who have sworn by their independence. The reality is that ultimately no one escapes the aging process, and very few never need help. In a recent one-year period, my husband and I weathered several medical episodes for two different parents that spanned months—involving hospitals, rehab centers, a move out of a family home and into assisted living, endless doctor's appointments, financial and insurance consultations, interim caregiving logistics, and much more.

Any level of caregiving for aging parents can essentially become a woman's third or fourth job, demanding time and attention alongside responsibilities for children, households, and paid professional work. Twenty percent of women involved in eldercare switch from full-time to part-time employment, 29 percent pass up a job promotion, 22 percent take a leave of absence, 16 percent quit their jobs, and 13 percent retire early.[27]

Eldercare not only reduces or eliminates paychecks, it also means fewer contributions to 401(k)s, Social Security, and other retirement savings vehicles. Most alarming is the fact that 63 percent of caregivers have no plan for subsidizing the cost of their parents' care over the next five years, and 62 percent say the cost of caring for a parent has impacted their own ability to plan for their financial future. These figures, from an *AgingCare.com* survey,[28] prompted its publisher, Joe Buckheit, to say, "With an estimated 34 million Americans providing care for older family members, the survey results indicate a financial crisis in the making."[29]

Women who leave traditional full-time jobs without searching for more flexible options pay a very high price. Working women age 50 and over who leave the workforce permanently to care for a parent lose nearly $325,000 in wages and benefits.[30] The loss is even greater when you account for the portion that could have been invested, saved, and compounded over a decade or more.

Joanna Gordon Martin, founder of Theia Senior Solutions in Princeton, New Jersey, helps both men and women juggle jobs and family eldercare needs through corporate-sponsored programs and referrals from financial and other advisers. Her clients, representing many different industries, are taking steps to help their employees manage their caregiving roles so they'll have more peace of mind and fewer work distractions—and not be compelled to entirely leave their jobs.

Gordon Martin explains, "People often think eldercare will be similar to childcare. The reality is that if you're blessed with a healthy child, children become easier as time goes on (teenage years aside), and the corporate support for mothers and now fathers is becoming more significant. With aging parents, the first episode is often the tip of the iceberg, and without the right tools and strategies, caregiving can completely overtake an adult child's life."[31]

Data shows that caregiving for aging parents can become both a time and financial burden for women who already have responsibilities for their own children and households:

- Nearly half of adults in their 40s and 50s are in the "sandwich generation": they have a parent age 65 or older and are either raising a young child or financially supporting a grown child. Only 28 percent of these multigenerational caregivers report their financial situation as "living comfortably."[32]
- Twenty-two percent of women spend 21 or more hours per week providing (and/or managing care for) ill or aging parents.[33]
- On average, caregivers of elderly parents are age 49. Nearly half are between the ages of 18 and 49.[34]
- The percentage of adult children providing personal care and/or financial assistance to a parent more than tripled between 2002 and 2017.[35]
- As Americans lead longer lives, some degree of cognitive decline is almost guaranteed. The prevalence and severity of impairment rises exponentially with age, with more than half of those over age 85 experiencing some form of this condition.[36]

Elderly parents who otherwise appear to be in good health can actually be declining because of cognitive issues. Ginger Nash, a naturopathic doctor based in New Haven, Connecticut, notes that a decline in brain function within the central nervous system can accelerate major organ deterioration (and conversely, a failing organ can speed cognitive decline). It's not only obvious health issues like cancer or heart disease that require eldercare: very common cognitive impairment issues can require long and expensive caregiving, too.[37]

If women believe they have financially secure elderly parents, they may mistakenly assume they'll never personally need to subsidize or cover eldercare costs. The high cost of eldercare (detailed in chapter 3) is probably not an issue for the wealthiest "one percent" demographic: the well-heeled parents who are able to support themselves through very long retirements, with any type of care and through any medical challenge. For the other 99 percent of elderly parents who may not have a huge retirement nest egg, an expensive home to sell or borrow against, or other significant assets to easily liquidate, funding for all the care needed at the last stage of life can quickly snowball and require help from adult children.

The hardest part of funding aging parent care is the unpredictability. You can plan to cover college costs at a definite date, but eldercare is a wild card. A big surprise happened in my family when my widowed 84-year-old uncle completely ran out of money. Like many adult children, my cousins didn't know his exact financial situation. They didn't think their father had robust retirement savings, but they also didn't think his resources would run completely dry. At the time, he was also facing two operations with only the most basic Medicare coverage. Initially, he strongly resisted selling his family home, but that was the only option that would not burden his adult children. He was fortunate to complete the sale quickly, but although my cousins dodged that bullet, there are likely to be other chapters in this story. The proceeds from the sale of the house (reduced largely by a reverse mortgage that had previously generated much-needed cash) will not cover all of my uncle's needs if he lives, as he intends to, until age 105.

With Two Caregiving Roles, There's No Perfect Time to Work

So often women tell me they'll leave work "for just a few years" and return when they feel they've put the requisite time into what I call their first caregiving job: raising children. But I caution them that this plan might just coincide with the time when their *second* caregiving job begins: helping aging parents. Most of the women I coach are in their 40s and 50s when they think about returning to work after a long hiatus— ironically at or close to the average age of 49 when women assume some or all eldercare responsibilities.

Few women realize that eldercare could force them out of the workforce—or delay a return—even more than the responsibilities of caring for children. With even the best of children we all experience bumps in the road, but the total transformation of parents from vitality to frailty; the often-long string of falls, illnesses, and general discomfort; the decisions of where to live and who will provide daily care; and the psychological toll of watching beloved parents slip away is more life-encompassing than making meals, carpooling, and overseeing homework day to day.

Possible care for aging parents needs to be factored into all work and financial planning decisions, and the demands of two often consecutive caregiving roles make it wise to *always* work in a flexible way. Make absolutely sure your own retirement expenses and your aging parents' retirement expenses will be sufficiently funded. The stress of suddenly assuming the financial burden of your parent's care or the risk of depleting your own retirement savings (thus passing on the burden of your own eldercare costs to *your* children) would have a far more profound impact on your family than finding a way to continually blend work and life today.

> ❝ *My ideal work evolves. When kids are young it's easier to work full time. As they get to middle school and high school, you want to be around more to see what's going on with friends. Then as they get closer to college, it's inspirational for the kids to see your career. But when children are older, aging parents start to need care, too—making flexwork necessary at every life stage.*"
> —Woman in her 40s, Connecticut, master's degree

Adult Children Can Get Too Comfy in the Family Nest

If the unexpected cost of supporting even one aging parent is not enough of a threat to your own retirement security, there is also the possibility that one or more of your adult children will take many years to become financially independent. The unemployment rate for the up-to-24-year-old age demographic (including recent college graduates) is more than twice as high as prime-age workers (ages 25 to 54) at 9.8 percent versus 4 percent. The youth unemployment rate is nearly three times higher than older workers (ages 55 to 64).[38]

Today's young adults are more likely to be at home for an extended stay (an average of three years) than previous generations. As of 2016, 15 percent of 25- to 35-year-old millennials were living in their parents' home. This is 5 percent higher than in 2000 and double the number of young people who lived at home in 1964.[39]

Many millennials return to their childhood bedrooms while they conduct a perpetual search for jobs. The jobs they find often do not cover the cost of living on their own. Entry-level salaries can be painfully low, and they're increasingly in short supply. Companies bruised by the Great Recession stayed lean by automating and outsourcing core entry-level functions while slashing training budgets and payrolls. Other companies have raised the bar for new graduates, who are expected to arrive job ready on Day One. The frustrating conundrum is that nearly all jobs with high education requirements (i.e., bachelor's degree and above) have significant experience requirements (i.e., two years or more of relevant work experience). As a result, recent college graduates often turn to nonprofessional jobs in an often futile attempt to make ends meet.[40]

When recent graduates are expected to have more experience, and employers have an abundance of older, more experienced workers to choose from, young job seekers are forced to seek out internships, which are often unpaid. Those unpaid months or years can require the financial help of parents to cover the cost of commuting, clothing, and daily living. The longer that unpaid employment—or underemployment—continues, the more parents drain their retirement savings.

Burst the Bubble: "It *Will* Happen to Me"

When I set out to write this book, my intent was not to put women in a state of fear about disaster lurking around every corner. We all face challenges in life, and we all try to work through them with positivity and grace. My point is simply "be aware and prepare" for possible contingencies as another form of life insurance. Women can cushion life's unwelcome surprises by finding ways to generate even a small income from college through retirement years.

❝ *It makes no sense to give up working at any age. We lost our home to fire, and I suddenly had to be the breadwinner and provide health benefits for my family."*
—Woman in her 60s, South Carolina, bachelor's degree

Every dollar counts when it comes to long-term financial security—and for women it's more about the consistency of earning, saving, and investing than the heft of a job title. To position yourself well for any life calamity, you don't need to be at the top of a corporation or building a startup that will achieve exponential growth. I've known women who worked steadily in moderately paid part-time jobs and kept households afloat when partners lost one or multiple jobs. I've seen women who turn hobbies like jewelry-making or gardening into profitable small businesses that send kids to college when partners lose jobs or become terminally ill. And I know women who became widows at a young age who paid every monthly bill without cash from a big life insurance policy or savings account—just because they had always worked and kept resumes current in some flexible way.

Generating an income—and learning how to make the money you earn grow—is an imperative for all women. Financial planning is a topic we need to bring to the forefront in our own families and for women as a whole. Eight in 10 women don't talk about their finances with friends and family, and half of women are nervous about making financial decisions (especially Gen X and Y women born in 1965 and later). Since nine in 10 women will be the sole financial decision makers for their household at some point in their lives, the potential for long-term financial shortfalls is a reality all women must face and embrace.[41]

> 66 *I had to reroute for a bit when our disabled child was born, but I always worked in some way and kept myself involved so I could work flexibly and care for my son.*"
>
> —Woman in her 30s, New Jersey, master's degree from Penn State

Ultimately, women do know that being in the dark about financial matters is not wise. "Do what I say, not what I do" is advice I'm hearing more and more women give to their daughters. Women in their 40s and 50s who took big caregiving breaks from the workforce and feel they are subsequently not as financially stable as they should be are now the biggest proponents of continual work. In my "Motherhood and Career Ambition Survey," fewer than 7 percent of mothers say they'll advise daughters to leave the workforce and care for young children. Most women say they'll encourage daughters to always find some kind of work that fits their lives—some way to generate even a small paycheck—so they always have current skills and experience to support themselves. (A 2017 Allianz Life study has related results that do not mince words: when respondents were asked how they would advise daughters about money, 72 percent said "do not depend on others for financial security."[42]) All this advice is not surprising: hindsight is 20/20 vision. Many women have made work and life choices that made them less resilient to financial challenges, and they want their daughters to do everything they can to avoid the same fate.

> 66 *My mom schooled me to be financially independent, given many of the unexpected life misfortunes she faced.*"
>
> —Woman in her 40s, Connecticut, master's degree

Chapter 3

Age with Financial Power (It Will Take a Lot More Money than You Think)

AGING WELL TAKES STRENGTH—NOT JUST hearty physical health, but also a solid block of financial assets that can fund what could be several decades of retirement. Too many women spend more time worrying about physical fitness than about financial fitness. It doesn't matter whether you can still fit into your wedding dress at age 70 or 80 if you don't have enough financial power to cover your expenses and enjoy a stress-free life.

Exercise for Financial Fitness, Too

- *Reach out* to family and friends for recommendations of financial advisers who listen to and fully understand the challenges and opportunities women face in all of life's ages and stages.

- *Jog* your memory about every facet of your finances: organize all account numbers and contacts, wills, insurance policies, etc. If you're in a relationship, don't be the partner in the dark about critical financial matters.

- *Stretch* your thinking beyond today: create long-term life plans and determine how much money you'll need in order to be able to fund your daily living, passions, dreams, and goals.
- *Cycle* away from haphazard spending and toward wise budgeting through easy online tools.
- *Flex* financial muscle through a regular savings discipline both within and outside employer plans.
- *Swim* against the current with confidence. Learn about the investment risk that makes sense at your age and life stage.
- *Build up* your resources so you can power through unexpected detours: all the twists and turns that could require funding from paychecks earned by *you* down the road.

Face the Reality: A Man Is Not a Financial Plan

I wish I could take credit for the clever slogan "A Man Is Not a Financial Plan." It's the tagline for the Women's Institute for Financial Education site, WIFE.org. Women who feel they will weather any life storm often are those who shift financial power away from themselves and put the responsibility for their own security in another person's (usually a husband's) hands. Cindy Hounsell, President of WISER, the Women's Institute for a Secure Retirement, told me[1] that many of the women who find themselves in financial despair following an unexpected divorce often hold their husbands wholly responsible for their misfortune—rarely aware that they played a role by relinquishing personal financial responsibility.

Women relinquish their financial power because they often feel less confident than men in their ability to save and invest. Despite the fact that the majority handle day-to-day household finances, 61 percent wish they had more confidence in long-term financial decision making, and

63 percent wish they knew more about financial planning and investing.[2] Interesting, though, is the fact that when women do have the confidence and knowledge to invest wisely, they tend to outperform men due to different personality traits—primarily the patience to trade less frequently and the discipline to adhere to an investment plan more faithfully.[3] This is evidence that with more guidance and information, women have the ability to be strong financial managers for themselves and their families.

Building confidence and actively participating in earning, saving, and investing is critical because women have many years to fund with—and also likely without—a partner. Only 27 percent of married women and 8 percent of unmarried women have $250,000 or more saved for retirement.[4] Low saving levels correlate to feelings of inadequacy in financial literacy: two-thirds of women feel that vast financial information and myriad investment options are overwhelming, leaving them unsure of how or where to invest.[5] Though financial literacy is a problem for both genders, women lag men in the ability to pass a basic quiz on how to make a nest egg last (17 versus 35 percent).[6] You can take the Retirement Income Literacy Quiz yourself at *http://bit.ly/2qhBtYk*

Clearly, there's a disconnect. To have the resources to cover expenses, women need to be financially savvy and participate in the process of earning, saving, and investing. Women at any age need a basic knowledge of life expectancy, healthcare costs in retirement, long-term care costs, how Social Security works, and savings withdrawal rates. All this knowledge contributes to *financial well-being,* the ability to

- fully meet current and ongoing financial obligations (including unexpected financial shocks);
- feel secure in your financial future; and
- make choices that allow the fundamental enjoyment of life.

Within this definition is a big focus on the future—not just any financial comfort that might be felt at the present time, and not only the financial comfort that might be provided today by a partner.

While we can't predict all of life's surprises, we can adjust our financial planning to accommodate the facts:

- Women typically work 12 fewer years than men over their life-time.[7] That means women, on average, have 12 fewer years to contribute to 401(k) plans or other tax-deferred retirement accounts.
- Women contribute less to Social Security over their working lives, resulting in a smaller benefit during retirement.[8]
- One in four 65-year-old women will live past age 90, making more than 30 years of savings for retirement a realistic target.[9]
- Many financial experts swear by the 4 percent rule, which allows you to withdraw 4 percent of your savings balance during your first year of retirement and then adjust subsequent withdrawals for inflation. Following this rule, they say, makes your nest egg last for 30 years. If a woman has $250,000 saved she would have only $10,000 to spend in her first year of retirement.

The need for careful planning hits home even more dramatically in this data on general pre-retiree expectations and retiree realities (affecting both working women and those who rely only on the income of a partner):

- The majority of retirees (60 percent) retired sooner than planned, and 66 percent did so for employment-related reasons, such as organizational changes or job loss. Twenty-seven percent retired for health reasons, and 11 percent for family responsibilities (e.g., becoming a caregiver). Only 16 percent retired because they found they had saved enough or received a windfall.
- Among those who retired later than planned, most (61 percent) did so for financial reasons or the need for employee benefits.
- Seventy-six percent of retirees wish they had saved more consistently, and 48 percent say they waited too long to concern themselves with saving and investing for retirement.[10]

You're Never 100% Covered: Plan for Big Healthcare and Eldercare Bills

There are two major reasons women need to think ahead and make sure they have the power to fund their retirements: the costs of healthcare and eldercare. Healthcare relates to medical needs and end-of-life eldercare relates to help with daily living needs. Many women need to worry about funding their own healthcare and eldercare—and the possibility of contributing to or covering these costs for elderly parents who may run out of money.

Insurance is only part of the answer. There's no such thing as a free ride, and it's especially important to know that employer help for the healthcare expense is declining: the share of large employers (200 or more workers) offering retiree coverage dropped from 66 percent in 1988 to 24 percent in 2015.[11]

Most people underestimate how much they will spend for both healthcare and eldercare during all their retirement years. Starting with healthcare, here is quick cheat sheet that addresses some common misconceptions; for more in-depth information, consult medicare.gov.

- There are three parts of Medicare and they are not cost-free. For Part A (hospital and nursing facility coverage), you don't have to pay a premium to participate in the plan, but there are deductibles and other forms of cost-sharing. For Part B (physician services) and Part D (prescription drugs), there are premiums if you choose to participate in these plans, and there are also deductibles and other forms of cost-sharing on top of the premiums.
- Medicare Part A does not offer unlimited coverage. You are covered for up to 100 days per benefit period of care, but only the first 20 days are covered in full.
- Retirees have the option of purchasing Medicare gap insurance—or "Medigap"—to defray costs not covered by Medicare, but these supplemental plans only cover medically necessary care,

not help with activities of daily living like bathing, dressing, eating, etc.

- Long-term care insurance policies (which are completely separate from Medicare) are the only plans that cover care for activities of daily living, but these plans are very expensive and often do not last for the many years daily nonmedical eldercare can be needed in the last phase of life.

Delving further into Medicare, this fact illustrates why it is not a government subsidized benefit without costs to you: Total projected lifetime premiums (including Medicare Parts B and D, supplemental insurance, and dental insurance) for a healthy 65-year-old couple who retired in 2017 is $321,994. Adding deductibles, copays, hearing, vision, and dental cost sharing, the number grows to $404,253 of out-of-pocket expenses.[12] If the federal government implements Medicare reforms, an even greater share of the burden could shift to retirees. Another critical reality is that these figures don't include the cost of ongoing daily living care outlined later in this chapter or additional costs you may incur if you decide to take—or are forced into—early retirement before Medicare kicks in. (To estimate the total healthcare costs you'll face in retirement, consult AARP's Health Care Costs Calculator at aarp.org.)

Most alarming is the fact that healthcare costs will continually rise at an annual rate of 5.47 percent for the foreseeable future—almost triple the United States inflation rate from 2012 to 2016 (1.9 percent) and more than double the annual projected Social Security cost-of-living adjustments (COLAs) at 2.6 percent. A 66-year-old couple retiring in 2017 required 59 percent of their Social Security benefits to cover their out-of-pocket retirement healthcare costs. This percentage also increases over time: a 55-year-old couple will eventually need 92 percent of benefits, and a 45-year-old couple, 122 percent.[13] Like Social Security, Medicare faces long-term challenges—with expected solvency until 2034.[14] Social Security and Medicare form the base of almost every American's retirement plan—and current projections threaten every woman's retirement security.

Average Americans who are many years away from retirement are not thinking about the fact that they could experience at best reduced Social Security and Medicare benefits. Even a healthcare professional at the top of her field looked at me quizzically when I pointed out in casual conversation that healthcare costs eat into a retirement nest egg. She said, "Well, that's what Medicare is for…" not realizing that this insurance does not cover every healthcare cost, and that the Medicare system overall is in peril.

Independence Isn't Forever: Know the Skyrocketing Cost of Daily Eldercare

It's clear that out-of-pocket medical care costs will eat into your retirement nest egg, but that's only the first big bite. The second major bite is nonmedical care—interchangeably referred to as long-term care, custodial care or eldercare. Many adults think they won't need to pay for daily living care at all. But the facts are clear: by 2050 the number of elderly people using paid eldercare services in any setting (at home or in an assisted living facility, for example) will double from 13 million in 2000 to 27 million.[15] Anyone reaching age 65 has a 40 percent chance of entering a nursing home in particular.[16]

The annual Genworth Cost of Care Survey[17] is a very useful reference with information provided by state (national averages are in the table that follows). My home state of Connecticut, for example, is one of the most expensive for eldercare, along with other states in the Northeast and Northwest, plus Alaska, Hawaii, and California.

This table shows the median cost of each type of eldercare *for only one year*. The average nursing home stay, for example, is almost 2.5 years,[18] and at median annual rates for a semiprivate room, that stay

Average 2017 and Projected Cost of United States Eldercare Services

	2017 Average Daily Rate	2017 Median Annual Rate	2027 Estimated Annual Rate	2037 Estimated Annual Rate	2047 Estimated Annual Rate
Community Adult Day Healthcare	$70	$18,204	$24,459	$32,871	$44,176
Assisted Living Facility	$123	$45,000	$60,476	$81,275	$109,227
Homemaker (In Home Services)	$131	$47,928	$64,419	$86,574	$116,348
Home Health Aide	$135	$49,188	$66,110	$88,846	$119,402
Semiprivate Nursing Home	$235	$85,776	$115,274	$154,919	$208,198
Private Nursing Home	$267	$97,452	$130,971	$176,015	$236,549

now requires about $214,000 in savings. Looking at cost projections, a 50-year-old today is facing about $520,000 for that same nursing home stay—an increase of 41 percent. It's also likely that the elderly will need to pay for one or more services as they decline, whether they're living at home or in a facility.

When I discussed my own concerns about eldercare costs for my parents with a friend (a midlevel executive woman in her 50s), she said she'll just have her widowed mother live with her family when her mother's own resources run out. That conversation was one of many that inspired this book, because I saw she was not thinking clearly about the cost she personally would assume. She and her husband both work and commute more than two hours each day. I pointed out that her mother would need in-home care at least 12 hours each day. At an average of $20 per hour, that's about $1,200 per week that this adult child would have to fund for her mother—a big nut by any standard. Another issue is that a sudden and rapid decline in independence and health often requires around-the-clock care.

Both as a personal preference and as a result of the high cost of elder-care facilities, many people want to "age in place" at their own home or in an adult child's home. (After a two-year stint in a lovely, upscale assisted living facility, my father secretly moved out and found an apartment "away from all the old people.") When the elderly have care needs, most (79 percent) can rely on family, at least initially.[19] Whether this is possible and for how long really depends on the situation: the type of illness and the ability to meet the elderly person's needs in a private home rather than a fully equipped institutional setting. For example, my father-in-law's downward spiral of health issues dictated the need for a facility despite his original intentions. When he broke his hip, staying home quickly became impractical. It would have taken the help of two around-the-clock caregivers to get his solid 230-pound frame out of bed.

Those who have long-term care insurance can defray the cost of nonfamily help when they are aged and infirm. As mentioned earlier, policies are generally very expensive, and they are offered by few providers. You will now find these policies more commonly offered as riders to existing life insurance policies. According to the American Association for Long-Term Care Insurance website (aaltci.org), the cost of these policies "depends." The factors that affect price are how much protection you buy, your age, your health, and which insurance company is the provider. As a quick example, a couple who buy a shared policy at age 55 will pay an average of $2,350 per year to each have the $150 per day maximum daily benefit. Premiums are much higher if you buy coverage in your late 60s or 70s, assuming you're not turned down.

You have to speak to various providers about your personal circumstances, assess what supplementary coverage you can afford, and do all the math—but my point is that at any price long-term care insurance will likely defray the cost of, but not totally pay for, your last phase of living needs.

There's No Magic Retirement Savings
Number: Just Save More (and More)

All the costs of healthcare and daily eldercare make increased longevity a double-edged sword. Of course, we all want to enjoy being healthy and active for as long as possible, but there are an increasing number of years we have to fund. "Catastrophic longevity" is the risk that people will live longer and need more money than they ever imagined.

Laura Carstensen, head of the Stanford Center on Longevity, says, "Most people can't save enough in 40 years of working to support themselves for 30 or more years of not working. Nor can society provide enough in pensions to support nonworking people that long. I'd like to see us move in a different direction toward a longer, more flexible working life."[20]

With a ripe old age of 100 a very realistic possibility, how much money you actually need to have saved for retirement is a matter of great debate, one that requires some research to find your own comfortable target based on your expected retirement age, life expectancy, likely Social Security benefits, inflation, and your healthcare needs. Great internet resources abound, including the *Forbes* article "The 25 Best Retirement Websites."[21]

There are many different retirement savings recommendations from reliable sources, but most experts agree you should save 10 to 20 percent of your income each year—and have a total savings of *at least* eight times your ending salary as of retirement. (I've seen recommendations as high as 11 times your salary.) Using the more conservative multiple of eight, if you and/or your partner end your working years with a total household income of $100,000, for example, you need a minimum of $800,000 in savings to cover retirement needs.

A target in the high six figures is very far away for most Americans. Even those who manage to save $1 million aren't guaranteed that the money will last if their retirement is 30 years or more. How long your retirement savings lasts depends largely on where you live: $1 million lasts for 26 years in Mississippi, for example, and 11 years in Hawaii.[22]

How much you need to save also depends on many factors, such as whether you've paid off your mortgage, the value of a home you might sell to downsize, an inheritance that might be more or less than you expect, and the status of your health. Some people who anticipate big expenses in retirement—either pleasant or unpleasant—may need to save even more.

All these numbers presume *normal* expenses throughout retirement—not the unexpected challenges discussed in chapter 2. With so many variables, it's hard to pinpoint exactly how much you should save, and it's a good idea to enlist the help of a financial planner. With that in mind, precise numbers are not necessary to assume you probably need to be saving more. There is not a headline that proclaims that the majority of Americans have adequate retirement savings. The US retirement savings deficit is between $6.8 and $14 trillion,[23] which includes many people who, on the surface, don't look like they will ever run out of money.

The savings deficit has a lot to do with the fact that the most well-intentioned savers often take costly steps backward. Those who do save—at any pace—don't always leave their savings accounts untouched. The early tap of 401(k) plans has replaced home equity loans as the "American piggy bank." Especially during the Great Recession, the lack of emergency savings forced millions of Americans who found themselves out of work, on the verge of losing their homes, or facing other financial emergencies to raid their retirement accounts. These accounts can't withstand the hits: the average 401(k) savings account at a high of almost $98,000 (and, by the way, a similar average of $100,000 in the other popular savings retirement vehicle, IRAs)[24]—is not a huge reserve. Most people do need to keep their retirement accounts intact and growing: though the wealthiest (top 1 percent) of Americans have $1 million or more stashed away in 401(k)s, even those in the top 90 percent have only $274,000 saved, and the average 80th percentile family had $116,000 saved in 2013.[25]

Many parents who have not saved enough for their children's college tuition also dip into retirement savings, thinking they have plenty of time to make up for early withdrawals over time. Though college tuition is a predictable expense, at a private institution it can go well beyond $175,000[26] for four years of room and board—*per child*—and just 39 percent of American families are saving in advance.[27] This ever-increasing astronomical expense (rising an average of 3.3 percent per year at all institutions)[28] is yet another incentive for women to always contribute to savings via flexible, lifetime work.

Don't Bank on Social Security or an Inheritance from Mom and Dad

As mentioned earlier, full Social Security benefits will not be paid out forever. That means that anyone in their 40s or younger can expect reduced benefits—or none at all. The average retiree benefit in 2018 is $1,404 per month[29] (significantly less than the most generous minimum wage monthly paycheck of $2,000).[30] Even if you're lucky to receive full Social Security benefits in retirement, it will likely be enough money to pay only a portion of your monthly bills.

If Social Security and all your savings are insufficient, you can't necessarily bank on Mom and Dad. In my conversations with women who as a couple or individually do not have enough money saved for retirement, an inheritance from affluent elderly parents is still a perceived safety net. Surely if there is enormous family wealth, then adult children could inherit a white horse to save their retirement day. But elderly parents are living longer and are often forced to spend money they might otherwise have left to their adult children. And when retirement savings are low, elderly parents often find themselves generating cash through reverse mortgages, which also makes it less likely that the sale of their homes will be the cash their adult children need. Sandra Timmermann, the former director of the MetLife Mature Market Institute and a recognized expert on aging, says that when it comes to inheritance transfers, "Expectation is greater than reality."

Is Retirement Out of Reach? Work Steadily (and Longer)

Knowing that they need to fund long retirements, 53 percent of women plan to continue working past age 65 or not retire at all.[31] Forty-five percent of workers planning to delay retirement say, for example, they are "not too confident" or "not at all confident" they can fully retire with a comfortable lifestyle, and only 19 percent have a backup plan if they are unable to work because of a job loss, health issues, or family obligations. Eighty-two percent say they lack faith in Social Security, and 45 percent are concerned about healthcare costs.[32] All these figures are reflective of women who are continuing to work; women who work intermittently with nonearning caregiving breaks are at a significantly higher financial disadvantage.

> 66 *My ideal is to always work in a full-time position*
> *where I can be committed to growing my career, but*
> *also have the flexibility to care for my family."*
> —Woman in her 30s, New York, bachelor's degree

If the traditional work-free retirement is far off in your future, you're not alone. Those over the age of 55 are expected to be the fastest-growing workforce demographic by 2024, with the population of older working women growing at a slightly higher rate than men.[33] Many employers are accommodating these older workers with flexible schedules, higher 401(k) matches that accelerate savings, and financial wellness programs to help employees mitigate savings shortfalls.

Many people who work during traditional retirement years do so for purpose and personal fulfillment, but also, largely, they work for financial reasons. Most Americans say they *should* be saving 25 percent of their income to catch up on retirement savings, but they are actually saving only 6 percent. Fifty-two percent of households risk not being able to maintain their standard of living in retirement if earners retire at age 65.[34] With an average price tag of $700,000, retirement has been called "the purchase of a lifetime." Few feel ready to make that purchase: only 10 percent say they are prepared for a retirement lasting 30 years. Shorter projected retirement periods do not engender much more financial confidence; only 16 percent say they could fund a 20-year retirement, and 27 percent feel comfortable about funding a 10-year period.[35] With so many financial concerns about retirement, it's prudent to work consistently to avoid frantic catch-up work in your later years. Women who extend a workforce hiatus for child or aging parent caregiving also can't assume they'll have the energy or health to work well past age 65.

Age Gracefully on Your Own Dime

When you're in your late 70s and 80s, you might not ski down the mountain with the same fierce abandon or travel with great ease around the world, but an older age doesn't mean your interests and general life preferences disappear. If you enjoy dining at restaurants and going to museums, there will be canes, wheelchairs, or people willing to wait for you as you walk independently at a slower pace. You'll still have hobbies and collections to fund, gifts you want to give to grandchildren, and donations you want to make to your favorite charities. You'll want to maintain your lifestyle—and not be a burden to your children in the process—until the day you die. To do anything else would be taking the life out of your life and giving up the experiences you most enjoy.

❝ *I left a full-time corporate career to spend more time with my children, but since then I've always freelanced. This decision has served me well financially, and it's work I can do at any age—until I decide I have the funds to retire."*

—Woman in her 40s, New Jersey, master's degree from Columbia University

A very small percentage of people retire with no financial worries, and when retirement funds are insufficient, the obvious solution is to turn to adult children, who may or may not have the means to provide support. Eric Kingson and Nancy Altman, codirectors of Social Security Works (a social justice nonprofit focused on safeguarding the economic security of those dependent on Social Security), predict a new phenomenon that plays off the term "boomerang kids" (the adult children in their 20s and 30s who return to live in their parents' homes). They say, "Get ready for boomerang parents, formerly independent middle-aged people who—10, 15, 20 years hence—will have no choice but to move into their adult children's homes because they cannot afford their own."[36] The catch is that if you're forced to rely on the help of adult children, you put them at risk of their own retirement savings shortfalls.

Realize You Can't Save What You Don't Earn

Once you stare at the big number you're supposed to save, it becomes clear that unless there is major independent wealth or savings from sustained sky-high earnings, a woman's consistent, lifelong income is a vital component in her own and her family's comfortable retirement and long-term financial security. The epidemic of small retirement nest eggs is due in no small part to the fact that more than half of retirees leave the workforce—and diminish their retirement saving ability—earlier than planned, or earlier than necessary. The reasons for forced early departure are a range of life's unexpected challenges, including health problems or disability (37 percent) and job loss (27 percent).[37] Factor in the many women who leave the workforce to care for children and/or aging parents, and it's clear how lost earnings and savings jeopardize your financial strength and take the shine off what could actually be truly golden retirement years.

Chapter 4

Prioritize Ongoing Professional Work Over Paycheck Size (Even Small Savings Grow Substantially Over Time)

A s A CAREER COACH AND speaker, I've met hundreds of stay-at-home mothers who spend months—and often years—weighing the pros and cons of returning to work. I've also met hundreds of professional women who contemplate a departure or actually leave the workforce for family reasons. Oftentimes, both sets of women think that only a hefty full-time salary makes a difference in long-term financial security, and they never pursue family-friendly alternatives that may have lower, but still significant compensation. It's hard to argue against the fact that some income is better than zero income: even in affluent communities, finances are tight in many one-income households. The monthly bills are paid on time, but there's not a lot of room for nonessential extras. There's also eventual concern about how to afford multiple college tuitions—let alone a long and expensive retirement.

Among those who do leave the workforce, most women I've coached have a general intention to return to the workforce someday. But unless there is a pressing financial reason to return immediately because of a negative life circumstance, most women feel they have plenty of time to reinstate their professional selves. Most want to wait until their youngest children are at least in middle school, and plenty don't make a move until every child is out of the house.

Any length of time completely out of the workforce does not make long-term financial sense. Each year that goes by is a year of lost income, savings, and investment potential; professional experience; skill development; and earning power. More to the point, every year out of the workforce makes a woman more vulnerable to life's uncertainties and less well-positioned to support herself and her family. The Center for American Progress has created a calculator to precisely determine the cost of a hiatus, and they offer an unsettling data point: *a woman who leaves the workforce loses up to four times her salary per year.*[1]

Add Up Your Earning Years: Don't Miss Out on Your Own Social Security

It's obvious that if you don't work you don't get a paycheck that can be invested and saved. But the ability to generate income to cover all of life's expenses straight through your retirement years does not only relate to a salary from an employer. Women in middle- to upper-income households often underestimate the lifetime value of Social Security benefits— which, for a couple, can easily reach $1 million.[2] (Though the agency's decline jeopardizes full benefits for women under the age of 40, for all others Social Security is still an important component of retirement income. Your monthly Social Security check will probably not pay all your monthly bills, but over a 30-year retirement period, the benefit adds up to quite a lot of supplemental income.)

It's not widely known that women at any age who leave the workforce to care for children or aging parents may never see any of their own Social Security benefits at all.

Women (and men) need *a minimum of 10 contributing years*[3] to earn enough credits for their own Social Security eligibility. They also need as many strong earning years as possible, since Social Security calculates benefits on the average of their 35 best earning years. Many low- and zero-earning years (from, for example, teenage summer jobs and employment gaps) yield lower benefit payouts. For this reason, it's wise to replace these lower-earning years prior to retirement.

> 66 *My early career positions offered little opportunity for advancement, and my husband's job had much more potential—so I worked professionally for only four years."*
> —Women in her 40s, New Jersey, master's degree

It may seem unlikely that the majority of well-educated women have not worked in a professional capacity for at least 10 years. It is, however, surprisingly true. I learned this eye-opening fact when I held a big event for 150 returning professionals who earned MBA degrees from the most prestigious business schools. Most of these women worked for a couple of years out of college, went to business school, and then worked only for another two or three years after they earned their graduate degrees. While this anecdotal data represents the work activity for just one demographic slice, there are certainly women who work in their early 20s, get married in their mid-20s, and leave the workforce when they start to have children in their late 20s. Within that time span, there are not 10 earning years.

Avoid the Professional Cost of a Work Hiatus

When women completely leave the workforce for more than two years, there is a professional cost: it becomes increasingly difficult for them to pick up where they left off. If they make a consistent effort to stay current—through occasional freelance work, for example—they have a better chance of recapturing their titles and salaries from the outset or soon after they return. This, however, is not the typical scenario: women on hiatus usually become immersed in raising children and running households, and they frequently fill any extra time in the role of mega-volunteer.

Though many resumé-worthy business skills are used for high-level volunteer work (such as serving on nonprofit boards or running the PTA), in the eyes of employers, the time out is still considered a hiatus from *professional, paid* work. This was very clear when I worked with a big investment bank that wanted to recruit returning professional women. The CEO was interested in starting a job-sharing program so that the seemingly endless investment banking business day could be covered by two women, not one.

Wow, did this sound great to the hundreds of ex-Wall Streeters in the women's network I cofounded. We created job-share pairs and hope was in the air…until it wasn't. The CEO's vision did not extend down the line. As we approached various departments about hiring our job-share teams, there was great resistance. Managing directors who had clocked 70- and 80-hour workweeks nonstop just couldn't fathom why women with MBAs had traded deal-making for child-rearing.

One male managing director who was openly critical of women "throwing their educations away by leaving the workforce" said that he thought long absences were ludicrous. To illustrate, he told the story of a male colleague who had decided to take only a very short sabbatical. Once this man left, he worried he had made the wrong decision. He called the managing director repeatedly in the three months he was out, always concerned that he was becoming "stale." It's no wonder this particular managing director and others like him had a cynical view of women who had been out of the workforce for a decade or more.

These attitudes are not unusual in many big corporate environments. To be fair, some of the big financial institutions, including Goldman Sachs, J.P. Morgan Chase, and Morgan Stanley, have since launched "returnship" programs and brought a limited number of women back to significant full-time positions that are similar to those they once chose to leave behind. However, this is the exception and not the rule. Women relinquish professional traction in *any* industry when they opt to spend years focused primarily on their motherhood or other caregiving roles.

Consider Total Compensation (Giving Up
Employee Benefits Costs You Even More)

Staying in the workforce or returning to work has the obvious benefit of a paycheck—and the often less obvious benefit of qualifying for full Social Security benefits. Too often women overlook the value of other employment benefits that can be worth thousands of dollars each year. Topping this list—most often for full-time workers—is a retirement account, like a 401(k), that allows you to invest pretax earnings. It's even more valuable if your employer matches what you contribute. A typical plan offers a match of 50 cents per dollar for up to 6 percent of your salary. This is essentially forced savings and free money that continues to grow and grow over time.

❝❝ *My ideal job has been a flexible full-time job so I can be available to my children and get health benefits since my entrepreneur husband doesn't have them.*"

—Woman in her 50s, Pennsylvania, master's degree

Also very valuable is health insurance, which for the time being is a required benefit under the Affordable Care Act if you clock at least 30 hours a week for employers with 50 or more employees.[4] Employers determine how much they pay toward the premiums, and out-of-pocket costs for employees vary widely. But receiving any money toward the premium is a big benefit, and insurance can also extend to life and disability coverage to increase your financial security even more. Even if your spouse receives health insurance from an employer, your employer may offer something additional or more generous, such as vision or dental care.

Then there are flexible spending accounts, which can stretch the money you have to shell out for work-related expenses or healthcare needs outside of traditional insurance coverage. Many employers offer workers the chance to direct pretax earnings into these accounts, which can be used to pay for commuting or healthcare expenses not covered by the company's plan.

Some employers who no longer hold fast to rigid work structures, like the accounting firm PricewaterhouseCoopers (PwC), offer an unlimited number of paid sick days. This gives employees the flexibility to sleep off their own cold, care for a sick child, and tend to other responsibilities, like caregiving for older parents.[5]

The list of possible employee benefits goes on and, in some cases, is trending to the amazing. Starbucks helps both full-time and part-time employees to become parents by covering up to $20,000 of in vitro fertilization (IVF) treatments.[6] The management consulting firm Accenture gives new mothers a pass on their industry's usual extensive travel, encouraging them to work locally for one year instead.[7] Goldman Sachs, Genentech, The Boston Consulting Group, St. Jude Children's Research Hospital, and REI are a few companies offering fully paid sabbaticals.[8] Companies like Netflix and GE offer *unlimited* paid vacation time.[9] Fairygodboss.com lists 80 companies that offer generous maternity leave (52 weeks at Netflix; 26 weeks at Adobe Systems and Etsy; and 24 weeks at eBay and Motorola, for example).[10] Generous parental benefits also include paid leave *during* a pregnancy, reduced schedules to ease back to work after maternity leaves, adoption benefits, errand services, lactation consultants, and "baby bucks" for new parents. Fifth Third Bancorp even has concierge services to plan your baby shower.[11] Genentech pampers sleep-deprived new parents and all other employees with on-site spa services.[12] Add in the very valuable but comparatively mundane performance bonuses, tuition reimbursement, full payment of healthcare premiums, health club discounts, financial-planning advisers, free or subsidized lunches, stock purchase plans, and more, and the value of working multiplies on and on.

Look Before You Leap or Jump Back In!
(It's Hard to Make Up for Lost Time)

Women who have already made the decision to leave the workforce and now want to return always ask me what they should expect to earn after many years at home and as a volunteer. There are no hard-and-fast benchmarks about what you should or will earn as a returning professional. Companies do not and legally cannot discriminate against returning professionals per se, but they often assume women on hiatus have not kept abreast of industry trends and practices and may need time to get back up to speed.

If your circumstances are different, it's up to you to challenge an employer's assumption. If you're a former marketing manager who is current with marketing trends, who has stayed involved with professional marketing associations, and who has worked on an occasional freelance marketing project, then there's a good chance you haven't skipped a beat and you meet all the requirements for a management-level position today. If you're hired, you can expect to be paid the full salary, regardless of the fact that you've spent time out of the workforce.

On the other hand, if you've been out of the workforce for 10 years and during that time the word *marketing* has barely passed your lips, it's a different story. You're probably not current and do not meet the job requirements. In that case you should expect to *initially* take a role a notch or two down and earn less as well. You have to be honest with yourself about how current you are in your industry; whether you now really, truly meet all the requirements of a higher-level job; and the amount of money you're likely to earn at the point you return.

When it comes to the earnings hierarchy, the business world hasn't changed: the highest compensation rewards usually come to those in sell-your-soul, more-than-full-time jobs. The flexwork that most returning professionals want—often part-time hours—generally does not at the outset generate high compensation. Women who do have flexwork coupled with high compensation are most often current professionals who have transitioned from a high-paid, full-time job to a correspondingly high-paid, part-time job, or they are independent consultants or freelancers who have current work experience and expertise that commands a high hourly rate.

> **❝** *I value flexibility and convenience over the size of my paycheck."*
> —Woman in her 40s, Vermont, master's degree

Many of the women I placed as a recruiter into coveted "permanent" part-time jobs pursued administrative or midlevel positions with 20-hour workweeks and salaries that frequently ranged from $25,000 to $45,000. ("Permanent" is in quotes because you'll be on the books as a permanent employee, but permanence is more and more fleeting in today's workforce.) Most often, the women willingly chose to scale back from previous higher-level and higher-paid careers.

Carol Fishman Cohen, founder of iRelaunch, a company widely recognized for helping women restart careers, agrees that women may intentionally return a level down because their prior role required spontaneous travel or "always available" accountability. These women may want a less stressful job that allows more room for integrating work and life, or they simply may want to try something entirely new, which most often requires a more junior starting role.[13] Though most of the returning professionals in my coaching practice continue to ask for advice on finding part-time work, Cohen says that within the group of about 6,000 women who have attended her company's 21 return-to-work conferences, 70 percent say they would consider returning to full-time work. In my experience, *consider* is the operative word; many women change their minds as they reacquaint themselves with the logistical implications of more-than-50-hour workweeks plus family.

❝ *After a long work hiatus, my ideal job is a part-time position that offers fulfillment and good compensation within predictable hours.*❞
—Woman in her 30s, Michigan, master's degree

Value a Professional Job with a Paycheck of Any Size

Women frequently tell me that it doesn't really matter if they leave the workforce for a few years "because I'm not earning a big salary." Similarly, many women stay out of the workforce because they don't think the salary they could generate is enough to warrant time away from home. In both cases, it's shortsighted to think only a certain salary number makes it "worth it" to work.

I see the origin of this thinking. When women do the math—adding up expenses like commuting, childcare, and maybe extra household help—the amount they're left with can appear to be an insignificant drop in the bucket for college, retirement, or other big expenses. I've seen many women wrestle with decisions about continuing to or returning to work, but often higher-earning partners step in with the closing argument: "Once your smaller salary is taxed in my bigger tax bracket, it just doesn't make sense for you to leave the house."

The fact is, though, that it indeed makes long-term sense for women to consider a professional salary of any size: to invest valuable time into their future earning power, build their resumés, expand their portfolio of marketable skills, and earn some amount of money that can be invested and saved. Women who think they will not earn enough money to return to the workforce—or current professionals who have "all or nothing" attitudes about high compensation—aren't thinking broadly about saving and investing. Financial advisers repeatedly tell me that many well-educated women don't consider how the basic concept known as the power of compounding increases even small savings over time.

Here's a quick explanation of the power of compounding, which is how you get any amount of money to grow and grow.

The Power of Compounding

The power—or magic—of compounding is the snowball effect of earnings continually generating even more earnings. You receive interest not only on your original investments, but also on any interest dividends and corporate gains that accumulate, so your money grows faster and faster as years go by. This is a particularly powerful phenomenon in 401(k) and IRA retirement accounts, where principal is allowed to grow for years tax-deferred or even tax-free.[14]

Obviously, the more you save, the more your nest egg grows over time. Even saving a small amount can make a big impact on your ability to fund life's unexpected challenges and a long retirement. Let's look at an example.

Nancy returns to work at age 45. She doesn't want a big corporate job, so she takes a part-time (20 hour per week), midlevel job during school hours at a small local firm. She earns $25 per hour, or $26,000 per year, and her husband's earnings put them in the 43 percent state and federal tax bracket (the highest federal tax bracket of 37 percent plus a 6 percent state tax rate, which is about midrange in most states). Since Nancy's earnings are not needed for current household expenses, she can save all the money she clears after taxes. To keep things simple, let's say she works for 20 years and her compensation stays the same. If she socks away her take-home pay, what will she have saved by age 65?

To get the answer, I consulted Galia Gichon of Down to Earth Finance, a financial advisory firm that counsels women.[15] If Nancy clears $14,950 after taxes per year, and she invests that full amount in, say, a Moderate Balanced Allocation Mutual Fund with a conservative return of 5 percent for 20 years, she'll have savings of $519,000 at age 65. That's more than half a million dollars in savings from a small, containable, moderate-stress job during school hours and close to home.

In terms of retirement income, Gichon went one step further to run some numbers for Nancy. The $519,000 nest egg gives Nancy about $40,000 a year for retirement expenses (assuming a conservative 5 percent annual interest rate and savings compounded from age 65 to 92). For most retirees, an extra $40,000 per year will be put to good use. One example would be unreimbursed medical expenses. The $404,253 out-of-pocket healthcare expense estimated for a couple who retired in 2017 (mentioned in chapter 3) could be more than covered by the savings from Nancy's back-to-work earnings.

The examples so far have focused on what women can *gain* by returning to or staying in the workforce via flexwork. I asked Gichon for an example of the potential savings women *forfeit* when they leave the workforce at a midcareer point.

In this example, Joan is a 35-year-old woman on the career fast track who has a full-time income of $90,000 per year. She's considering a work hiatus to spend more time with her young child. Her husband is a higher earner (and they are in the same 43 percent tax bracket as in Nancy's example), and she feels that, at least for a couple of years, her family could live comfortably on one income. Joan lives and works in a city, so she doesn't have big commuting expenses. Her big expense is full-time day-care for a young child, which is $1,500 per month. So, after paying taxes and childcare, Joan clears $2,813 a month.

If Joan stays in the workforce she can save half her take-home pay—or $1,406 per month. That's a total of about $16,875 per year in savings. If she actually stays out of the workforce for the average 12 years, she gives up a total of $282,032 in compounded savings (again assuming a 5 percent interest rate) that could have been generated in that period. Over 30 years (from age 35 to 65) Joan's savings could have kept growing—giving her a final total of $1.3 million in savings. So, if Joan gives up her job, she loses a huge amount of money—and, most of all, she loses a great deal of earning power that could be difficult to recoup when she wants to return.

The ability to keep skills current and earning power growing, the long-term financial security from even small compounded saving and investing, eligibility for full Social Security benefits, an expanding menu of employee benefit perks, and personal fulfillment are all good arguments to keep your status "employed".

Chapter 5

Follow Your Own Path to Financial Security (It's Okay to Lean In-Between)

To some degree, women working professionally and women at home caring for family believe the grass is greener on the other side. There will always be pros and cons to every work and life choice, but it's safe to say that life can be less stressful and more satisfying when it is not at one of the extremes. There's an acceptable middle ground between the 60-hour workweek that gives you only a glimpse of your children and full-time caregiving that involves no paycheck at all.

> 66 *I've been focused on advancing my career since I graduated from college. If I get to the top, fine. I'm okay being an essential leader in my organization. Being in the C-suite isn't necessarily the goal."*
> —Woman in her 40s, Ohio, bachelor's degree

Too many women have subscribed to the all-or-nothing approach to work and life. Either you're "leaning in" to the big career, chasing the highest titles and compensation, or you're home, "leaning out." The next section of this book shows that decisions about working don't need to be so black-and-white; women need to give themselves and others permission to move to that middle ground. Jumping off or being wary of returning to the traditional corporate ladder is not a sign of weakness or defeat. Leaning in only to the degree that actually fits your life can bring you the most solid and sustainable professional success of all.

For mothers, perhaps the greatest reason to find this middle ground is to be a positive role model for daughters—and sons. When mothers choose to stay home, their children can have gender views that belong in 1952. I often tell the story of a day I was at my daughter's swim meet, where both boys and girls were competing. It was an informal practice meet, so the children were just getting the hang of the procedures. In each heat, the girls were slated to swim before the boys. One 6-year-old boy was sitting near me, watching the girls dive in. He was undone that the boys were not the first swimmers.

"Hey, why aren't the boys first?" he demanded of the coach.

> ❝ *My ideal is a full-time position that allows me to juggle both family and work commitments while setting a positive, strong example for my daughter.*"
> —Woman in her 30s, Massachusetts, MBA degree

The young female coach, obviously thinking he was just being playful, gave a hurried, off-the-cuff answer, "Oh, I don't know...ladies before gentlemen."

The young boy clearly did not like that answer. I could see him intently working on a powerful retort. Finally, he blurted, "But men go to work!"

This view that important "work" is a man's job persists among young women, too. Halfway through one of my presentations on how to return to the workforce, a woman in the audience added both a bit of humor and a more somber reflection to the lively discussion.

At the time, I was speaking about the controversial "lean in or lean out" debate and advising that, first and foremost, women should lean in the direction of financial security. The woman in the audience agreed, but then she took the discussion in a different direction. She told the story of her 7-year-old daughter, who had recently said, "You know, Mommy, when I grow up I want to be just like you. I'm going to find a nice guy to marry—one who makes a lot of money—so I don't have to do anything." This story elicited howls of laughter, especially when the woman ended with, "Apparently, I'm not a mother, I'm a hooker." But then all the women in the room realized the story is not so funny, and the discussion moved to the subject of role models and how children view the "work" you choose to do each day.

Even though running a household is no cakewalk, children of stay-at-home moms downplay the job. A woman at a school coffee told a group of mothers that her teenage daughter begged her to do some errands, with the rationale that her stay-at-home mother has "all her days free." Just as kids don't consider Dad's Saturday grass cutting his real "work," they don't think Mom is really "working" when she is cooking meals.

There's a value to showing sons and daughters that women can both nurture and provide financial support for the family. One working mother's 9-year old son said he wanted to be a *businesswoman* because business<u>women</u> make the money. This young boy knows his father goes to work and earns money, too, but his mother has spent a lot of time talking about the value of *her* work to the family, and a strong impression has clearly been made.

❝ *My ideal is a flexible job that shows my kids I have an equal partnership with my spouse and equal ability to be a professional."*
—Woman in her 40s, Maine, master's degree

The positive role model influence is also very evident in an essay one of my former interns wrote about her own experience having a working mother. She wrote, "Girls look up to their mothers as role models for what they'd like to be when they're older and have families. For me it will not be an issue of whether I can work and be a good mom. I saw my mom doing more than one thing well. I know my kids will not need me to be home all the time to succeed in life. I look up to women who work and successfully run their families."

Indeed, the ability to generate an income to pay for daily expenses and fund all of your financial emergencies is an essential and admirable life skill that should be demonstrated and taught by both mothers and fathers. Young women who see their mothers do *only* housework do not have a role model when later in life they question whether they have what it takes to assume professional roles and gain financial independence. Being a role model for professional work does not necessarily mean you need to pursue big corporate jobs: even a small part-time job that requires only a few hours a week can be fodder for pragmatic conversations about balancing work and life—a skill as valuable as instilling kindness, integrity, honesty, and all the other character traits parents want their children to adopt.

As flexibility fuels the new feminism, the smartest and most creative women will be role models who carve out flexwork that accommodates caregiving. They'll raise their children, but they'll also be active participants in building financial security for their core family, and they will be prepared for life's financial surprises. They'll capitalize on their educations, and they will always continue to grow intellectually and professionally. Most important, they'll make money consistently and learn how to save and invest that money wisely over time.

The new feminists will find work that fits every aspect of their lives.

To get to this new feminism, we're going to need a lot of help from the everyday sisterhood. Not the power sisterhood that thinks the only way forward is up and has a tendency to pass judgment on women who aren't striving to shatter the glass ceiling, run corporations, or run the country. The new sisterhood will be everyday women who want to work for professional fulfillment, for financial security, and to make a difference, but who also want enough quality time to care for themselves and their families.

In this new sisterhood, women will be more transparent about the flexibility they've wrangled from employers. They will share more tips and strategies for finding sustainable flexwork, and they will be role models who smash stereotypes about who is ambitious and who is not.

As you figure out your own work and life path, start the conversation. Tell lots of women about your own hopes, dreams, and fears—and ask them to share theirs as well. You'll find that few women have mastered the perfect work and life blend, but with a broader definition of ambition and the wider world of flexwork, many are getting very close. My coaching clients speak to me freely about the work and life choices they've made, but on a larger and more public scale, they're less apt to touch the highly charged issues of financial security or work versus family. It's largely a fear of being judged, but we can help each other get to the middle ground that is often the most palatable and life-friendly choice for all.

A New Definition of an "Ambitious" Woman

An ambitious woman is *any* woman who finds a flexible way to blend work and family, always building her own and her family's long-term financial security—and insuring against life's "you never knows."

In the process of speaking to more and more women about today's many work and life possibilities, you're likely to learn quite a lot from others' regrets, triumphs, reinventions, and many instructive stops and starts. To get this research started, the next section of this chapter offers great collective wisdom; in personal interviews more than 40 everyday women shared with me "What I'm Glad I Did" or "What I Wish I Had Done." (You'll see one from me attributed to K.S. on page 90.) There's no one solution, and there are many different viewpoints about the path to professional fulfillment and financial security, but the universal message is that when it comes to blending work and family, *it can be done and it's never too late.*

Draw on the Wisdom of the Everyday Sisterhood

Don't Make Your College Degree a Life Sentence

"Although I began my career as an attorney, I'm glad I didn't make myself stay in that box. I dabbled in many areas—taking on part-time roles in TV, publishing, real estate, retail sales, substitute teaching, and more. When I was blindsided by divorce, and alimony didn't cover all my expenses, I could build on many different experiences to find flexwork and support my family.

"Ironically, I've now come full circle after many reinventions to practice law again. Had I told myself I could only be an attorney, I never would have had so many interesting experiences, which will now give me different perspectives and insights for my entrepreneurial practice."

—B.S., age 56

Avoid the Perfection Trap

"I wish I had not brought my female perfection guilt to the workplace. In retrospect, I was so diligent about being there early and staying late—while many of my male counterparts took more vacation, left at 5:30 p.m., didn't answer emails at night and on the weekends. They didn't have the guilt and insecurity I did about being available and present all the time, and they better protected their personal lives without negative repercussions. Women need to be confident about the value we bring to the workplace, and not feel obligated to let our employers own our time."

—L.S., age 52

Do Personal Work Before Professional Work

"I'm glad I did 'personal work' before I returned to professional work. Discover, understand, develop, and embrace unique gifts and talents that are central themes in your life and work story. All that internal work helps you find your authentic self, true passions, and ability to support yourself and your family. It's also what will bring you happiness because you'll know you've built a solid foundation and found the right place.

"It's also important to believe there are always new opportunities at any age. At age 62, for the first time in my life, I was fired from a job. I had been a top producer and never imagined it would happen. Six months later, after tenacious job searching, I landed a more senior-level job that offers tremendous personal and professional growth. In addition to my day-to-day role, I've found a way to help my employer create philanthropy programs, giving women the chance to follow their passions and change the world. I see many professional chapters for me in the years ahead."

—H.O., age 64

Beware the Vortex of the Mega-Volunteer

"I wish I had gotten off the volunteering treadmill earlier. Volunteering involved often massive and uncontrollable hours. I realized I needed/wanted to bring home a paycheck for all my time and effort—and a long professional hiatus made it difficult to regain my foothold in the workforce and return to challenging paid work."

—G.R., age 52

Volunteer Your Way Back to a Paid Job

"After more than 20 years at home, with a long resumé of volunteering at my children's schools and at three nonprofits, I started my first full-time job since I left work to have my first child.

"Getting to this full-time position was a multistage process. Despite a bout with cancer, major surgery, and post-surgical complications, I first returned to work through a part-time job in a new field. After this part-time job ended, I posted my resume on LinkedIn, thinking, 'No one will EVER look at this.' Then the hiring manager at one of the nonprofits where I had volunteered invited me to run a four-month project, saying,

'I saw your profile on LinkedIn, and you're the perfect candidate!' Then that four-month project turned into the full-time job I have now— including enormous flexibility.

"This job at a small nonprofit has been challenging: the organization has had financial difficulties, and I wasn't able to negotiate a competitive salary. But I saw the opportunity to add significant current professional work to my resumé, and I know if my salary doesn't improve, I have an excellent track record I can capitalize on elsewhere.

"I'm glad my view of the time I spent volunteering has evolved. I focus less on the fact it was 'volunteering' and more on the actual work and my accomplishments. My change of attitude helped me get into the paid working world again. I know the advice to stay-at-home moms is to build on your volunteer experience. I've heard if you volunteer in the right place at the right time, you'll be the first in line for a paid job opening. I'm still amazed it worked for me."

—L.Z., age 61

Keep Your Hand in the Game; Win Financial Security for Life

"I'm glad that even during years my family lived abroad, I always found ways to keep my hand in the game. I've been a writer, researcher, PR specialist, and photographer, sometimes for four hours and other times for 40 hours a week. If I could have predicted my divorce, I would have returned to consistent full-time work much earlier, but the transition was easier because I never fully left the workforce.

"I'm glad I was 'selfish' about investing time in one personal passion while my children were young. Having the proverbial '10,000 hours' in a specific field leads to surprising opportunities. My photography paved the transition from stay-at-home mother, to part-time and then full-time work.

"I'm glad I was always willing to take a chance, to see where something might lead, to put experience before prestige, to make a little less money than I hoped—and to see that work is not only a traditional, black-and-white, full-time job. This flexibility has always given me the ability to earn a paycheck—in the years when it was a nice extra and in the years when it paid the rent.

"And I'm glad I didn't think my return to work required a long *Eat Pray Love* analysis and transformation. You can find your career and life paths through the actual doing, not just thinking. Don't delay the process: keep jumping in. And know when to jump out. It's like a sailing race: knowing when to change tacks is just as important as rounding the mark. You don't have to make a lifelong commitment—but you do have to keep moving toward the next reasonable step."

—E.L., age 54

Stay at It ... Despite All Life Changes that Come Your Way

"I'm glad I kept working, even though my husband's job moved us three different times, which was very disruptive to my career. It was challenging to explain to employers why my marketing career was not linear and why I took two breaks because of kids and the various moves.

"Despite that, I concentrated on staying in the workforce. I worked at two startups, wrote a blog, and was lucky to get into an amazing return-to-work program in a global innovation position. Be kind to yourself and realize how much you have to offer. Focus on what's ahead and keep learning. Brush up on skills you'll need in the workplace, like PowerPoint, Excel, and social media so you hit the ground running. It has been incredible returning to the workplace at this time in my life, and I probably appreciate it more now than I did in my 20s and 30s."

—E.D., age 56

Work in Different Ways at Different Times of Your Life

"I'm glad I listened to my mother's sage advice: 'You can have it all, just not all at the same time.' This advice from a woman who had been, at different times, a professional and a volunteer helped me reconcile the difference between the financial success I had early in my career versus the work I pursued as a mother. I started out in a male-dominated, deal-oriented, elite finance firm that I relished. More recently I've pursued flexible, but also high-impact, opportunities I created for myself in the nonprofit world while raising a family and caring for aging parents.

"The cost of that career change in terms of earning power was substantial, but the earnings from my nonprofit job have still enabled me to share the burden of school tuitions with my husband. The family and community relationships that will enrich my life forever were worth the sacrifice of the finance job. If you're blessed with a long and healthy life, there's time for all of it. Now that my children are grown, I look forward to building upon my experiences and creating a capstone phase of my career that may build greater financial security and tie all my career experiences together."

—M.W., age 57

If You Take a Career Break, Do It Wisely

"I'm glad I built a good, solid career and met several professional goals, so I could step away from work for four years during my daughters' teen years. By then their school schedules, extracurricular activities, and teen emotional needs were more complicated than ever. It was great to drive my girls to various activities—time in the car was valuable talking and listening time.

"I planned ahead and was able to save enough money during my working years so that time off didn't mean we had to change our lifestyle. In addition, and important to me, I still had my own money to spend as I wished.

"I had every intention of returning to work, and I made a concerted effort to stay in touch with a strong network of professional contacts during my hiatus. When I left work, I was very specific—telling my network I'd be looking for a job in three to four years. I stayed abreast of work in my field over a monthly lunch with various contacts. Before I knew it, my youngest daughter had her college acceptance, and I was ready to go back to work. Within six months, I had a new job with the same title—though less responsibility/stature and a slightly smaller, but very acceptable salary. Having been back to work for a year now, I think I can start to look at positions where I could increase my responsibilities and salary. At this point in life, though, I'm not sure I want to! I'm glad I have a decent income, interesting work, and a better work-life blend.

"I obviously gave up several years of income, but now that I'm back to work we have increased our savings schedule to make up for time lost by maximizing contributions to our 401(k) plans, including taking advantage of the over-age-50 'catch-up' contribution limit."

—K.C., age 54

Become Financially Literate Early to Fund Life's Dreams and Disappointments

"I wish I had taken it upon myself in my teens and 20s to fully understand how to be financially literate. Foolishly, I listened to my parents, who told me I'd marry and be taken care of financially by a husband. When I married, I let my husband handle all the details of our home purchase, only to realize later he didn't fully understand or consider all the surrounding financial obligations, such as property taxes! While I figured out how to manage my expenses and stay within a budget, it wasn't until much later in life that I realized how valuable it is to really know all about personal finance for the present and future. Especially when life can be unpredictable or difficult, there's peace of mind and security knowing I have options.

"Now on the edge of a divorce, with two college tuitions to share and the challenge of living in one of the most expensive regions of the country, I know options come in the form of having money in the bank and investments that provide income to sustain me through life's dreams and disappointments. I'm optimistic, but I also know there are many yet unknown variables that could affect my financial situation. Had I been more financially savvy and less dependent on my husband earlier on, I think I'd be more prepared for the storm I'm in now."

—A.M., age 58

Bind Your Marriage Partnership with Work

"I wish I had continued to work in some way throughout my marriage. In the early years, when my ex-husband and I were both working, we had more of a partnership and we shared the responsibility for our finances. When I stopped making money, I left it to my husband to manage all the finances. Not only did this leave me clueless when we divorced, but also I discovered that my husband had mismanaged—and lost—most of our money and even stopped paying for life insurance.

"I never wanted a big, demanding career, but I now realize that if I had always worked in some flexible way, it might have saved the partnership within my marriage. I think women need to do some form of work to have a say and a voice—and keep a relationship balanced."

—K.J., age 59

Shed a Bright Light on Your Personal Finances

"I wish someone had taught me about money when I was growing up. This would have helped me develop a financial partnership in my marriage. Instead I fell into the 'fairytale complex'—not working and thinking my ex-husband would take care of me and our children forever. I should have had very conscious conversations with him about money and finances, but I lacked the courage and confidence to collaborate on a financial plan from the beginning of our marriage.

"Now, as a certified financial planner, I'm empowering other women through education and awareness so they stay on track financially. My work is flexible and fulfills my passion for helping people—especially women, who often need a nudge to develop an empowered relationship with their money."

—C.B., age 50

Save for a Rainy Day So You Can Take on Any Life Challenge

"I'm glad I never felt the pressure to keep up with my friends and buy the McMansion. I invested more in my relationship with my husband and children than in material goods. My biggest priority was to save for a rainy day—and this turned out to be a good strategy.

"Despite the unexpected life challenge of my career ending at a Fortune 500 company after 16 years of employment, I had saved for a rainy day. I was able to dance and sing in the rain. I was able to help my ailing mother, who was moving from my childhood home to a nursing home. Because I had been conservative, I had the financial stability to take on these challenges of job loss and a sick parent without any regrets."

—R.C., age 52

Rekindle an Early Professional Passion at Any Age or Life Stage

"When my daughter left for college, I viewed my newly empty nest as an opportunity to spread my wings. The communications degree I attained four decades ago had been useful for many years, but it had languished. I had always longed to sharpen my pencil again, but this time in creative writing. Building on local and online writing classes, I worked toward enrolling in an MFA program—eventually earning my master's degree in creative nonfiction two years after my daughter's graduation.

"As a working writer, my schedule is flexible and full. I'm teaching classes, writing a memoir, editing a literary journal, and attending writing conferences, book festivals, and residencies around the world. Meeting new friends at all ages and stages—from beginners to bestselling authors—is my favorite perk to starting over. At a time when many of my friends were choosing to retire, I'm glad I took a risk to revive a lifelong passion that I hope will keep me young and current as I grow older and wiser."

—R.Z., age 62

Let Life and Work Take You off the Highway of Established Routines

"I truly believe if you pursue something you're passionate about, you'll significantly increase your chances of having a successful career and fulfilling life. I also believe that as long as you are of sound mind and body, and you are comfortable embracing the beginner's mind, it's never too late to pursue newfound passions that will take you places you never imagined. I'm glad I embarked on an improbable second-career journey from corporate strategy to oncology RN and now PhD candidate in nursing research. Along the way I was inspired by these words I heard in a sermon from Rev. Galen Guengerich:

> 'Once in a while, if we are very fortunate, life invites us to leave the highway of our established routines and turn onto a side road leading to new places and new possibilities. Often the road gets bumpy. Sometimes we're forced to a complete stop. But if we keep going, scrambling up the trail as best we can, we eventually find ourselves out in the open with everywhere to go.'"[1]

—I.B., age 62

Stress that Both Mothers and Children Have "Work" to Do

"My daughters have never known me as anything but a working mother. When they were toddlers, I had an office in our home with a door that was often closed. They knew that when I went into my office I was doing 'Mommy work,' and they went off with the babysitter to do some of their own work with paint, puzzles, or books. Later they had their own homework to do, and they've always respected and understood my professional life. I'm glad I never gave them the impression that work was only something that I did without them—they also had work they needed to do independently, too."

—K.S., age 59

Recognize that Feeling Motherhood Guilt about Working Is a Choice

"I'm glad it has never occurred to me to feel guilty about being a working mother, because to ensure financial security for my family, I didn't have a choice. Quite simply, we would not have been able to meet our mortgage payments without my paycheck. I would feel guilty if I didn't return to work and left the financial burden of being the sole breadwinner on my husband's shoulders. Even if our financial situation would have allowed for me to seriously consider staying home, my husband and I are in complete agreement that we want to provide our children with the best life possible—piano lessons, summer camps, family vacations—and in this regard, two paychecks are better than one."

—E.F., age 34

Add to the Love Your Children Receive through Caregivers

"I'm glad I kept working. It's been a great role model for my two sons to see that both their parents have a life and purpose in addition to our family roles. Of course, it has been crucial to have the right caregivers; we've had amazing nannies and two terrific male *au pairs*. Our kids have loved having these people as part of our extended family."

—L.S., age 52

"I had nannies for all my childhood. I have fond memories of the women who cared for me, and I'm sure if you asked me as a child I would have said I loved them—but I loved my mother the most. I would argue that you can't—and shouldn't—be all things to your child all the time. I'm glad I feel I'm enriching my son's life by giving him exposure to other people who love and care for him. I'm proud he has his own schedule of activities with other adults and children. I cherish the time I have with him in the mornings, evenings, and on weekends, and I know I'm the best mother I can be because of the added fulfillment I get at work."

—E.F., age 34

Seek Out Childcare Options with Enlightened Employers

"When I had my babies, I'm glad I worked for a company that had onsite daycare. It made me feel confident as a mom that my children were being cared for nearby, and it made my transition back to work a little easier as I was able to continue to nurse. Although the decision to stay at home or go back to work is a difficult one with tradeoffs, I'm glad I continued to pursue a career to support our family. I'm also glad I continue to make career choices with my family's needs in mind; I prefer a job closer to home with flexibility rather than a bigger paycheck with long hours and/or a grueling commute."

—J.G., age 41

Do What **You** Think Is Best for You and Your Children

"I wish I had not been so focused on society's view of 'doing the right thing' for my infant while neglecting myself. After eight months of a high-risk pregnancy that grew more physically demanding each week, more than 40 hours of induced labor, an unplanned C-section, a week in the hospital, and two months of recovery at home, I was in no condition to nurse six to eight times a day. I spent too much time worrying about how I could possibly express enough milk to nourish my infant—while I was trying to spend time with my active toddler. My baby has been fed bottles by me and by her father, grandparents, our friends, and her big sister. And she loves sitting in my lap as I work on a writing project at home. The opportunity to care for both my daughters in a positive way and take care of myself at the same time gave me the energy to make a career transition into the human resources field.

"I'm also glad my husband and I made the decision to place our toddler and infant in school at an early age. Not only does this allow both of us to pursue our professional goals, also it provides superb developmental environments for our children. Every school day, they return home happy and smarter than the day before, and they sleep soundly almost every night. Outside observers have questioned why our children aren't at home with me—yes, *me*. They never ask why my children aren't at home with my husband. I tell them honestly that my children love school, and I leave it at that."

—M.J., age 35

Buffer Unexpected Financial Challenges with Part-Time Work

"I'm very glad I always worked part time. In the beginning, I would contribute something for extras. Then, when it became necessary, my part-time experience allowed me to get a much more challenging, higher-paying job to help with household finances and contribute to college costs. Without my consistent presence in the job market from early on, I would never have qualified for the rewarding, lucrative part-time job I have today."

—K.C., age 62

Don't Delegate Your Own Financial Security

"My life started out as I had hoped, and after a 30-year marriage that ended in divorce, it took a dramatic turn. I've been left financially compromised and had to re-enter the workforce after a 25-year hiatus. After the birth of my first child, I stopped working to raise a family. My husband traveled all the time, and my three girls needed a parent. I wish I had never completely stopped working. While a tremendous amount of volunteer work gave me many skills, it never looks the same as a paid job on a resumé. Finding a job in my initial career area of arts management has proven to be very difficult—and I need an income. Though I have found an administrative job that pays the basic bills, I would like to love what I do. It has been a struggle, and I'm still on that journey."

—E.S., age 57

Cultivate the Ability to Support Yourself in Any Situation

"I wish I had followed a more serious career path when I was younger. I grew up in the late 1960s and 70s when women's roles were changing. My mother always told me I should be able to support myself, but I didn't take her seriously. I also grew up around privileged women, many of whom did not work. I've worked full or part time most of my life, but many of the jobs were not building toward a real career I could feel passionate about. Even though I was not the main breadwinner, I was able to ease the family finances and support us somewhat when my husband lost his job—several times. I was the one with the stable income and health insurance. Then when my husband died in his early 60s, I wasn't nervous about finances. I have a small amount from a life insurance policy, but it's not enough to live on for the next 20 years—so I continue to work. I'm lucky I found a company that allows me to do what I love: travel. I've taught my daughter that she must have a career and a definite skill, and she is now a nurse."

—C.T., age 64

Stand Up for Yourself and Your Financial Security

"I went through a difficult divorce at age 48. Then I received no alimony and little child support. Like every woman in this situation, I revisited my career and life choices. In my 20s, I had built a successful writing career, on staff at magazines and authoring a book. I gave it up when my children were born, and at that time it seemed like the right choice. My husband and I could afford for me to stay home, but I wish I had not given in to my husband's view that motherhood should be my only role, and kept my hand in freelance writing. I've gone through periods of paralyzing financial anxiety. I guess I was too submissive and not confident enough to stand up for myself. I've lived and learned, re-established that freelance writing career later in life, and emerged stronger and wiser."

—E.K., age 64

Network to Help Others…and Yourself

"I'm glad I learned the importance of maintaining a strong network. Many years in the career advising industry taught me the importance of networking and gave me opportunities to build a personal community teeming with leaders in their fields. I've helped hundreds of executives navigate their career paths, and now, as I move through my own career transition, that support is coming back to me and helps me get through more days than I care to admit. Everyone has value, and moving forward in the spirit of giving yields a far greater return than focusing on 'what's in it for me?'"

—L.R., age 52

Take A Risk and Give Yourself a New Path to Financial Security

"I worked full time, part time, took a break, and then left my journalism and writing career to take an interim job at a local college to be close to our two children and pick them up if they were ill at school. I always planned to return to journalism, but the world I came from had changed so much and I no longer had the contacts I once did. I'm glad I convinced myself to take a risk in a totally new area—marketing—because the next job I took turned into the career I have today. The skills I use in my current job are skills I used as a reporter. I've learned to go with the flow and not be bound by what I once thought was my ideal career path. It wasn't always easy. I made mistakes. But I have learned so much along the way."

—C.R., age 52

Take Small Steps to Hit Your Next Professional Stride

"I'm glad that when I realized I was not going to be offered a job I really wanted after a long workforce hiatus, I did not give up. I wrote to the CEO suggesting some specific areas where I could add value on a project basis. I had a sense of the company's top-of-mind concerns through the interview process. The CEO had a pressing project need, so she hired me to work as an independent contractor for two months. It got me in the door and I worked at the company for five years.

"I put my ego aside with this first back-to-work job and took a salary that was a lot less than the one I had at the big corporate job I left behind. I didn't obsess about the money; it was a great chance to get back to work in a cutting-edge sector working with bright, creative people.

"I'm also glad I held out for the right part-time opportunity with a company that was okay with me working from home a day or two a week. This made a huge difference for my family and me. My employer's flexibility made the more-than-one-hour commute (three days a week) manageable. Loving what I did helped, too. I was willing to compromise on my ideal situation (total work from home) because I had the chance to redefine myself professionally.

"When I returned to work, I dialed back my volunteering—only helping (in small ways) causes that held a special place in my heart. I needed to clear the decks to give myself the space and confidence to perform in a very different role than anything I had tried before. I knew if it wasn't right, I could move on to the next. The wonderful thing about our humanness is our capacity for reinvention."

—G.R., age 52

Freelance as a Great Foundation for Possible Full-Time Work Down the Road

"I worked through college, then as a freelance journalist, marketing communications specialist, conference planner, and financial analyst. I never, never, never wanted to end up in a corporate job. I was not ambitious, according to my mother—who despaired of my ever being what she considered 'successful.' However, when I had a child, I could fit my schedule around his. When my aging mother became ill, I could fly across the country to visit, take her to doctor appointments, and help her move. I'm glad I continually took on freelance projects and earned money.

"When I was divorced, I was almost 50, had a child in elementary school, hadn't worked in-house in more than 20 years, and desperately needed a steady income and health insurance. It took a very frightening two-and-a-half years, but through networking I met a man who had been looking for the right person for almost a year. It was in a field I'd never heard of, but my skills—strong writing, ability to interview people at every level, fantastic organizational skills from running my own business, and comfort with financial and business issues—were just what he wanted. His boss was skeptical because of my lack of long-term corporate experience, but my soon-to-be boss insisted. I took the job at a lower title and salary than I wanted, but it had great benefits and lots of flexibility.

"I was there for six years, and then during the recession our entire department was laid off. Throughout my time in that job, I continued to keep in touch with lots of former colleagues and always made the effort to expand my network. One of my contacts ended up at a rival company with a big title. He heard I was looking for a new position, and he offered me a job, with a promotion and a significant salary increase. Of course, I said yes.

"While this work is not what I dreamed of doing growing up, I'm financially independent, I supported my son and got him through college, and I have a nice retirement account going. I'll have to work longer than I might have liked because I started seriously saving for retirement late, but I'll be okay. I probably won't head my own department before I retire, but you never know. And it really doesn't matter, anyway. I'm well-liked and respected in my profession; I'm earning almost twice what my ex-husband does; and should I lose this job, I have a wide network of professional contacts who know my reputation and would be happy to help me find something else. It's not the 'lean in' definition of ambition, for sure, but I've been able to have a real life and help the people I love when they need it. I call that a win."

—R.W., age 60

"Do It All" through Flexwork

"One thing I'm glad I did was find a company that respects working parents, gives you the opportunity to still work hard and succeed, but also offers the flexibility and support to be a great mom. I'm contributing very much to my team, see tons of opportunity to learn and grow, and definitely look forward to doing more and more for the company in a family-friendly environment. I genuinely believe I'm setting an example for my daughter as a woman and also contributing to our family and our future in a meaningful way that will hopefully give her a better life than I could ever imagine. I looked up to my own mother very much when she worked all day and came home to take care of our family.

"I'll always maintain my ambition to have a challenging and rewarding job where I can contribute and have an impact on my business and others. However, success right now doesn't look like a certain job title or promotion (which it did 10 years ago). Now success is doing an amazing

job at the office and getting home at a decent hour to play with my daughter before bedtime. Success is a good balance between work and home
and knowing both sides feel my positive impact. Success is being in the
moment and feeling the power and liberty to be where I'm needed most,
whether that is at home at 2:00 p.m. holding a sick baby or in the office at
8:00 a.m. because there's a big meeting I'm leading."

—D.S., age 36

Downsize a Big "Career" and Keep a Nest Egg Growing

"I'm glad I chose to spend many years as an advertising director for a
major publishing company, which involved a lot of late hours and constant travel. Those years were fun and often crazy. I was there for all the
big moments with my two sons, but I certainly missed a lot of smaller
ones. I look back with pride about what I accomplished, even though I
often felt alone as so few women in my social circle worked full time. I've
recently transitioned to the nonprofit world, working as a development
officer for my alma mater. My corporate friends assumed this job would
be easier…that I would be paid a lot less and that I had shifted down a
gear. On the contrary, I'm still working a very full week, including some
weekends and nights. I do have more flexibility in this remote position,
and for the first time, I don't have to worry about face time. I earn a salary I'm proud of, and I'm continuing to add to my retirement nest egg.
This is the perfect situation for me at this point in my life, and it is no less
challenging than the years I spent in the corporate world.

"Some may question why I've stayed in the game all these years.
I've always taken the position that I answer only to my family, and my
full-time work has worked for us. I continue to be excited and challenged
every day and feel I'm living my authentic self.

"Not every woman wants the big job, but I've always felt that some
type of work is important."

—L.S., age 55

Don't Assume Big Corporate Jobs are the
Only Path to Professional Growth

"I left a vice president-level job at a Fortune 500 company after 15 years to find a better work-life balance. At the time, I had a baby and two young children, and the long commute to a more-than-full-time job eclipsed my time at home. After leaving my big job, I kept my business skills current through consulting projects and high-level volunteer work. I was the treasurer for a nonprofit, led the PTA, interviewed candidates for my college alma mater, and took classes to stay sharp. I also kept in touch with my former colleagues.

"Though I gained valuable time with my family, I was concerned about leaving my professional self behind. I wanted as few years as possible in my resumé gap—and I was always thinking about when the opportune time would be to step back in the game.

"Then the unexpected call came from my former boss, offering a big job with an even better title and money—and the same big commitment. As incredibly tempting as this job was, I had just started working as a part-time COO for a growing entrepreneurial venture near my home. I realized I could still do some very resumé-worthy work flexibly, without compromising my family, my marriage, or my health.

"Though I was not working for a big-name company, I'm glad I made the decision to spend two years expanding my portfolio of skills in a new and exciting way. This small company gave me the opportunity to wear many hats. I had always had broad duties encompassing operations, marketing, finance, social media, and branding, but this experience was more accommodating to my work-life balance goals. The experience of working with the small company ultimately led me to my next professional role: a flexible full-time job with high-profile professionals in the media world. Every step I took along the way led me to this ideal scenario. I no longer feel there's only one very traditional corporate way to find a professional, resumé-building challenge. Someone once said to me, 'It's a jungle gym, not a ladder.' Knowing it's not a straight and predictable path is an important part of the process."

—L.K., age 44

Let Go of the Big Corporate Career when You Find Flexwork with More Meaning

"I'm glad I wasn't afraid to make a change away from a big corporate career. I had a terrific more-than-30-year run in wealth management, dealing with interesting people and families all over the world. In my late 50s, I realized I really wasn't enjoying my work anymore. I started to feel less authentic, and this was my giant wake-up call.

"I had always volunteered either with the senior citizen community through pet therapy programs or initiatives empowering women. It took a while to figure it out, but 18 months later, I'm very happily on my way with my own for-profit company with a social mission. I connected the dots between my personal interests (culinary arts) and desire to empower women. A total win-win, and I love every minute of it."

—E.I., age 61

Be Your Own Boss and Have the Flexibility for Family Caregiving

"I'm glad that for 30 years I've had my own business. This always gave me the flexibility to care for my two sons and elderly mother while pursuing a career.

"It seems like I've been a caregiver my entire life. First taking care of my two sons and then taking care of my mother. The boys had just left the house when my mother started to need my care.

"At the beginning, it was long-distance care for my mother; she lived in Florida and I lived in Connecticut. This added to the time required to be sure she had proper care. She eventually moved to Connecticut, and I thought this would make things easier. In fact, it added to my workload. I had to take her to doctor appointments, make sure she was eating properly and bathing—as well as simple things like taking her to a hairdresser. I was the point person when she was in the hospital, which was often. If I had been in a traditional corporate job I would not have been able to give my mother as much time.

"There were days when I felt tired, alone, frustrated, and guilty. I felt guilty because I believed I should not be feeling any of these things. After all, it was my mom I was taking care of. I knew my business was taking a back seat, and I also knew this would have major financial consequences. I finally sat down and identified ways to best utilize my time and energy, while being sure my mom was being taken care of.

"Delegating improved the situation, but it did not erase the need for oversight care. With some juggling and work flexibility, I was able to take care of my mother, my business, and my own financial security."

—K.M., age 58

Set Yourself Up for Lifelong Flexible, Independent, and Plentiful Work

"When my husband decided he didn't want to be married to me anymore, my priority was to keep my 12-year-old son in his home and school. Since I was the primary earner and could afford to own the house on my salary, I agreed to buy my husband out. The day after he signed the quit claim deed, the president of my company laid me off (and yes, he was aware I was going through a divorce).

"What a blow. Certainly not part of my original plan.

"I had found a copywriting course a few months earlier. I heard people could make a six-figure income working from home in their slippers. So, when I lost my job, I dove into it. And I loved it!

"My intention was to find another corporate job as quickly as possible and to study copywriting on the side. But every time I went on a job interview I felt drained, even nauseous. Yet I would bound out of bed at 3:30 a.m. to get to my copywriting program! So, I took a closer look at what I thought I could do with copywriting, and I liked what I saw. I'm glad I decided to go for it . . . and I haven't looked back!

"As a former global brand strategist and marketer, copywriting is the perfect way for me to blend my business background with my love of writing. I work from home, and I decide how much I want to work. Never in my wildest dreams could I have imagined doing what I am now. I always felt I needed the security of a predictable paycheck. In the 1980s, when I entered the workforce, I believed company loyalty was rewarded. I had just two employers during the first 17 years of my 29-year corporate career. But then I was laid off four times in 12 years. The job market had changed.

"I'm still building my copywriting business, but I've had steady paying work for six months. My goal is to surpass my corporate income. It will take a while, but it's definitely possible. So instead of a traditional 'retirement,' which I think would make me bored out of my mind, I can simply dial back my writing."

—N.P., age 53

Know There's No Ideal Life Stage for Work: Eldercare Is Even More Consuming than Childcare

"For five years I had a full-time job at a church in town, where I worked longer hours Monday through Thursday (a compressed workweek) so I could spend every Friday with my elderly mom. It worked out very well for all that time, and I stayed in the job for the flexibility even though I didn't really make enough money. My job was eliminated, and I then worked at a nonprofit 35 minutes away and not as flexible. This made it very difficult with my mom, who at age 95 needs more and more help. The good news is that I now have a new, very flexible job close to home with a good salary and the ability to work at home on Fridays.

"Looking back, I wish I had paid more attention to my financial future when I was young. Retirement and old age seemed so far away when I was in my 20s, 30s, and even 40s—and I didn't factor in time that would be needed to care for my parents. I should have been more focused and prepared for the future back when I still had time on my side."

—B.W., age 58

Work Because Life Has Many Unexpected Twists and Turns

"I'm glad I've always worked—not only because I enjoy it, but also because I never wanted to rely on someone else for financial security. When out of the blue my husband was diagnosed with brain cancer at age 43, I realized my career was essential to our survival. That also changed my ambition to strive for a big title. Instead I decided to do a great job in a business development role and be more available to my husband and our boys. Today, as a single parent, I love my job, I'm compensated nicely, and I'm financially secure."

—A.F., age 60

"Life and work require resourcefulness, because things don't always go the way you planned. I'm glad I had a commitment to continuous learning and strong networking, and the flexibility to try many different career paths, including big corporate, consulting, and nonprofits. I continually found flexwork that helped me build long-term financial security—and gave me the room to manage an unexpected bout with breast cancer."

—C.M., age 58

Take Baby Steps toward Reinvention

"I'm glad I've always been a big believer in positive thinking and planning. My career path has been inspired by a 'vision board' that illustrates how I want my life to unfold. I have the vision, but I don't hold myself to a deadline for change. I've had many reinventions: as nursery school teacher, regional manager of a large childcare company, operations work for several biotech startups, and now a new entrepreneurial venture as an integrative health counselor with a popular online women's health program. I've always zeroed in on my transferrable skills and boosted my confidence for change through careful research. I kept my 'day job' in the biotech field for 14 years before I fully launched my health venture."

—J.V., age 56

Find Your Own Definition of Career Ambition

"Ambition to me is not a quest to make the most money, nor to add to the number of women at the top. It's about learning, growing, and evolving as a woman, a professional, and a mother."

—K.B., age 59

PART 2

How to Find the Flexwork that Fits Your Life

Chapter 6

Explore the Big New World of Flexwork Freedom (The Corporate Grind Is NOT Your Only Option)

A S WE'VE DISCUSSED, ONE OF the greatest threats to the long-term financial security of women is a persistent belief that professional, paid work is limited to the traditional, more-than-full-time, sell-your-soul corporate job. Even today, stay-at-home mothers often look at me cross-eyed when I ask if they plan to return to work. These are women who have several children and busy households to run. They tell me they can't possibly work long hours, commute a long distance, travel overnight, and do everything they believe work entails without sacrificing the mother they want to be.

Similarly, women currently working in a traditional full-time job feel they have a binary choice of staying on the fast track (and answering emails until 2:00 a.m.) or completely derailing their careers, packing it up, and going home.

The fact is that **women can now work in purposeful moderation**— avoiding both the all-encompassing, high-stress climb up the corporate ladder and a complete professional hiatus. Purposeful moderation is where part-time, freelance, and entrepreneurial opportunities are continually growing, offering many alternatives for building long-term financial security, current financial freedom, and ongoing personal fulfillment.

> **❝** *Being at the top of my career doesn't necessarily mean working full time or around the clock for a major corporation.*"
>
> —Woman in her 50s, Georgia, master's degree

Because workforce-dominant millennials are unwilling to work in the same relentless, stress-inducing ways their parents did, workers of all ages are now benefitting from an increasingly more magnanimous and employee-centric workplace. Flexibility is no longer seen as something a less-career-oriented mother wants so she can spend more time with her children. As Sophie Wade, workforce innovation specialist of Flexcel Network and author of a book on the future of work, *Embracing Progress,*[1] noted at my "Make Work Fit Life" event, "At some companies, happiness is now a corporate objective." Employees of all ages and in all circumstances can find happiness in blending work and life in their own way. Happier employees are typically more engaged in their work and more productive, so it is a win for employers, too.

The data Wade has compiled on the future of work and current employer efforts to attract and retain the best employees bears this out:

- Millennials may comprise up to 75 percent of the workforce by 2030. Unlike previous generations, they're less likely to feel that work defines their lives.
- Lack of flexibility is one of the top three reasons people leave jobs. Most employees will be more loyal to their employers if they have flexwork options.
- The continuous and compounding "linear career" is fading, and by 2030, PwC forecasts one future scenario where only 9 percent of jobs are long-term "full-time" or "permanent."[2]
- Companies are tapping flexible workers to staff up for project

demands and to find niche skills not available in house. In an Upwork study,[3] 80 percent of hiring managers attributed increased productivity to freelancers.

- Employers are asking, "Who works better and when?" Talent will increasingly be allocated when and where needed, better aligning with individual strengths and working preferences.
- Portfolio careers are emerging, giving workers the chance to apply skills in various ways at various times. The ability to follow multiple passions and interests over time will improve loyalty, retention, and productivity.
- We all need to know how we want to work and how we work best. Working independently isn't the answer for everyone; it can be isolating for some. We need to test ourselves in different environments and set ourselves up for success.
- Technology allows employees to (a) work remotely, (b) work during what they feel are their most productive times, and (c) work more effectively and efficiently.
- With online videoconferencing like Skype, collaborative tools such as Slack, and rapid technological advances that change how employees communicate with colleagues and engage with work, managers need to acquire virtual leadership skills.

Alexandra Levit, a futurist and author of *Humanity Works*,[4] advises Fortune 500 companies on workforce trends and estimates that by 2030 professionals will work mostly from home using super-fast data terminals. To cut down on overhead costs and productivity-sapping long commutes, employers will have fewer physical office locations. Coworking spaces will more than double from 11,000 in 2016 to 26,000 in 2020. Those who prefer not to work at home will have access to interconnected hubs or coworking spaces. Meetings will routinely occur virtually, with videoconferencing and Skype being replaced by virtual reality (VR) and augmented reality (AR) technologies by 2020, allowing meeting attendees in different locations to appear to be in the same conference room. Women will increasingly be able to work closer to home, and they will no longer need to worry about the family impact of overnight travel, since client visits will become far less frequent and necessary. **Flexwork is now much more widespread than most women realize:**

- Flexibility exists in some form at 80 percent of US companies,[5] including either widespread initiatives or individual employee arrangements.
- The flexibility wave is across industries. A survey of advertising and marketing executives, for example, reported that 76 percent of their firms offer some form of alternative work arrangement; 61 percent of the time it is part-time hours.[6]
- One of the largest flexwork job boards, FlexJobs, posts jobs across 55 categories.[7]
- From 2005 to 2015, "telecommuting" (work from home at least one day a week), grew 115 percent. A total of nine million US workers telecommute at least half the week (2.9 percent of the total US workforce).[8] Telecommuting is rising not only because employees want this perk, but also because employers realize they can save more than $11,000 per telecommuter per year.[9]
- More than one in five people employed in the US work part time.[10]
- Fifty-five million Americans are freelancers (workers who make money on their own terms), accounting for 35 percent of the US workforce,[11] and experts believe their share of the labor market could be as high as 50 percent by 2020.[12]

Though the trend toward flexwork is clear, it is still not discussed openly by the majority of CEOs who actually have the power to implement—and publicize—large-scale efforts to help women blend work and life as the first step to taking on greater titles and responsibility. The blind spot that CEOs appear to have is evident in a *Women@Forbes* interview,[13] where Lynne Doughtie, chairman and CEO of the global professional services firm KPMG, stated that to ensure advancement for women, leaders must be held accountable for identifying and sponsoring high-potential women to get them to the next level. Doughtie's method has merit, but greater flexibility is the imperative to keep more women in the pipeline and advancing in professional knowledge, capabilities, and experiences—and the endgame for leadership efforts cannot be limited to shepherding women toward executive suite roles.

In a January 2018 *Freakonomics* radio episode, PepsiCo CEO Indra Nooyi does acknowledge the competing work and life forces that get in the way of a woman's quest for senior-level positions:[14] "As you get to middle management, women rise to those positions, and then that's the childbearing years. And when they have children, it's difficult to balance having children, your career, your marriage, and be a high potential out-performer who's going to grow in the company in an organization that's, every one of them is a pyramid. So it starts to thin out as you move up. We have to solve for that. How are you going to attract women to the workforce, where we need them, but allow them to balance having a family and taking care of aging parents and still allow them to contribute productively to the workforce? Don't have an answer to that. It's got to be a concerted effort on the part of governments, societies, families, companies—all of us coming together."

Nooyi is right that it will take the collective thinking of many constituents to create programs and pathways to help women blend work and life on a large, senior-management-supported scale—especially across huge corporate entities. Though flexwork may not be the only "future of work" answer Nooyi and other CEOs are searching for (they're likely thinking at 30,000 feet about the promise of collaborative technologies, mobile workforce connectivity, and artificial intelligence, for example), here on the ground flexwork is a huge answer to the challenge of keeping women in the workforce. Right now as straightforward flexwork continues to expand and evolve, you need to be well versed in the kind of work structures you can seize upon—sometimes in small pockets of companies still trying to figure it all out and increasingly part of the culture of many companies ready to put their flexwork stake in the ground.

Savor the Full Menu of Professional Flexwork

When most women hear the word *flexwork,* they immediately think "part-time job." This is one great option, but there are actually *six* major categories of professional flexwork that can be successful when clear benefits are established for both you and an employer. Let's look at each type in more detail.

Full-Time Work with Flexible Hours

For many women, a "permanent," full-time position is desirable because it offers professional fulfillment, access to the full range of employee benefits, and maximum compensation. Today, however, you can have a *flexible* full-time job that does not limit your career potential or earning power. What makes a full-time job flexible is as varied as the many individuals in a company. Some women just want the flexibility to start the workday a bit later so they can get children on the school bus. Others want to work from home a couple of days a week, or they want to leave early every day, making up work time in the evening hours.

> ❝ *My ideal is a job that has a full-time, flexible schedule compatible to taking care of all generations of my family as best as possible."*
> —Woman in her 60s, Connecticut, master's degree

All these flexible schedules—and more—are possible, and they are showing up in some of the most unlikely places. My career coaching practice has been filled with a disproportionately high share of ex-attorneys who swear they will never return to the endless hours and unrelenting partner-track pressure at big city law firms. Things are looking up, however; now *Working Mother* magazine publishes an annual list of the "50 Best Law Firms for Women."[15] On this list are many of the big, top-ranked law firms my clients exited—now touting flexwork arrangements (reduced hours and remote work) and increased parental leave benefits (16 weeks). Most of these firms ensure that lawyers who take advantage of family-friendly programs are not cut off from partnership or leadership positions. I've seen this sea change firsthand: a smart and savvy attorney I know works remotely in Vermont, travels to her New York office occasionally, and still snagged the partner title at a prestigious firm.

    ❝❝ *When I was working at large law firms, I quickly realized I had no interest in 'making it' there. I've always sought balance and meaning in my work and personal life—both before and after marriage and kids."*

             —Woman in her 40s, Florida, law degree

> ❭ **TIP**
>
> Craft a professional proposal or employer-employee contract (read more about this in chapter 8) that very specifically outlines how your work arrangement will play out every day. If you're hired into a full-time, in-the-office role, your colleagues will pretty much expect they'll find you down the hall every day. A flexible full-time role goes much more smoothly when everyone can easily anticipate when and how often you'll be out of the office and the fastest ways to communicate with you.

Compressed Workweek

An efficient way to keep your full-time salary and benefits and get some flexibility into your schedule is through a compressed workweek. This option is for those who regularly work 40 hours but can "compress" all those hours into fewer days. The most common compressed workweek is four 10-hour days and the fifth day off. You could also work eight 9-hour days with a day off every other week. Like any other flexible schedule that gives you the freedom to have days off, there's always the risk that employers will call and interrupt your negotiated free time. Still, the compressed workweek option, offered by companies like Progressive

Insurance, Quicken Loans, and Plante Moran,[16] gives women a day when they know they can be home taking care of family responsibilities.

> 66 *I work seven hours for four days plus some hours at night, adding up to 40 hours. I get to put the kids on the bus and be there for field trips and doctor appointments—and still have a fulfilling job I love."*
> —Woman in her 30s, New York, bachelor's degree

> ### TIP
>
> Choose a compressed workweek if you have a fairly light family and household schedule in the evenings. A nine- or 10-hour day plus commuting time can be difficult and exhausting if you have older children who need your unspent brain for homework help or younger children who look forward to you to playing house with them before bed. The long days in a compressed workweek can still be a reasonable trade if your day off allows you to do something special every week—like volunteering at your child's school or spending the day with your elderly parent.

Permanent Part-Time Work

In 2017, FlexJobs identified 50 companies that had the most part-time job openings on their site. The list is diverse in company size and industry, and it includes many big corporate names, such as Hilton, AT&T, Apple, and Wells Fargo; nonprofits and educational institutions like the American Red Cross and Johns Hopkins University; and many less-well-known employers familiar to those in their local areas.[17]

A part-time job is usually defined as at least 20 hours a week, and this number can fit neatly into school hours. A woman working part time can usually get her children off to school, work four hours, and be home in plenty of time to meet the bus. Though there was once a bias against part-time workers (a criticism that they were in more junior-level or dead-end roles with less influence), FlexJobs has seen a shift toward professional-level, part-time jobs with titles like pediatrician, graphic designer, accountant, attorney, and finance director.[18]

The big consideration with part-time work is healthcare coverage. Under the Affordable Care Act, employers must offer health insurance to employees working at least 30 hours per week (a number that could change if and when "Obamacare" is repealed and replaced). To date, this mandate has not included smaller companies (less than 50 employees), which can decide whether to include part-time employees in some or all of their healthcare and other benefit programs.[19] Many women are happy to work the minimum 30 hours to get healthcare coverage.

> 66 *After my first child was born, I dropped to part*
> *time at a large firm, then to lesser part time after*
> *my second child, and then to part time at a small*
> *firm after my third child. I've only gotten happier*
> *with each part-time arrangement."*
> —Woman in her 40s, Washington, law degree

〉 TIP

Beware of part-time jobs that are full-time jobs in disguise. You have to make sure you're not paid part-time wages for what creeps into full-time hours. This involves clear communication with your boss (an outline of what you're expected to do each week and an agreement that the expectations are reasonable) and careful time tracking. It's best to focus on your total monthly hours rather than worrying about sticking to your contracted hours each week. If your agreement is to work 20 hours a week, you are required to work no more than 80 hours in a month. As an employee who practices "two-way street" flexibility, one week you might work 30 hours and another 15, but you have to speak up if your monthly total is regularly exceeding 80 hours.

Telecommuting

Telecommuters are most often hired to be 100 percent "work-at-home" employees who are connected through mobile telecommunications technology to the employer's office. Many large companies, including United Health Group, Hilton, Xerox, Wells Fargo, and Cigna,[20] have legions of telecommuters, and smaller companies with the least bureaucratic structures often allow employees to telecommute all or part of the time.

While telecommuting can sound like a dream come true for many women, it does require a high level of self-motivation and discipline to stay focused on work and not be distracted by household chores or friends who call to chat. The most successful telecommuters also have a professionally equipped, designated workspace. In most cases employers provide computers, phones, and other equipment, but they're not furnishing home offices with desks or chairs.

The average US telecommuter works at home two to three days a week. For many employers and employees, this is a best-of-both worlds arrangement balancing concentrative work at home with collaborative work at the office.[21] Companies like IBM[22] and Yahoo[23] rescinded work-at-home policies largely because of communication and collaboration challenges that can be mitigated when employees have more frequent time alongside colleagues.

66 *My ideal is to work full time in my home office, and this telecommuting arrangement has not hurt my chances to get raises and promotions."*

—Woman in her 30s, West
Virginia, bachelor's degree

Telecommuting happens nationwide, but larger companies and employers based in the New England and Mid-Atlantic regions most broadly offer this worker benefit. Arizona, California, Colorado, Florida,

Georgia, Illinois, Massachusetts, Minnesota, New Jersey, New York, North Carolina, Ohio, Pennsylvania, Texas, and Virginia are top telecommuter states.[24] Texas-based Dell encourages employees to telecommute as much as possible, going so far as to set a goal for 50 percent of their workforce to be remote by 2020.[25]

The top four career fields for telecommuting jobs are medical and health; computer and IT; customer service; and education. Opportunities for telecommuters range from the entry to executive levels and include both part-time and full-time schedules.[26]

When you see postings for work-from-home jobs, you'll no longer see only sketchy get-rich-quick schemes. Telecommuters have an array of professional job titles, such as accountant, case manager, territory sales manager, writer, engineer, analyst, account executive, business development manager, project manager, and developer.[27] The FlexJobs site has case study examples of individuals who have found flexwork with these titles and more. Some of the jobs tell an interesting story about the future of work. Nurses, for example, no longer work just in hospitals or doctor's offices; at-home job responsibilities for these professionals include reviewing medical records, providing patient education services, and more.

Telecommuting is also not just a junior- or middle-management activity: FlexJobs regularly lists executive-level remote jobs, including chief financial officers, chief operating officers, chief people officers, chief development officers, vice presidents in many disciplines, nonprofit executive directors, and interim CEOs.[28] Correspondingly, compensation for remote positions is competitive: 75 percent of remote workers earn more than $65,000 annually, the high 80th percentile of all home or office-based employees.[29] On average this is the same as compensation for on-site workers, and it can reach into six figures. FlexJobs lists top salary ranges for remote medical directors (up to $317,000); internal audit directors ($192,000); directors of analytics ($178,000); data engineers ($142,000); clinical data managers ($134,000); and project managers ($111,000).[30]

> **TIP**

Before you sign on for a telecommuting role, make sure you've given work at home or in a local shared workspace a dry run. It's unrealistic to think that you'll set up shop every day in a local coffee shop so that you can be around other people. I've known quite a few women who need face-to-face interaction (not technology) to feel very connected to their colleagues; many others feel distracted in shared workspaces that can become very "neighborly" and noisy. Women also tend to fantasize about the convenience of working at home and think they'll feel less "motherhood guilt" about work if they're always available in the house. The fact is that to be a successful telecommuter, you have to keep your eye on the ball during your designated work hours. It's unrealistic to think that you'll have time to dip in and out of your family's routine—and it actually undermines babysitter relationships and authority if your kids think you're always around to step in and take charge.

Job Shares

Job shares between two people are probably the most difficult flex-work positions to obtain and the least common to find. Work Muse, a Texas-based recruiting firm, is unique in its singular focus on creating an impressive number of job shares for women (workmuse.com).

Each job-share partner usually works two days solo and one overlap day together. This arrangement can work very well if two people are already sharing responsibility for a certain job function or client. It requires a lot of coordination so that the job share is seamless and team members and clients begin to think of the two partners as one unit. Employers can be very wary that job shares will cause many important details to fall through the cracks, so potential partners have to make a buttoned-up case for their masterful organization and communication skills. It's a bigger challenge to get the green light when two prospective employees suggest that they share a job, since both partners do not yet have a track record with the company.

> ### TIP

View a job share like any other business partnership and be painstaking in your choice of whomever you will entrust with 50 percent of the responsibility to keep your job and your income. There are lots of people who would be the wrong choice to start a business with…and also many people who could sour the business of your job share. Most of all, job-share partners need to share similar values, work ethics, and goals. An instrument like the Myers Briggs Type Indicator can pinpoint all your overt and underlying strengths and make it easier for you to articulate the combined skills and attributes of your job-share team. But to make sure you're teaming up with the right person, you have to do even more: go straight for the jugular and address the worst of the worst case scenarios: talk frankly about how you would handle difficult situations—for example, if a family member gets sick and one partner can't work 50 percent of the hours for weeks or months, if one member of the job share team is responsible for a major error, or other situations that would strain even the best of relationships.

Independent Freelancing or Consulting as an Independent Contractor

In official IRS terminology, an individual is an independent contractor "if the payer has the right to control or direct only the result of the work and not what will be done and how it will be done."[31] Independent contractors can work with multiple clients on a per-project basis, or they can work with one company at a time for an extended and specified "contract" period.

Though they use a different title, at the end of the day, most consultants are technically freelancers, too. Both are considered independent contractors, but freelancers and consultants often have different objectives. Those who establish themselves as "consultants" often want to build an actual business, forming an entity through a Limited Liability Corporation (LLC) that offers personal protection if they are sued and other possible tax benefits. Consultants are more often viewed as entrepreneurs who offer specific, seasoned expertise, often broadly advising departments, business units, or large, ongoing initiatives. Freelancers tend to be more project-oriented, providing a certain skill (even at the entry-level) for a series of assignments without the objective of establishing a "practice" or "advisory." Many people who lose jobs and find themselves in a long job search use the "consultant" title as a placeholder on their resumés so they appear to have a company and current work experience. (Recruiters are quick to call out these mock consultants when it is obvious there is infrequent or limited "consulting.")

When freelancers of any kind land long-term on-site assignments, the greater employment stability they gain has to be weighed against a frequent reduction in flexibility. Often, on-site freelancers are expected to work full-time schedules during normal business hours, and they face the same challenge of negotiating flexibility as the company's permanent employees. More flexibility does come into play when freelancers can rejigger their schedules and find, for example, longer-term assignments that are not active during summer months or the holiday season.

> ❝ *I worked furiously until my 3-year-old was diagnosed with developmental problems, and then things had to change. Giving up work was not an option... I had seen the unpredictability of life. Instead I found the flexibility I need in an independent consulting career."*
> —Woman in her 50s, New Jersey, master's degree

Freelancers report their own income to the IRS and pay a 15.3 percent self-employment tax for Medicare and Social Security in addition to regular income taxes.[32] If they are placed in the contract by a third-party agency, they receive a W-2 from that agency at the end of the year for hours worked (and they do not pay self-employment taxes for these hours).

Completely independent workers (called 1099 contractors) do not receive employee benefits. Agency-placed independent workers (W-2 contractors) often have access to a limited menu of benefits, such as a nonmatching 401(k) or a Flexible Spending Account.

Depending on the legal structure of an independent worker's business, a home office may make it possible to deduct the actual square footage used for work. Routine deductions for all independent workers can include office equipment and supplies, use and maintenance of the car for business purposes, and even health insurance.[33]

Evidence that employers are migrating toward a flexible, on-demand labor model appears in the 2017 Workforce Productivity Report:

- Nearly all (96 percent) of the chief financial officers and line-of-business managers surveyed say they engage independent contractors.
- Eighty-three percent of these business leaders believe contract workers are more or equally productive as full-time employees.
- Independent contractors account for 21 to 60 percent of the workforce at half the companies surveyed.
- Seventy-two percent of business leaders believe the increase in specialized labor on demand is increasing company productivity.[34]

The skills that are always in hot demand for more seasoned consultants include marketing and communications, project management, business analysis, accounting/finance, and a wide range of information technology expertise.[35] Working independently overall has become an increasingly viable and respected career option as employers see that they can choose the best talent from a wider geographic pool and save about 30 percent in payroll costs.[36] The freelancing platform Upwork features job listings from 20 percent of Fortune 500 companies.[37] Full-time freelancers work an average of 36 hours per week,[38] and, at a time when "permanent" employment is tenuous, they feel more security depending on several clients rather than on just one employer.

A big development in the freelance economy is the passage of the "Freelance Isn't Free Act" in New York City. The first of its kind, this legislation gives freelancers legal protection against wage theft. Companies are required to sign contracts with freelancers and double the wages if they are not paid on time.

Freelancers work in all industries, but there's a growing need for on-demand help at companies focused on language services, research, education, marketing, insurance, journalism, and e-commerce.[39] Also fueling increased demand are unemployment rates that are starkly lower than the Great Recession era. These rates have created "the recruitment market economy," where employers like Apple, Calvin Klein, The New York Times, Airbnb, Google, and many other Fortune 500 companies are in competition for highly skilled freelancers.[40]

When freelancers have dry spells, matchmaking websites such as Upwork, 99 Designs, Freelancer, Guru, Elance, People Per Hour, and Fiverr make it possible for more than half of independent workers to find new projects in less than three days.[41] However, while these sites save freelancers marketing time and aggravation, they're not without cost: many sites take a cut of your earnings. A great one-time-fee resource I've personally used is LinkedIn ProFinder. This huge networking site brokers freelance projects for members who upgrade to a premium subscription. Individual employers like PwC are offering no-cost alternatives—their Talent Exchange connects independent workers with available projects firmwide (talentexchange.pwc.com).

There are many motivations driving freelancers beyond the freedom to be your own boss, including supplementing primary income from a "day job," replacing a conventional job that is no longer in large supply, or simply avoiding the often-grueling task of finding a permanent job. Job seekers can also use freelancing as a steppingstone to more permanent work down the road.

With strategic planning, freelance compensation can definitely pay the rent: 20 percent of freelancers earned more than $100,000 in 2017, an increase over the 12.5 percent recorded in 2011. The income for full-time freelancers averaged $65,300,[42] with social media management (up to $94,000 annually); business consulting ($71,000); accounting ($66,000); and content writing ($41,000) serving as examples of average compensation for specific skills.[43] Older workers (age 53 and over) who have more experience had higher average earnings at $77,000. LinkedIn found that average freelancing rates are in the $50- to $150-per-hour range.[44] One young woman I know earned more than $90,000 in a yearlong freelance entry-level advertising job—and it was her very first job out of college. The most compelling data point is that the majority of freelancers who leave a full-time job earn more money within one year.[45] Also very interesting is the fact that 25 percent of freelancers work in an entirely different field than they pursued working for an employer.[46]

Because freelancers can't always bank on a steady flow of work, financial planners often advise them to have an emergency fund that covers six months of living expenses. Health and disability insurance are especially important for women who are not covered under a partner's plan. The Affordable Care Act gave many independent workers alternate access to health insurance; plans are also offered through the Freelancers Union (freelancersunion .org) and The National Federation of Independent Business (nfib.com). As a replacement for company-sponsored 401(k) plans, independent workers can purchase "solo 401(k)s" from brokers, a mutual fund company, or organizations such as the Freelancers Union. Other options are individual retirement accounts (IRAs) or simplified employee pensions (SEPs).

Freelancing is a great option for women who do not have sole responsibility for paying all the household bills on time. Most freelancers can pick and choose where and when they want to work without the burden of establishing a full-blown consulting business. This is especially attractive for women in heavy caregiving mode who just want to stay current in their field through occasional freelance projects—filling resumé gaps with paid, rather than just volunteer, work.

Though many people may once have viewed freelancing unfairly as a stop-gap for misfits who could not get a "real job," today these independent workers command full respect. The 2016 Field Nation Freelancer Study proclaims that "freelancing has become the domain of the educated, experienced and the expert."[47]

> **TIP**

If you have ever said "I'm not a salesperson" or "I don't like net-working," independent consulting or freelance work as a source of significant income is not for you. Though there is a big sales element to every job search (landing a job is essentially making the sale that your skills and experience are the right fit for the employer), a permanent job is the result of only one big sale that reaps a paycheck each and every week. Earning a consistent income as an independent worker requires you to be in sales mode 100 percent of the time. Assignments have a way of disappearing for a stretch and then bunching all together—you can never bank on perfectly spaced out work or when a dry spell will end. And when you're deep in the throes of an assignment you always have to be thinking, "who is my next prospect?" Though LinkedIn and freelancing job sites can make your life easier, you still need to be comfortable with the sales hustle.

Shop Around for Your Best Flexwork Options

It's not enough to say you want a flexible job or to pick one type from the list above that sounds like the perfect fit for your busy life. Most women jump quickly to seeking some variation of part-time work. But before you give up on or rule out full-time hours—and a full-time salary that could greatly impact your long-term financial security—ask yourself these key questions:

1. **Do you need a full-time income ... but prefer flexible hours?**
   A full-time, permanent job with flexibility is still the easiest, most predictable route to a full-time income.
2. **Do you need employee benefits?**
   Other than a full-time, permanent job, you're also eligible for employee benefits at larger companies (50 or more employees) if you work part time (currently at least 30 hours a week). The only

other possibility is some freelance assignments—but these situations are less frequent, and without a "permanent" job you will always be at risk for losing benefits.

3. **Do you need a consistent, predictable income?**

Permanent full-time or part-time jobs are your best bet. Or, if you feel confident you will have instant, continuous (and loyal) clients as a freelancer, it's possible you can bank on a more predictable income. Generally speaking, not being on an employer's payroll is not a great option for anyone who needs a consistent income, since you never know when and where you'll get your next project, and not all employers pay their bills on time.

4. **Do you want control over the number of hours you work per week?**

With all the flexwork arrangements described earlier in this chapter, it's possible, with careful negotiation and a true give-and-take attitude, to manage or limit the number of hours you work each week. You have the most control over your schedule, however, when you have multiple clients as a freelancer.

5. **Do you want to be home by the end of the school day?**

In this case, all flexwork options are a possibility—but there are more challenges with a permanent full-time job, where it's harder to leave the office at the same time every day and it's likely you'll need to catch up with work in the evening hours. This is also the case as a freelancer working on a full-time assignment at an employer's office. You have a bit more control, but you have a full-time workload and colleagues will still be looking for you at all hours of the day. Your best bet if you want to meet the school bus and shut down your work brain for the day is a permanent part-time job with designated daily hours in the timeframe you need, or shorter-term freelance assignments conducted in your home office.

6. **Do you want to work at home all or part of the time?**

All flexwork options may allow work at home, but the likelihood you can work most or all of your hours at home is built-in to freelance work. There are times that freelancers may be asked to work in an employer's office, but for the most part they're free to work at home, in a coworking space, or anywhere they choose. Telecommuters are also by definition 100 percent remote workers who work from home and may go into the employer's office for the occasional meeting. The term *telecommuting*, however, can more loosely refer to a certain amount of time employees are allowed to work at home (e.g., "I telecommute two days a week in my home office").

7. **Do you want control over which months of the year you work?**
   If you want to take summers off while your children are young, then your best work options are shorter-term freelance assignments. Permanent full-time or part-time positions do not afford this time off, and it's often difficult to avoid working in the summer months with longer-term, on-site freelance positions. Even if you are able to schedule short-term projects within the school year, you will have to turn on your business brain and start networking for new assignments well before Labor Day.

8. **Are you looking for a way to "keep your hand in" the workforce and generate an occasional income—without a huge work commitment?**
   Freelance work is great for women who want to keep current work on their resumés but are not necessarily looking for consistent, week-after-week work. Even a project once a quarter can keep you from looking like you've been totally absent from the workforce for many years. Consultants can also limit and space out projects, but many want to create a consistent income through a busier "solopreneur" practice, a professional brand, and a strong client base that continually taps into their expertise.

Though there is now a burgeoning freelance economy, if you think you might someday pursue work inside a company as an employee, be aware that employers often think that those who work solo for many years have rusty management and team-building skills. Landing a longer-term freelance assignment is considered a major resumé plus, since recruiters know these contracts often require you to engage continually with colleagues on site. I always advise freelancers to seek out projects where they have a lot of client interaction and the opportunity to manage both people and process.

Decide if a Home Office Would Be Your Heaven or Hell

Diehard telecommuters, freelancers, consultants, and entrepreneurs think the best flexwork involves a two-minute commute to a home office desk without the hassle of trains, planes, or automobiles—and no coworkers who interrupt them with tales of kids or pets. As great as a home office seems, though, it's not for everyone. Before you sign on for any amount of professional solitude, think hard about whether it's the work structure in which you'll thrive. If you're starting your own business or considering an independent or telecommuter career, here are 13 things women need for home office success.

66 *I've been fortunate to have several flexible work-from-home opportunities—and it wasn't hard to create a quiet and productive workspace."*
—Woman in her 40s, New York, MBA degree

1. **No passion for pajamas.** Serious at-home workers rise early in the morning, get dressed, and "go to work" on time. It's hard to keep a professional energy level and mindset in slippers and loungewear.
2. **Independence and a love of solitude.** When you work at home, you have to motivate yourself. And you have to be comfortable with "me, myself, and I." Usually there are no other adults around to chat with about your weekend, and you don't have the time to fill any lonely lapses with calls to friends.
3. **Discipline, discipline, and more discipline.** Even the most successful professional women can't help but keep a running mental checklist of the hundreds of nonwork things that vie for their

time. When you work at home, it's very tempting to "just take a minute" here and there to fill out school forms, get a head start on dinner, or throw in a load of laundry. All those minutes add up—so you must have laser concentration and the ability to keep both eyes on work.

4. **Big chunks of scheduled work time**. Working at home often means you can set your own schedule—especially if you're the boss or your employer has an "as long as the work gets done" attitude. But you'll never maximize your intellectual mojo if you're constantly dipping in and out of work to shuttle children, exercise, or take elderly parents to appointments. High-quality work requires long stretches of uninterrupted time.

5. **A designated workspace with a door that closes**. Working in a high-traffic area—like on the kitchen table—is a productivity buzzkill. You need a tightly closed door to deafen the sound of barking dogs, crying children, lawn mowers, and general household mayhem. You also need a workspace that accommodates a proper desk or work table, a sturdy chair that won't lead to back problems, a place to file papers, a bookshelf, a computer, a printer, and everything else at the typical office worker's disposal.

6. **Childcare**. Even the best multitaskers with eyes on the back of their heads can't tend to wide-awake children and employers at the same time. It's likely you'll need at least a part-time baby-sitter for infants and other young children. Your boss is always sure to call when your baby is NOT down for a nap.

7. **Respect from your children**. Children will need to know that your workspace is out of bounds during work hours (unless the house is on fire). Without boundaries, you'll endure endless requests of "Mom, can I do this?" or "Mom, can I have that?"

8. **Respect from your spouse, extended family, and friends**. Just because you work at home doesn't mean you'll be able to drop everything in the middle of the day for a walk or coffee with a friend. Your partner also can't expect you to run to the dry

cleaner, oversee the house painter's every brushstroke, or plan the family vacation when you're busy with work. Like all other professionals, at-home workers need to do nonwork tasks during nonworking hours.

9. **Up-to-date technology.** If you don't have an employer-owned laptop computer, it's not likely your boss will spring for one if you're only working from home a few days a month. You need a secure, current model computer with high-speed internet access to log on to your employer's network and facilitate conference calls and the ability to install other communications tools to help you stay connected.

10. **A computer that is yours and yours alone**. For at-home workers, the family computer is a disaster waiting to happen. Multiple users—especially those with little hands—can erase your presentation draft, use up your memory, or visit crazy websites that invite computer maladies of the worst kind.

11. **The ability to be your own IT department.** When you work at home, there's no tech department or staff guru down the hall. The ability to troubleshoot and solve minor problems on your own leads to less frustration and hiccups during your day.

12. **An artistic flair for drawing the line between work and home**. At home, your business becomes an 800-pound gorilla tormenting you constantly for "one more thing." Instead of taking the kids to the park on Saturday, you could prepare for that presentation next week. Instead of going for a run on Sunday afternoon, you could get a jump on a looming project. Think about whether you'll be able to stand up to that gorilla: you'll need a mental "do not enter" sign on your office door to preserve your sanity, your health, and valuable family time.

13. **A sense of humor**. Working at home is not for the tightly wound or easily stressed. The dog *will* start barking when you're on the phone with an important client. Your child *will* get sick on the day you have to finish the proposal. And roofs will leak, babysitters will cancel, and the car won't start whether you have a

critical deadline or not. When you work at home, you need to roll with many punches and know your workday may not end until you're burning every last drop of the midnight oil.

Smart Shortcuts to Flexible Jobs

The most surefire way to find any kind of job—flexible or otherwise—is to make networking an extreme sport. You can make great headway among people you know and new connections you continually make via LinkedIn and other resources. Here are some more valuable shortcuts to consider.

Business specialists: A frequent concern I hear from aspiring independent workers is how they should price their services. In addition to your own research, SCORE, a nonprofit advisory service supported by the Small Business Administration, can help you learn the business of being a freelancer or consultant. The organization has more than 300 local chapters offering free or inexpensive workshops that can get you to clients faster and on more solid footing.

Association job boards: Many industry association job boards list competitive consulting work and freelance assignments. These organizations give you concentrated networking opportunities in your field as well—rather than dealing with more mass-market, industrywide resources.

Inside scoop: One great shortcut is the Fairygodboss Work-Life Balance Guide (fairygodboss.com), a marketplace where professional women looking for jobs, advice, and the inside scoop on companies meet employers who believe in gender equality. A crowd-sourced database gives women insider perspectives on employers who have part-time or telecommuting jobs, compressed workweeks, allowances for some work-from-home days, or flexible workday start and end times.

Women who review their jobs on the Fairygodboss site rate their employer's flexibility culture and policies, and half the employers are rated as somewhat or very flexible. Encouragingly, less than 10 percent of women contributing to the site consider their employers very inflexible.

Recruiting firms: The Gig Economy has spawned a growing number of boutique recruiting firms specifically focused on matching women to a wide range of family- and life-friendly jobs. Representing a huge reserve of untapped talent, these firms attract very impressive women who opted out of the corporate rat race but have not yet found a more flexible alternative. Top-tier companies of all sizes and in all industries use these firms as resources for challenging, lucrative, short- and long-term assignments.

Many of these recruiting firms have a national focus, working with clients either in one specialty area (like law or technology) or across a wide range of industries and job functions. It makes sense to register with these firms, which could possibly have opportunities that fit your profile and your life. The caveat is that they generally do not have *thousands* of available jobs for the thousands of women who want flexwork. To help get the word out about these firms (which are primarily focused on women and listed in the Recommended Resources section), I formed The FlexWork for Women Alliance. On kathrynsollmann.com, you can find the full list of companies with contact information, types of flexwork offered, and geographic concentrations.

Boards focused on flexwork: There are many job boards featuring freelance and other kinds of flexwork (Google the *Forbes* article "79 Websites to Get Freelance Jobs Fast" for a very comprehensive list[48]), but FlexJobs is one that stands out in terms of quality and mission. This job board was started by Sara Sutton Fell, known as the "Queen of Remote Work," who is widely known for her commitment to providing education and awareness about the viability and benefits of remote working and work flexibility for both employers and employees.

FlexJobs.com publishes an annual list of the top 100 companies offering remote jobs. These companies are largely on the East and West coasts, with a good number in the Midwest as well. As you will read in chapter 9, flexibility is much more widespread among smaller employers, so companies like IBM, Verizon, and American Express are in the minority on the FlexJobs list. All the companies are vetted as great places to work, but not all are household names.

The cost to use the FlexJobs site is reasonable ($14.95 a month at the time of publication), but the biggest selling point of the site is the fact that every job is screened for legitimacy. That is the key problem with job boards in general: too often the jobs listed aren't even truly available opportunities. (In many of those cases, large companies operating as "equal opportunity employers" post jobs only so they can prove that the broader public was notified of openings; there are often many strong internal candidates and little intention to hire anyone from the outside.)

If nothing else, looking through the FlexJobs lens, flexwork is more plentiful than most women would imagine. On one random day, their website touted 33,454 job postings at 4,711 companies. These numbers still don't make flexwork standard practice across all employers, but with strategic networking, you can find many smaller companies that truly have the flexibility to be flexible.

Beware the Entrepreneurial Option (Unless You Can Take on "Caregiving Role No. 3")

The perceived emphasis on profits over real-life employee needs drives many women out of corporate America. Of course, the most flexible work option is an entrepreneurial venture where you're the boss, you set the schedule, and you can come and go as you please. This is the route that I have taken for most of my career, and when you read this section it may sound at times that I am not promoting entrepreneurial roles. The fact is that I am a huge supporter of women business owners—as long as they really know, from the earliest idea stages, what it means to be an entrepreneur day in and day out. When you are employed by a company, your job has an immediate infrastructure, support system and paycheck—a situation which may or may not be the better fit for you.

> ❝ *I started my own company and became my own boss to create a schedule and work-life balance that would work for me, not an employer."*
> —Woman in her 40s, New York, master's degree

Before you seize an enterprising idea and start printing new business cards, step one is to very, very carefully consider if you are what I call "Type E." Type E is the Entrepreneur type—requiring all the skills and attributes to be your own boss. This critical first step is missing from the vast resources that show women *how to start their own businesses.* In my view, a lot of people have Walter Mitty dreams about being an entrepreneur, especially as they near retirement. In reality, there are lots of good ideas, but good ideas need good execution from people who can play the multifaceted, life-encompassing role of entrepreneur.

> ❝ *Autonomy rules. It's much easier to balance work and home when I only answer to my clients and myself."*
> —Woman in her 40s, Washington, law degree

I know this because I've owned and operated a variety of businesses since I was 18. Along with the catering business I had in college, I've had my own "sole proprietor" marketing communications consulting business, I've helped high-profile executives launch and run their own start-ups and I've run two ventures focused on women and work—*9 Lives for Women* now on my own and another with a partner for 10 years. All these entrepreneurial ventures have had one major thing in common: the need to work days, nights, and weekends to earn consistent and significant income. In your own business, you work harder than you've ever worked in your life because it's yours, it's always staring you in the face, and if you don't exert a 150 percent effort, it's hard to get past the startup phase.

Many people are not Type E because they don't have the interest, ability, tenacity, or energy to wear hats of every shape and size every single day (including times when you wish you could pack it in and have a more predictable job). When you have your own business—especially in the solo startup stages with lean resources—delegating is often not an option. So that means you do everything until you can afford to outsource or hire. You may love your core business, but not bookkeeping, facilities management, mailing, errands, and the 99,000 details that only you are available to do.

> 66 *My professional ambition waned in the face of the masculine corporate environment, while my creativity and entrepreneurial energy flourished."*
> —Woman in her 30s, California, bachelor's degree

Then there's sales and marketing. All business owners have to attract customers and grow their businesses. If you don't think sales and marketing is your forte (including all that needs to be done via multiple social media platforms), you may have a hard time pinpointing your competitive advantage and continually getting the word out about why your products or services are the most cutting edge.

The most successful Type Es can sell and promote—and they have the money to do so. It's the rare story that highly successful entrepreneurs started their businesses on a shoestring (like Sara Blakely, the woman who famously started the blockbuster Spanx line with only $5,000). One of the biggest reasons most entrepreneurs fail is related to their bank accounts. Many startups never reach prime time because of limited financial resources. It's simply a fact that it takes money to launch, build out, and expand a business. (This is true even when you're a creative professional starting a home-based business you intend to keep small and manageable: a stationery designer, for example, has to buy tools and supplies, pay for printing, and build enough inventory to create even a limited a line of products.) Most often initial business costs are financed with your own wallet, because many banks and investors are wary of lending to startups unless they see you're willing to risk your own money, too. The increasing number of venture-funding-backed angel investors focused on women can be the answer to your financing prayers, but to attract these dollars you need to prove that your business idea has the real potential to sell—and scale in size as well.

> 66 *When I left my corporate job, I started my own business so I could work at home part time around my children's schedule. I'm planning to go back to work full time in an employer's office when they are in school full time."*
>
> —Woman in her 40s, California, bachelor's degree

The other side of the money issue is how long you can endure little or no income, forgoing not only a paycheck but also earnings you could otherwise save and invest. Few entrepreneurs turn a profit in the first year, and sometimes it can take many years to make serious money. Some try to offset this by keeping their "day job" or taking on part-time jobs to provide another source of income, but this eats up critical time you really need to spend developing your own business.

Despite the many challenges, more and more women have the fortitude to try their hand at running their own show: they are the majority owners of 38 percent of US businesses, up from 29 percent in 2007. In 2016, there were an estimated 11.3 million women-owned businesses in the United States—a 45 percent increase since 2007.[49] And all these startups are not the brainchild of young professionals. Women-owned businesses are launched by many seasoned professionals: 57 percent are age 40 and older. These are women pursuing second or third careers at the same time they are caring for children and aging parents. Seventy-nine percent have one or two children, and 80 percent started their businesses as mothers.[50]

One major reason women want to be entrepreneurs is related to the fact that working for yourself can rightfully be considered the new job security. With millions of workers serving as employees at will, subject to layoffs at the drop of a hat, employers no longer offer long-term stability. Assuming you can ramp up your own small business and attract some loyal clients, having your own company with varied income streams can be a safer bet than relying on one organization for your total compensation.

Entrepreneurial ventures carry their own uncertainties, however, in the form of longevity and sustainability. Having your own business is also a risky business: although 80 percent of businesses survive their first year, the survival rate at two years is 66 percent. At five years, it's 50 percent, and at 10 years, it's 30 percent.[51] While women are certainly more than qualified to launch a business with the staying power to multiply in size or attract a buyer at a big price, sky-high entrepreneurial goals can involve the same (or more) relentless pressure and work-life imbalance as top corporate jobs. Among female entrepreneurs there can also be similar judgments about what kind of business models

> **❝ *I've always worked—and what fuels my ambition is being in the driver's seat as an entrepreneur.*❞**
> —Woman in her 50s, Connecticut, master's degree

constitute true ambition—with some disdain for pursuits that are, for example, limited in scope and headquartered at home. In the entrepreneurial world, as well, ambition comes in many forms, and there is huge opportunity for women who are truly Type E to create home-based or smaller-scale businesses that generate very respectable incomes and build long-term financial security. The entrepreneurial life is not for the faint-hearted, though, and upon further consideration many women looking for more work freedom find they are better suited to a flexible job at a company that someone else loses sleep over and funds.

Are You Really Type E?

- Shadow some entrepreneurs for a few days to see how much of their time is NOT spent on the fun part of their core business.

- Decide if you're interested in a full-fledged business or just a hobby. You can compartmentalize a hobby. A business is life-consuming.

- Think back to your corporate days, and assess how much you really enjoyed rolling up your sleeves and doing the menial work that needed to be done to meet a deadline.

- Take your sales and marketing temperature. If you're someone who likes to do the work—not sell the work—an entrepreneurial venture may not be for you.

- Give your finances the stress test. Assess (a) how long you can wait to earn real money, and (b) whether you're willing to risk at least some of your money to fully establish, promote, and expand your business.

- Decide if you can go it alone. Can you find a truly compatible partner? Do you thrive only when there is interaction with teams of people?

If you're still convinced you're Type E, look into the many organizations that help women business owners succeed like NAWBO, the National Association of Women Business Owners, which has many regional chapters.

View Work as an Evolving Money-Making Activity, Not a Ball-and-Chain Career

Whether jobs are flexible or not, in our society, the labels "working woman" or "working mother" connote "career woman": a woman who works very long hours at a paid job, travels the world, and spends time with her family on the fly. This stereotype covers only one extreme end of a very large spectrum. The number of high-powered "career women" at the very senior levels is actually a very small percentage. There are many reasons for this fact, and they do not all have to do with gender inequalities, pay gaps, or the fact that few women have the support they need to reach the executive suite. In reality, there are many working mothers who *choose* to keep their work within a manageable, life-friendly realm.

Women tend to get tripped up on that emotionally charged word *career*. It's a word that implies that you strive relentlessly to achieve fame and fortune for a sustained period of time. A career has the potential to overtake your life, but "work" that is fulfilling and fits your life can enhance the person you are for yourself—and your family. Careers might be the realm of movie stars, athletes, and the relatively few women who crave the ultimate power and prestige. For the rest of us, it makes sense to explore many different kinds of flexible "work" we can do and many different skills we can use to achieve personal fulfillment and financial security over an entire lifetime: freelance or on staff, employee or entrepreneur, at home or in a corporate office, five hours a week or 50, moving sideways or maybe up—with endless possibilities that accommodate life's uncertainties at every age and stage.

66 *I was very career-focused until I had my baby. Now I'm rethinking the idea of a career and considering many interesting types of flexwork I can fit around family and still save money for the future."*
—Woman in her 30s, Illinois, bachelor's degree

But in all this work freedom there lies a caveat: a path that resembles more of a complex "labyrinth" than a rung-by-rung ladder heading up does not mean women can leave their professional development and financial security to chance. In fact, in this new flexwork environment, planning is more essential than ever because next steps are not clearly marked. To navigate a labyrinth successfully, women must deliberately map the direction toward their goals—taking even small steps in paid and volunteer roles and keeping on track throughout caregiving periods.

Opting for work over career does not in any way suggest mediocrity or passionless, low-energy activity—just work that doesn't compete with life. Interesting and fulfilling flexwork that capitalizes on educations and leads to financial security is in fact what most women who responded to my "Motherhood and Career Ambition" survey indicate they have always wanted. The majority agree with the statement, "Getting to the top of an organization has never been and never will be important to me," and their answers also indicate that as soon as they started families, their push toward hard-driving, life-encompassing careers waned.

> 66 *I've always had the ambition for a solid professional career, but I've hoped it would never come at the expense of family. Many people I've seen at the top of corporations have made lifestyle and family choices I don't want to emulate."*
> —Woman in her 30s, District of Columbia,
> bachelor's degree

Remember, though, that motherhood—or any caregiving responsibility—is not a ticket to work only on your own terms. Flexibility has to work both ways—for employer and employee. Just as there are unforeseen circumstances in big volunteer projects that require extra hours at inconvenient times, paid work has unpredictability, too. A flexible schedule is most successful when, within reason, you'll take that call or log on to your computer on off hours or days. As long as you're willing to put the extra time in when projects exceed your usual hours (at home or in the office), most employers will be flexible, generous, and respectful about your personal time, too.

Chapter 7

Don't Let the Cost of Childcare Keep You Out of the Workforce (It Costs Much Less than a Big Resume Gap)

Y OU WANT THE FREEDOM OF flexwork, but even with a less traditional schedule, you'll probably still need some form of care for any child who cannot yet drive. Though nearly one in three families report spending a whopping 20 percent or more of their annual household income on childcare,[1] it's not a reason to stay home. Most data relates to challenges mothers face when they need childcare that synchs with a traditional, inflexible full-time job. With flexwork, childcare is a problem most women can more easily solve.

Before we get to the cost issues, first, let's focus on the more pressing reason so many women feel they must stay out of the workforce: concern about leaving their children in the care of others. In all the years I was working in a flexible way and raising my two daughters (who thankfully are now able to care for themselves), I always thought the hardest part was not the actual work; it was finding, keeping, and feeling good about childcare. Though I was bound and determined to always work, I was also worried and guilt-ridden when I would set off on the train to New York City, leaving my infants in the care of babysitters.

My husband was always the voice of reason. He reminded me, often, that countless women have no choice but to work and have children who turn out just fine. My daughters grew up and, from all indications, love and respect me, and they are leading productive and happy lives. We tend to forget that responsible and caring nannies, *au pairs,* babysitters, and daycare centers can give our children valuable educational and life experiences that augment what we give them ourselves. If you need childcare and you're on the fence about its safety and positive influences, take a look at the Child Care Aware of America Family Voices Blog Series (usa.childcareaware.org), which features many mothers talking about how they have made childcare work in many admirable ways so they can ensure financial security for their families.

Another reassuring fact is that childcare as an industry is expanding to include a significant educational component. As a result, many providers feel pressure to become certified as more highly qualified childcare development associates. Washington DC is going a step further by offering a public preschool program free to all residents, and they have also created a city-funded career and technical education program called "First Step," which aims to build a pipeline of highly trained providers who can help transform the quality of care and education for the district's youngest learners.[2]

Women mired in work and life tend not to see positive changes in an industry that receives so many negative reports. The exodus from the workforce continues: nationwide as many as 43 percent of high-potential, midcareer women leave the workforce[3] in peak childcare years (their late 30s and early 40s).[4] Often this is due to limited knowledge of positive childcare trends, fears they will miss a childhood milestone (I feared that my children would love the babysitters more than me), and frustrations about high costs. In my experience, these women leave more-than-full-time, rigid corporate jobs behind before fully exploring flexwork and the possibility of more creative childcare options. As earlier chapters have shown, they do so at great peril to their financial futures.

" " *As soon as I started a family, I realized it wasn't possible for both my husband and me to pursue careers at the top of our professions. I didn't want to rely totally on babysitters, and my husband didn't want to work fewer hours, so I made the choice to work part time and hire babysitters on a more limited basis."*

—Woman in her 50s, Texas, bachelor's degree

Warm Up to the Cost of Locking in Long-Term Financial Security

Now we'll delve into the cost issue: there's no way around the fact that any type or amount of childcare carries a big price tag. Many women decide to avoid childcare expenses and stay home when they calculate their take-home salary (which is often less than a partner's) compared to the cost of childcare. *But this is not the right calculation!* The real cost of childcare is the woman's salary multiplied by the likely number of years she'll be out of the workforce.

The Center for American Progress (CAP) runs all the numbers with their interactive childcare costs calculator. Using the example of a 30-year-old woman who earns $50,000 annually, the tool illustrates that leaving the workforce for three years would cost her $150,000 in income, $140,000 in lost wage growth, and $125,000 in retirement assets and benefits over her career lifespan.[5] That total $415,000 loss would be even greater for women who have higher salaries and/or who stay out of the workforce for many more years. Compare just the $415,000 loss to the average cost of full-time daycare for five preschool years ($54,860) or the average cost of a full-time, in-home *au pair* ($95,420) for the same five preschool years.[6]

In reality, **women are not saving money** by eliminating the childcare cost: in no way is the care a woman provides for her own children "free" of a financial cost. When women see these numbers the vast majority say that given a do-over, they wouldn't make the same shortsighted financial decision to give up working again.[6]

These eye-opening calculations also show that it still makes sense to work even if you currently pay out more in childcare than you earn in salary. The cost of staying home today poses the greater financial loss down the road. From both a psychological and professional standpoint, it may be more palatable to reframe the dilemma: **for a defined period of years, childcare is the cost of doing the critical business of building a portfolio of current, valuable skills and ensuring your ability to earn an income in the event of any unexpected financial struggle.**

Here are some examples of how this kind of pragmatic thinking pays off. A single mother decided to continue her work as a secretary at IBM. Over the years, she brought her three children to a patchwork of child-care arrangements in three different towns, even though this childcare swallowed most of her paycheck. She persevered because she saw her work as an investment for the future. Eventually, her bit-by-bit approach brought her many benefits in career advancement, compensation, and the ability to save. Today she is the CEO of a highly respected non-profit organization. (In this case, the woman was working a traditional full-time job, long before flexwork was commonplace. It's important to emphasize again, however, that today *a full-time job with flexible hours* is an attractive flexwork option for many women who need a full-time income and health benefits. Flexible hours would have made it less hectic for the woman in this example to have different childcare arrangements in different towns.)

When I broke my wrist, my physical therapist, who was pregnant with her second child and worked two days a week, mentioned that she barely had any money left over from her part-time salary after paying for in-home childcare. She did not focus on this depressing arithmetic, however. Instead, she recognized that a big resumé gap in a fast-moving industry would set her back in continuing education credits and very quickly make her skills out of date. She saw her part-time work as a valu-able placeholder: a time in her career when she was not losing ground, even though she also was not advancing rapidly in title or compensation.

She kept her eye on the future, knowing she was making deposits in her bank of experience that would pay off in later career gains and earning power when her young children came of age for school.

I also know a young human resources professional who shares a similar view. She has three young children, and childcare (particularly expensive in her area) now eats up almost 50 percent of her take-home salary. To minimize childcare costs, she has a live-in *au pair* for the two youngest children and takes only her eldest child to a more expensive local daycare facility that has an educational component. A flexible full-time job with predictable hours allows her to keep to daycare facility drop-off and pickup schedules and relieve the *au pair* at the designated hour. Though she says her childcare arrangements "bleed money," her continued employment allows her and her husband to maximize contributions to not one but two 401(k) plans, reap the benefits of two pension and life insurance plans, and save in other ways for their retirement years.

Even though childcare will always take a big bite of your earnings, you'll see later in this chapter that flexible work—especially part-time, freelance, and entrepreneurial roles—can minimize the childcare you need. When your children are young, it may always be the case that your leftover income is lean, but it's well worth it to stay in the workforce, making wise investments in your portfolio of skills, future earning potential, long-term marketability, and lifetime financial security.

Think Outside the Usual Sandbox

The reality is that even when mothers recognize that work, paychecks, and other benefits are important add-ons to their caregiving roles, they still face the challenge of finding the high-quality, affordable childcare that accommodates their work schedule and family dynamics at a time when the government has not stepped in with widespread funding and solutions. (It is simply not true, however, that it is now *impossible* to find good childcare—there are many innovative solutions that rarely make the headlines.) And even if the government at some point intervenes, it's unlikely that childcare will ever be *free*. In any scenario women will always need to research their most cost-effective options and think carefully about the *minimum* childcare they need for flexwork.

For example, when my daughters were young and I was working as an independent consultant, I learned about a very reasonably priced, licensed, "as needed" babysitting service that was located at the home of an acquaintance. I would never have found this woman's services in the phone book or on the internet; she was well-known in the community, and I found her through word-of-mouth.

> **❝** *Childcare was never easy, but it worked well for me when I had excellent support from a reasonably priced babysitter who lived in our neighborhood."*
> —Woman in her 60s, New Jersey, MBA degree

During a later childcare phase, I found another professional woman to share the cost of a babysitter who cared for both our daughters after kindergarten dismissal. The situation was comparable to play dates with adult supervision, and the girls got to enjoy the company of a friend at each of our homes. This arrangement took some creative thinking and negotiating. We didn't want to pay a full-time salary, so we helped the babysitter fill up her morning (and generate full-time earnings) by arranging for her to care for the children of other friends.

Our local high school also helped me find babysitters who were not overloaded with sports and other activities. When my daughter was in elementary school, a lovely high school senior met her school bus every afternoon and played games with her until I returned at 6:00 p.m. The high school student was probably the easiest to work with and least expensive babysitter we had.

Though I give myself credit for some resourceful childcare options, the most creative solution I've ever seen was a young, high school-educated woman who was determined to work but who lacked the earning power to cover the cost of childcare. She became a school bus driver, and the first seat was always taken by her daughter—in a portable baby carrier clearly within her mother's sight.

Although few jobs allow parents to bring their children along, with more creative thinking and more informal babysitting co-ops, more mothers can work and pocket more of the money they earn. For example, since most women want flexwork and many want part-time jobs, it's possible to find one in-home babysitter who makes childcare more affordable for two mothers, working two days for one mother and three days for the other. And not all reputable and loving babysitters come through agencies or demand top dollar per hour. Many professional women have turned to babysitting as extra cash income while they're pursuing another degree or working part time in a new career and a lower-paying, entry-level job.

The part-time self-employment route also opens many doors to a work situation that does not necessarily require many hours of childcare. While it's difficult to work and care for a baby at the same time, it really depends on the type of work you choose and whether it involves a lot of phone time. For example, with one baby who is not yet walking, it's possible to carve out 15 to 20 hours of work a week without childcare if you work at home. During the day, a mother could find two hours to work at times when the baby is napping and another hour each evening after the baby is asleep. Add in a few hours over the weekend when a partner might take the baby to the park, and she's found enough hours for a reasonable part-time job. I've known many former corporate women or lifelong creative professionals who have segmented their day, avoided childcare, and earned significant at-home income designing stationery, making jewelry, selling designer clothing lines, creating websites, and more. Often women tap into an entirely different interest and skill set (putting more "corporate" interests on hold), like the former hedge fund professional who still uses her business development skills operating a popular online vintage goods Etsy store whenever her toddler and infant nap.

Avoiding a commute can also lessen your childcare bill. Average one-way commute times are 25 minutes,[7] but women who live in suburban areas often commute to big cities that require up to four hours round-trip. In that case, working at home could reduce the need for a babysitter by 20 hours, a potential significant savings. (On the topic of how much babysitters cost, Care.com has a great babysitting rates calculator to zero in on the going rate for your area.[8])

The bottom line is that women can't make blanket assumptions about how much childcare they will actually need, how much they will need to spend, and the options that are available—privately or, as you'll see in the next section, through employers. With creative thinking, collaborating with other mothers, and strategically choosing flexwork that fits with their best childcare options, women can ensure that both their children and their nest eggs receive the proper care.

Find Employers that Ease the Childcare Pain

The good news for mothers is that many employers now realize that some form of childcare assistance is a powerful way to attract and retain top-quality employees—and keep them present, productive, and focused on their jobs. Check the *Working Mother* magazine list of "The 100 Best Companies for Working Mothers"[9] nationwide, and similar lists of family-friendly companies in your local area. The criteria for getting on these lists often includes a company's willingness to help employees with childcare needs.

Many companies large and small, in and out of corporate America, now offer ways to help parents reach childcare peace of mind. Here are the most typical examples.

Dependent care flexible spending accounts (FSAs): When employers offer an FSA, employees can direct up to $5,000 of their annual salary to a pretax spending account that can be used for childcare or costs not covered in typical healthcare plans. This includes the cost of preschool, summer day camp, or after-school care for children younger than 13.[10] Unbelievably, this is an underused benefit; one in three parents are not aware that this cost-cutting tactic exists.[11]

FSAs are the alternative to the Child and Dependent Care Credit parents can claim on their annual income tax. Only a portion of the money they spend on child and dependent care (same eligible expenses as FSAs) while they're at work can be claimed. Depending on your income, the credit covers 20 to 35 percent of childcare costs up to $3,000 for one child and $6,000 for two or more (lower earners get a higher credit). If your income is $43,000 or more, the credit is worth 20 percent of eligible childcare expenses, with a maximum credit of $600 for one child and $1,200 for two or more. The general rule of thumb is that those in lower tax brackets benefit more from the Child and Dependent Care Credit.[12] In some circumstances you can use both the FSA and the Dependent Care Credit, but it depends on income, number of children, and other factors that your HR department and accountant can help you assess.[13]

Care resource and referral benefits: Some companies offer family care benefits through a program like Care.com Workplace Solutions. These resource and referral benefits help parents find the best childcare solution for their families—substantially cutting down on the amount of time, frustration, and confusion that searching for quality childcare can entail. On a larger scale, Bank of America offers employees a full range of financial counseling services, and their Benefits Education & Planning Center includes free guidance on the costs of childcare and FSAs.[14]

On-site child care: Though on-site childcare (sometimes subsidized) is far from the employer norm, it's worth researching which companies in your area offer this convenient benefit, which puts you and your child under one roof. The retailer Patagonia is widely lauded for their very-forward-thinking childcare benefits, including subsidized on-site facilities, which draws 95 percent of new mothers back to work.[15] SAS, a global leader in analytics, also credits low employee turnover (less than 5 percent) to their subsidized on-site daycare and preschool, which have cared for 600 children over the course of almost 40 years.[16] Employers who do not have the space for on-site facilities sometimes do the next best thing; Princeton University built a daycare center near their campus for the children of faculty, staff, and students.[17]

The *Fortune* "100 Best Companies to Work for 2017" includes many well-known names. These organizations, which include Google, Quicken Loans, Capital One, Marriott, USAA, Allianz Life Insurance, and Campbell's Soup, make their employees' lives easier with on-site daycare.[18] Cisco Systems capitalizes on their technology prowess to allow parents to view their children throughout the day via high-resolution cameras.[19] All University of California campuses have employee childcare centers,[20] and much smaller, less well-known employers are getting in on the on-site childcare act, too. Examples include Pure Growth Organic snack food in New York, Outreach in Seattle,[21] and the Murfreesboro City Schools in Tennessee, to name a few.[22]

Collaborations with leading daycare companies: Employers who would prefer not to reinvent the wheel sometimes collaborate with leading daycare companies to create cobranded facilities specifically for their employees. An example is the prominent law firm Alston & Bird, which has teamed up with Bright Horizons in Atlanta to subsidize care for infants, toddlers, preschool, and school-age children.[23]

The childcare-in-a-pinch backup: Some employers, like Brigham & Women's Hospital in Boston, provide subsidized backup care so parents don't panic when school or a daycare facility has a weather closing or a babysitter is sick. The hospital offers a reduced rate for six days of emergency care at home plus access to a backup childcare center.[24] Companies are also contracting with outside services such as Trusted at Work, which is like an on-demand Uber for babysitting. Trusted at Work uses background and DMV checks, along with reviews of terrorist and sex offender registries, to give parents peace of mind.[25]

Child-friendly offices: For women who have a hard time separating from their newborns when maternity leave ends, more than 200 companies in 35 different industries have bring-your-baby-to-work programs. These companies, which allow parents to care for their infants while they work, include credit unions, law and technology firms, consulting and manufacturing companies, retail stores, schools, dance studios, libraries, and government agencies with up to 3,000 employees. Babies at work have been cared for by parents in a wide range of positions, from secretaries and call center personnel to lawyers, teachers, bank tellers, logistics professionals, and many others at the executive level. Companies like Palo Alto Software in Eugene, Oregon, let older kids come to the office, too.[26]

Join the Childcare Sharing Economy

Most mothers would agree that the scariest part of childcare is not the cost; it's the prospect of leaving your children with strangers. Though it's the norm for agencies to put their reputations on the line and present you with vetted candidates, there is plenty of questionable caregiver behavior that can slip through the cracks. That's why there is nothing more comforting than leaving your child in the care of trusted family and friends. Creative parents are finding ways to leverage these "inner-circle" resources—without letting the goodwill well run dry.

Grandparents are the first go-to resource for parents who are lucky enough to have these family members nearby. Since a growing number of people past the age of 65 do not have enough money saved for a long retirement, the problem is that many grandparents work part time and are not available to provide free care for their grandchildren while parents work full-time schedules. (I have heard of mothers who pay grandparents for childcare, which is a great way to help grandparents boost their retirement savings and have your children cared for by trusted family, too.) With some strategic thinking, grandparents who don't have full-time availability can still anchor a patchwork childcare arrangement. Even if financially secure grandparents can babysit on an unpaid basis only one or two afternoons a week, their involvement cuts down on the cost of paid resources. It's considerably less expensive to hire a part-time babysitter or bring a child to daycare for less than five days each week.

If care provided by extended family is not possible, two parents could try to get flexible scheduling that would reduce childcare costs. When two parents compress their full-time jobs into four 10-hour days a week, they can coordinate separate days off and pay for childcare only three days a week. Another option is negotiating staggered schedules. One parent, for example, works 7:00 a.m. to 3:00 p.m. and the other works 9:00 a.m. to 5:00 p.m.[27] The parent who goes to work later does the daycare drop-off, and the parent who leaves work earlier does the pickup—another way to shave a few hours off the daycare bill.

66 *We completely underestimated the high cost of full-time daycare. Luckily, we worked with our provider and our employers to do some creative scheduling— which eased the financial burden."*
—Woman in her 40s, Wisconsin, bachelor's degree

Local friends can also be cost-effective resources, especially when it's possible to create informal co-ops among a group of mothers who know each other well or socially from neighborhoods, schools, religious organizations, companies—or anywhere that they share community visibility and a common bond. The typical parent co-op allows you to share care with four other parents, who each take one day a week to watch all five (or more) children. This is a viable option for a group of mothers who work part-time: with some schedule engineering, each mother can be the group babysitter on a regular day off. Generally, childcare centers are required to obtain state licensing, but some states allow families to care for their children through a cooperative arrangement.

Stay on Top of Childcare Trends: Tap into the Growing Cottage Industry

For generations, the most well-known options for childcare have fallen into two basic categories: some version of a daycare center where you bring your child, or some version of a babysitter you bring in to your home. Recognizing that so many families struggle to find and afford childcare, many smart and enterprising people are applying their business skills to the problem, offering innovative alternatives to traditional care. All these new services should give women assurances that it will become increasingly easier to find good quality, affordable childcare options—and that even now there may be similar offerings in your local area. Here are just a few of these developing possibilities.

Coworking and coparenting spaces: The growing freelance economy brings with it a growing desire for office space away from the distractions of home. Coworking spaces are popping up all over the country, and many, like Workafrolic[28] in Washington, DC, offer affordable childcare on the premises. At the Women's Business Incubator coworking space in Seattle, the childcare facility offers even more: a flexible, drop-in preschool for children between the ages of 2½ to 5. A similar setup can be found at Brooklyn Explorers Academy and Nido in Durham, North Carolina.[29] A Fort Walton Beach, Florida, office offers an attractive incentive for working parents to rent private and group office space with on-site babysitting at the very low cost of $3 to $5 *per day*.[30]

"Pop-up" childcare: Two Pittsburgh mothers launched Flexable-care.com, a service that brings on-site childcare to groups of parents at work (e.g., childcare provided for a company's employees on a snow day when daycare facilities may be closed) and at networking and professional events that take place in the evening outside of normal childcare hours.[31]

Websites that link parents with caregivers: Automating the recommendations-among-friends model, Sitterfied uses Facebook to help parents find babysitters whom their friends have used and liked. The company, which services families in New Jersey and Manhattan, hosts rapid-fire "meet and greets" (similar to speed dating), which give parents the chance to meet babysitters in person and see if they click.[32]

My Child Care DC is a Washington, DC–based, one-stop-shopping website that makes it easy for parents to search for licensed childcare and compare home-based and facility options (childcarereconnections.osse.dc.gov). On a more personalized basis, Sittercity in Chicago helps parents find babysitters on a regular schedule or on occasion (sittercity.com).

The larger-scale site Care.com operates in 20 countries (and boasts one parent-caregiver match every two minutes), and Urbansitter.com helps parents find childcare in 60 US cities.

All-in-one in-home daycare and preschools: Wonderschool is a San Francisco startup that facilitates a network of high-quality, in-home early childhood daycare/preschool hybrids. The startup helps educators and childcare providers launch their own schools out of their homes (even in apartments), and it provides help with licensing, program setup, and marketing—as well as software for teachers to track the progress of students.[33] Wonderschool has more than 50 programs in cities throughout California, and they are opening 150 boutique programs in the New York City area that are priced more competitively than private preschools.[33]

A childcare concierge: As the name implies, services that act as the intermediary for parents seeking high-quality childcare usually cater to higher-income families. Kid Care Concierge of Bridgewater, New Jersey, (kidcareconcierge.com) offers "kid care assistants" who manage the busy afternoon schedules of today's often over-programmed children. Zum (ridezum.com) in Southern California and the Bay Area keeps parents away from endless shuttling, offering rides via a Lyft-type service.

With increasing innovation in the childcare industry, don't assume that you'll never find safe, reputable, and affordable care. Yes, with any option, childcare will always be a significant expense, but focus most heavily on the fact that it's a declining cost as your children age. With a part-time or flexible full-time schedule, it's also possible to reduce child-care costs when infants need all-day care, toddlers need care when they're not in preschool, and older children need care when the school bus drops them off. Be resourceful and open-minded about finding the childcare that gives you the comfort to pursue the work that fits your life. Without question, childcare is an investment than can reap big long-term financial security returns.

Chapter 8

Break the Traditional "9 to 5" Mold (You Can Make a Full-Time Job Flexible, Too)

YEARS AGO, WHEN I HEARD Gloria Steinem speak on my college campus, she did not suggest that you can "have it all" because someone is going to *give it all* to you. Finding full-time work that fits and funds your life takes effort—and a positive, not defeatist, outlook.

If you're currently employed in a full-time job you enjoy, or you're interviewing for a new full-time job, the first step toward finding an easier way to "do it all" is to explore the possibility of work flexibility within a full-time schedule (especially if your weekly hours expand well past "9 to 5"). Most women have a truncated conversation with current or prospective employers about flexwork options, and as a result they conclude prematurely that it's not possible to make it work. It is, however, very possible when you put the time in to map out a mutually beneficial arrangement.

Aim for a Healthy Work-Life Blend, Not Balance

Work-life "balance" is a bit of a misnomer, and it's an ideal few if any women will actually achieve. Regardless of where you work, how flexible your job is, or how many hours you log, the work-life balance seesaw is always uneven. We are imperfect creatures with many competing responsibilities, so a fulfilling, productive, and lower-stress life requires an ongoing series of adjustments and tradeoffs. The time you spend at home will never equal exactly the time you spend at work. You'll never feel exactly the same level of contentment, passion, and fulfillment for both your work and home life. The key, instead, is to *blend* your work and life in a way that reduces stress and guilt.

Former Xerox CEO Ursula Burns is widely quoted for her no-nonsense work-life wisdom: her pragmatic spin is that work-life balance is something to aim for *over a lifetime,* not in a single day.[1] Stewart Friedman, founding director of the Wharton Leadership Program and the Wharton Work/Life Integration Project, goes a step further, advising both men and women to integrate the four domains of their lives—themselves, their work, their families, and their communities. He calls the quest for balance a zero-sum mindset that could shortchange enriching parts of your life. Friedman finds that people who feel "out of balance" are not focused equally on all parts of their lives, and that a more holistic approach leads to less stress.[2]

It's easier to reduce stress when women ease up on what is "supposed to be" work or nonwork time. With great regularity, there are home and family issues that will come up at the office, and there are work issues that will come up at home. The fact is that at certain times work or home will drain most of your energy. As a working mother, rather than continually striving for work-life balance, it's much more realistic to make sure that work and home alternate to the highest end of the seesaw with reasonable regularity. This does not suggest there would ever be a time that you neglect your children, your spouse, or your home. But *neglect* is an extreme word: there may be certain times you go through the regular routines with your children, but not all the extras like bedtime stories and movies. Carol Bartz, former CEO of Yahoo and Autodesk, made this point very well; she noted the importance of setting realistic expectations and keeping communication open with your family about times when you have a huge work project and won't be home much. The flip side is that you give your family confidence that when the big project is over, you'll turn off the technology and be fully present.[3]

Women also create unnecessary stress when they buy into the stereotypes that full-time working women are *always* fully consumed by their jobs. Time management expert Laura Vanderkam, author of *I Know How She Does It*,[4] is certain that women underestimate the time they have available during nonwork hours. Vanderkam suggests that women first realize they have a large weekly time palette—a full 168 hours—rather than struggling to fit everything they want to do into one 24-hour day. In her keynote address at the *9 Lives for Women* "Make Work Fit Life" conference,[5] she highlighted her data from senior-level female executives, which revealed that they worked, on average, 44 hours per week and slept 54 hours per week—leaving a full 70 hours a week for everything else, including commuting as well as personal and family time. Vanderkam challenges women to stop the universal "I don't have time for it" lament and admit that many things that are not done actually fall into the category of "this is not a priority for me."

Vanderkam's best piece of advice is that "done is better than perfect." It's not possible to be a perfect mother and a perfect professional—and striving for perfection in all aspects of life is the fastest route to burnout and stress. She advises women to take a cue from the hit Disney movie *Frozen* and "let it go." She says, "We have the choice to make life easier or to make life harder. If you want to make it harder, do so for a really good reason. Making the choice to work—and making long-term financial security a priority—allows all the other less important 'priorities' to shrink away."[6]

Ultimately, a work-life blend is up to all of us to manage—and it is something we can achieve with better awareness, strategy, and planning. Brad Harrington, executive director of the Boston College Center for Work & Family, agrees: "Whether you're fortunate to have a supportive workplace culture or not, the responsibility for achieving a work-life fit comes down to each of us individually. You can and should ask for modifications whenever necessary. But if they aren't forthcoming, you can only blame your employer for so long. Assuming you have marketable skills and the courage of your convictions, at some point you have to say, 'It comes down to me to fix the situation.' "[7]

Snag Flexibility from Interview Square One

As we have discussed, many women want to work full-time for professional and financial reasons. But they want that full-time work within a flexible schedule. The easiest way to get flexibility is from square one—at the point when you start a new job. Once a boss or a team is used to seeing your face every day in the office down the hall, it can be more difficult to switch to a schedule of working all or part of the time at home.

Your first priority is to direct your job search toward family-friendly companies that truly embrace flexibility on a companywide basis. This requires research and networking among company insiders—current or former employees. Don't rely only on lists that tout the best companies to work for in terms of flexwork advances. It's true that most of these companies have *some* form of flexibility within their work schedules, but that could be a single, small department or a particular initiative that accommodates, in reality, very few employees. I once complimented the head of human resources at a midsized company that was listed as one of the most flexible employers in Connecticut. She brushed off the compliment, saying that a couple of people had been hired into part-time positions, but it was in no way the norm. She went so far as to say that flexibility was not part of the company culture and that all employees were expected to work more-than-full-time hours at their office desks.

Once you have ferreted out the companies that truly offer widespread flexibility, the question is how to broach the subject of a nontraditional schedule. Recruiters will tell you not to mention flexibility until you have an offer on the table. I had a different view during my time as a recruiter: I told women that flexibility won't magically be injected into a full-time job after you sign the onboarding papers. If flexibility is a deal breaker for you, it's something you need to address diplomatically from the first interview. You might say something like, "I'm totally committed to the full-time responsibilities of this job, but I'm looking for a flexible schedule. After an agreed-upon period of time when I can prove my productivity and results, would it be possible for me to work at home two days a week?"

The answer to a question like this will be very telling. If the employer immediately responds that everyone works full-time in the office, then you know you're at a dead-end. If there is a noncommittal "We'll see," then there's a big risk you'll never get the flexibility you want. But if the employer cites examples of how flexibility has worked within the company and gives you a timeframe for implementation, it makes sense for you to continue the interview process.

Whatever you ask for, though, be specific. *Flexibility* is a big, ambiguous term. When employers hear the word, they often think *mayhem*—worrying they will never know where you are or what you're doing. I've learned to many women flexibility can mean very slight tweaks to a full-time schedule, like leaving early every Thursday afternoon. When employers hear that women have reasonable, specific, and predictable schedule adjustments in mind (rather than blanket requests for flexibility), they put their guards down and negotiate.

There are limits, however, to what would be considered a reasonable flexibility request. Here's what you *should not* ask for in an interview for a full-time position:

The equivalent of a part-time job. A full-time job description requires full-time hours. You can ask to divide your work hours between employer and home offices, but the required hours rarely shrink in the interview process. As a recruiter, I encountered many women who believed if they could just get their foot in the door they could convince employers the job could be done in fewer than 40 hours. This tactic is a waste of everyone's time.

A full telecommuting arrangement. Life and work are all about compromise—and it's particularly true in job negotiations. If the company doesn't have a broad telecommuting policy, it's unrealistic to expect that you'll be granted the opportunity to work entirely at home before you've developed relationships with your boss and your team and proven that you can get the job done well. An increasing number of jobs are advertised from the start as full telecommuting (lots of information technology jobs, for example), but for all others it's best to propose an introductory period of time that you work all or most of the time in the employer's office.

Get the Ideal: Flexibility with Predictability

Whether women ask for a nontraditional arrangement in a new job or in one they have been in for many years, they're not just looking for a flexible job, they're looking for a *predictable* flexible job. In reality, a great deal of intermittent flexibility exists:

- Eighty-one percent of employers allow employees to periodically change starting and ending times.
- Forty-two percent allow at least some employees to change start and end times on a daily basis.
- Eighty-one percent allow employees to take time off during the workday for important family and personal needs without loss of pay.
- Sixty-six percent allow at least some employees to work from home occasionally.
- Forty percent allow at least some employees to work some of their hours at home on a regular basis.[8]

It's first important to acknowledge that these numbers represent a big increase in flexibility since 2005. The ability to change start and end times has increased 13 percent, and to work regular office hours at home is up 32 percent.[9] Progress is being made, but by no means is there complete flexibility in the workforce or flexibility that is always predictable. The problem is that all this occasional, irregular flexibility makes planning for childcare, doctor appointments, school volunteering, and other personal matters difficult. The ability to take time off as needed for sports games or recitals is great, but it is a more fragmented blend of work and life. The point is that you should feel emboldened by the increase in flexibility and do what it takes to get the predictable work structure you need. The onus is largely on you: more routine, built-in flexibility is granted when it's clear that the arrangement is a "give and take" with a schedule that works for your boss, your team, and your department.

> ❝ *My ideal is a flexible, full-time job that predictably begins and ends early: 6:30 a.m. to 3:00 p.m. so I can be home for soccer and dinner.*"
> —Woman in her 40s, Virginia, master's degree

Carve Out Flexibility that Works Both Ways

In my seminars for current and returning professional women, I've often said "put yourself in the employer's shoes" and realize that flexibility can be, as I've joked, "the other 'F' word." Women who are fortunate to work flexibly—and many of those who are trying to negotiate a less rigid schedule—have no idea what it's like to manage a team that is coming and going all hours of the day.

I do know what it's like. For many years I managed a team of 10 women—all mothers of children from teenagers to tots. My business partner and I decided to walk the talk. We were recruiters who worked with employers to create flexwork opportunities for women, so we gave our team the typical small-company flexibility mandate: "We don't care when you work or how you work...just get the work done."

As it turned out, the lack of specific parameters was a big mistake. There was a fair amount of chaos and productivity that waned and occasionally waxed. One woman didn't work on Tuesdays, and another never worked past 3:00 p.m. Some women arrived in the office as soon as children were put on the school bus, and others came in late in the morning after a doctor's appointment or two. Half the team worked well into the night, and the other half never checked their email past 5:00 p.m. Some women worked only at home, and others practically slept at their desks. Without some simple flexibility guidelines, we spent a lot of time chasing down our team, and figuring out when to hold a staff meeting required an email round-robin that lasted for days.

After this experience, I understood why many employers would balk when we proposed flexible jobs. Clearly, flexibility can have a bad rap—and when clear guidelines do not exist, many of the criticisms are true. My argument, though, is that there is a compromise between freewheeling flexibility and being chained to a desk. How can the boss and all members of the team bank on when, where, and how they can reach each other—and when they can expect a response or work to be done? That's the question you have to think hard about before you broach the subject of flexible hours.

Don't Give Up Too Soon
(The Flexwork Request Is Not a Simple Ask)

Nearly all of my "returning professional" coaching clients tell me they left their jobs because flexibility was *definitely not possible* at their companies. When I dig deeper, I find that they made premature assumptions or exerted very little effort to negotiate. A stressed, overworked boss who is asked one question on the fly (e.g., "Would you mind if I work a day or two at home?") is not likely to react in a positive way. It takes a more professional proposal (ideally a written one that a boss can consider quietly and carefully)—detailing how the flexibility will actually work and how there will be safeguards so that nothing falls through the cracks.

> 66 *There was no flextime in the company I worked for (I realize now I didn't look too hard), so after my second child, I still worked full time, moved to the suburbs, commuted on an early train, etc., until my mother got sick and we moved her into our home. That was the end of my career."*
>
> —Woman in her 50s, New Jersey, bachelor's degree

One important note: a formal flexibility proposal is not very common in the interview process, because as a prospective employee it's difficult to know exactly how the department you would work in operates and how all the team members interact. It is still a good idea to review all the aspects of a professional flexibility proposal, however; there are likely to be some key points you could raise in conversation that would help you inject flexibility into your work structure.

For women looking to switch to a flexible schedule in a current job, the first step in creating a professional proposal is internal company research. Read your employee handbook to see if your company has a formal flexibility policy. If there is no written policy, don't immediately approach the HR team; they could thwart your efforts. Unless companies have adopted universal flexibility as a formal employee benefit, you're much better off trying to work out an arrangement directly with your boss.

Once you know the company line on flexibility, gather as much information as you can from colleagues in various departments about where flexibility actually does exist, how employees approached the request, and how it works best for individuals or teams. It's also a good idea to speak to friends and colleagues at other companies to see if they have flexibility approaches that could possibly work at your company, too. Focus on the metrics and productivity gains that will calm the fear of the unfamiliar and untested. The objective is to find—both within and outside your company—the best practices that will prevent a flexwork failure. If you jump in without the requisite research, and your flexibility arrangement is on shaky ground, it won't take long for your boss to shut down and call you back to your office desk full time. ·

An internet search will give you competitive research on peer companies that have adopted flexwork policies. One great shortcut is fairygodboss.com, where you can see the kind of flexwork that exists at various companies and employees rate the flexibility of their workplaces overall.

In your research you'll find numerous studies that document the fact that flexibility leads to higher productivity and lower employee turnover.

There's plenty of data on major cost savings and even data related to reduced greenhouse gas emissions as more people work at home. I'd advise staying away from data like this because it will likely fall on deaf ears. Employers tend to be very myopic—believing their companies have the most unique challenges—and they're only likely to listen to trends within their particular industries and peer groups. A manager is much more likely to be swayed by more anecdotal examples of how flexibility is working right in your own company, or at client or vendor companies closer to your fold.

Craft a Bulletproof Flexwork Proposal

The formality of your flexibility proposal will depend on your company and department culture and the relationship you have with your boss. At a minimum, you want to be armed with well-prepared talking points for a thorough discussion. If you think your boss would react favorably to a written proposal that can be reviewed after your meeting—and perhaps shared with senior management or HR—it makes the most sense to take this more formal approach.

The most critical part of your proposal is the topic of accountability. Any successful flexibility arrangement is completely transparent so you can manage the expectations of your employer. Your schedule can never be loosey-goosey; you need to set regular hours—always big blocks of time when your employer will know you're on the job. It's also best to set regular times for daily and weekly catch-up calls or meetings. The more your boss can predict how and when you'll be working, the more trust will be built into your flexible schedule.

Develop your pitch carefully so your boss knows you've thoroughly considered all aspects of a new work structure from collaboration, trust, and communication angles. The following is a general framework for your thinking that you can customize to your needs.

Zero in on your "ask." Decide exactly what you're proposing as your new work arrangement. "I'd like to work in a more flexible way" is a vague request that puts the onus on your boss to figure out possible scenarios. Because most managers prefer to have the people they manage always in their line of vision, take the lead in crafting an arrangement you and your boss can use as a starting point for discussion.

Begin by asking yourself, what is my major flexibility objective? If your answer is simply to achieve a better work and life blend, you need to get much more specific. You'll feel more control over your work and life if you establish and meet certain goals. What, specifically, will give you greater work and life satisfaction: a consistent eight- or 10-hour workday, fewer commuting days, the ability to drop your children off at school every day, a weekly volunteer morning for an organization you support, a part-time arrangement that gives you half the week at home?

Build your flexibility structure. Once you know your flexwork goals, the next step is to see how these goals translate to an actual work arrangement. Put more structure around your proposal by asking yourself questions such as these:

- Do I want reduced hours (something less than 40 hours) or a more flexible full-time schedule? Or is what I really need a full-time focus on making my work and life fit—not necessarily a part-time job?
- How important is it for me to advance to more senior levels? If that is a goal, will a flexible schedule get me there more slowly (or not at all)? Is a better work and life blend ultimately more valuable to me?
- What is my ideal flexible schedule—for example, beginning or ending the day earlier or later?
- Am I consistently working 40 hours a week, and could I compress all my hours into fewer days?
- Can I afford to earn less than a full-time salary?
- Could I successfully do all the most important aspects of my job in a part-time schedule? Could I work three days and be

paid 60 percent of my salary—a substantial savings for my employer and two free days for me?

- How would a part-time schedule affect my eligibility for employee benefits?
- Are there known busy periods throughout the year when I'd be willing to forego flexibility?
- Is the ability to work from home one or more days a week my objective?
- Do I have—or can I create—a home office setup that will be a productive, professional, quiet space?
- What equipment or software would need to be duplicated in a home office—and what would my employer likely provide?
- Which regularly scheduled meetings require my presence on site—and which could I participate in virtually?
- Should I be on site for predictable monthly responsibilities requiring last-minute coordination among many people and departments?
- How much on-site training or oversight is needed by the individuals and teams I manage?
- Do I need the buzz of a busy office to be truly productive?
- Would a job share be viable? Who would be a likely partner?
- Would my current childcare arrangements fit with my ideal flexible schedule?
- Would my childcare provider also be flexible when I need to give my employer extra time or handle emergency work situations?
- Would I prefer to cut back on or eliminate business travel? If this isn't possible, does day or overnight travel affect my desired flexible schedule?
- How does client interaction and oversight—especially for those in different countries or time zones—affect my ideal flexwork?

Decide where the work will get done. When women ask for my help in creating a flexwork proposal, I most often recommend an arrangement that includes time in both the employer's and the home office. In my experience, employers and employees find this arrangement a palatable happy medium. Working totally solo at home can be an isolating, distracting, and a less energy-charged environment. When the home office is not the only office, women appreciate the days they don't have to commute and the days they can be part of a more stimulating, interactive environment. Opportunities for advancement are also influenced by personal relationships, which can be harder to cultivate over email and Skype.

66 *My ideal job is a flexible full-time job where my expertise is respected and I don't need to put in excessive face time."*
—Woman in her 30s, New York, bachelor's degree

The trick is to decide which responsibilities are not compromised in a home office setting and which are best handled at your employer's office. To decide the optimal percentage of home office time, make a list of your major responsibilities, noting when you're working solo and when you're collaborating with the team. Highlight key accomplishments and the amount of solo time that was involved. If you find, for example, that 20 percent of the time you're getting significant work done completely on your own—and that the work is portable—then you have a solid argument for one workday at home. As you decide where work will be done, factor in all the communication tools that can make work at home easier, such as document sharing, the cloud, and conference call resources.

Ensure liberty and fairness for all. The reality is that in most offices, because of client meetings and travel, entire teams are rarely in the office together day in and day out. The fact that you're proposing home office work should not be considered an anomaly unless your team truly never leaves their desks.

If you're working on a very small team, there's wisdom in creating a flexwork proposal for everyone. Flexibility can backfire when only one or two employees appear to be getting special treatment, and employers often avoid individual flexibility deals because they don't want to invite an onslaught of disparate requests. If you take the extra step to think about how flexibility could work for the team overall, then you have much more firepower for a positive response.

Fairness is an especially critical issue when you're the manager of the team. If only the boss gets the perk of working at home, there will be a lot of friction. As the boss or a team member, create simple parameters for flexibility that accommodate all. Here are some ways to do that.

- Designate certain required "in the office" days for the entire team. Those are the days you can always schedule the team meeting.
- Choose core hours each day that team members should be available and engaged. Tell employees they have to make every effort to schedule their doctor's appointments, teacher conferences, and other personal matters, for example, before 11:00 a.m. or after 3:00 p.m.
- Keep technology as your friend, not your foe. The downside of flexibility is work that never ends. Let your team know they can unplug without penalty. Consider suggesting no emails after 9:00 p.m. or on Sundays, for example, to promote a culture that is not "all work, no play."

Show what's in it for your employer. It goes without saying that flexibility helps employees manage and blend work and life. From a negotiating perspective, however, don't dwell on how a more flexible schedule will allow you to do this or that with your family. Say simply that you're committed to and enjoy your job, but you think a more flexible schedule would help you increase your overall productivity.

Keep the major emphasis on your company and what they can gain from the arrangement. Since some employers will be wary because they can't see what employees are doing when they work at home, a good strategy is to think of ways that your productivity could very visibly increase and operational costs could decrease. Consider issues such as these.

- What might you be able to do better and faster without the distractions of a busy office?
- How much time do you spend commuting? If you're proposing to work two days each week at home, and you commute one hour to work each way, you've just gained four hours—the equivalent of a half-day each week—that could be used to make a dent in back burner or special projects.
- Are you a very early riser? Focus on all the routine tasks you could have done at home before 9:00 a.m.
- Where could you cut out the fluff of your job? Every job has wasted hours on tasks or projects that aren't big contributors to the bottom line. Propose dropping or streamlining some of your responsibilities. You may be able to get the real meat of your job done in fewer hours—saving your company money.
- Could allowing another person to take over some of your responsibilities provide a developmental opportunity for a less experienced, but high-potential, colleague?
- Could shifting your schedule so you come in earlier or stay later than usual allow your company to extend the hours it services global clients?
- Could working from home free up space in a crowded office or help a growing company avoid the cost of moving to a larger space?

Speak openly about your support system. Employers fear that women will juggle at-home work with the care of young children. Explain that even when you're home, you will continue to have childcare.

Stress your communication skills. To less technology-minded employers, working at home can be akin to working in Siberia. They need to be reminded you are "Jenny on the Spot" when it comes to communicating with the boss and the team. But it's not just about the speed of your response; they also need to be comfortable you'll have the right tools to communicate. Especially if you're suggesting a partial telecommuting arrangement for all or part of your team, look into technologies like Zoom or Click Meeting for videoconferencing, Slack for instant messaging, and Trello, Teamwork, or Weekdone for transparent workflow and project management—and other collaborative tools like Google Docs, Hootsuite, and GitHub.

Dodge the curveballs. Because every office culture and every manager's personality is different, only you know the objections you're likely to hear. Think about how your boss generally reacts when someone suggests a new way of doing things. You're likely to hear a similar brand of objections. Here are some I repeatedly heard when, as a recruiter, I asked if some full-time jobs had flexible hours:

> **"We have problems when people don't work full time in the office."** It's true that some people are more productive and bigger contributors than others. But point out that this has more to do with their work *ethic* and overall commitment to the business than their work *arrangement*.

> **"If we open that Pandora's box, the whole company will want to work flexibly, and it will be mass chaos."** While redefining company policy might be biting off far more than you can chew, you can address this objection by proposing how flexibility could work for your immediate team.

> **"Business is unpredictable. What if there are last-minute client requests or meetings, or an unanticipated trip out of town?"** This is an employer's worst fear: that you won't be available in an emergency situation. The best way to calm this fear is to give the assurance that your childcare will be flexible to cover last-minute situations when you have to be in the office or travel overnight.

"People aren't as productive or accountable when they're working on their own." With this objection, you again have to emphasize your work ethic and the volume of work you produce. It's also a good strategy to propose a trial period so your boss will see you still deliver high-quality work on time. In her remarks at my "Make Work Fit Life" Conference, Karyn Twaronite, partner and global diversity & inclusiveness officer at Ernst & Young, noted that her firm has had success with 30/60/90-day check-ins. She says, "Manage expectations. When you first arrange a flexible schedule, treat it like an internship, because you really do not know how well you will work in a flexible situation, and how well it will work for your employer."[10]

"Some jobs just can't be done at home." It's true that some jobs are better suited for telecommuting than others. But this objection usually relates to full telecommuting. Even high-intensity investment bankers or corporate attorneys have work they can easily do productively at home. Your boss will be more comfortable if you designate work that can be done well anywhere at any time.

Keep the likelihood of objections in mind as you prepare your proposal, and rehearse answers to the objections you think you'll hear.

Create checks and balances. Any big change needs some tweaking along the way. Your check-in meetings need a well-crafted agenda as well, covering topics such as these:

- Key accomplishments in your more flexible role
- Objections or accolades from colleagues and senior management with regard to the flexible structure
- Communication breakdowns
- Overall project coverage
- Team morale and fairness issues
- Seamless client interaction
- "Two-way street," mutual benefit issues

As you prepare your proposal, be flexible about flexibility. You'll never find the perfect work structure (or the perfect overall life structure!), but it is possible to find one that is a better work and life blend. Your goal is to make your boss feel that your flexibility arrangement will be seamless and transparent, and that it will never adversely affect the bottom line.

Salary and career negotiation consultant Katie Donovan of Equal Pay Negotiations recommends approaching the flexwork discussion as a routine negotiation.[11] She notes that 84 percent of managers expect employees to negotiate their employment packages, and there is the greatest wiggle room with salary, vacation, and flexibility. While she does not advocate an overt threat of declining a job offer or leaving a job, current or prospective employees should diplomatically make it clear that work flexibility—now available in some form at most companies—is one of their top priorities. Employers know all too well that women often decline offers or leave jobs when their flexibility requests aren't granted, and most will make some effort to compromise.

The price tag for employee turnover has been estimated as high as two times the employee's salary, so it's usually in the employers' best interests to retain the staff they've got. But many employers will be willing to bear the cost of replacing you if they think your flexibility proposal is skewed in only your favor. Donovan says that thorough preparation and careful research—especially at an employee's own company and at key competitors—drives successful outcomes most of the time.

Though a successful flexibility negotiation can initially appear to be a win, the pitfall to avoid is the job that is classified as part time but actually requires full-time hours to complete all the assigned work on time. Many women sell their value and negotiate a part-time schedule and salary, but then they actually end up working full time at half-time pay. One possible way to avoid this is to ask employers if they are willing to pay you on an hourly basis. Though this may seem like a junior-level solution, it works well for a senior-level headhunter at a top 10 executive recruiting firm who realized that she was not being compensated for all of her "part-time" hours. Most weeks she works her negotiated 20 hours and during busy times she works many more, but now she never runs the risk of "donating" her time. She has proven her value, and that trust and dependability have created an easy give-and-take situation with her boss. If you can give your employer the same comfort level of knowing that you're willing to bend and accommodate, then you may be able to change diapers and corporate history at the same time.

Some women who read this chapter may say it's too much work to get a flexible, full-time arrangement in their current jobs. While it's not a simple process, it's well worth the investment of time if it allows you to stay in your current full-time job or find a new, more flexible job that has full-time compensation and benefits. In my coaching experience, I've found that women who thrive when they are "all in" to professional work rarely are satisfied with a part-time job or a childcare hiatus with life as a mega-volunteer. If you use your well-honed business skills to convince employers that you won't miss a beat on a flexible schedule, you'll keep your professional life moving, blend work and family, and never jeopardize your long-term financial security.

Chapter 9

Target Small Employers that Have the Flexibility to Be Flexible (Corporate Giants are Slow to Change)

W HEN I WAS A SENIOR in college, there was great excitement when
big corporate recruiters came to campus looking for the next crop
of entry-level candidates. Every company was a household name, and I
remember feeling pretty special when I made it to the second round of
interviews with IBM. Thinking back, I have no idea why I was interviewing with IBM—other than I liked the prestige of the very well-known big
company name. It made little sense otherwise: I was an English major,
the editor of the campus newspaper, and not at all interested in selling
behemoth business machines.

Some version of that story has been told to me by current and former professional women many times. I've met left-brain, creative
women who were lured by the prestige of right-brain, big-bank training programs; journalists now earning a fraction of the big law firm
salaries they pursued on the strong suggestion of hard-driving parents;
and ex-consumer product marketing executives turned nurses who
finally came to the conclusion that healthcare has more meaning than
account management. For a variety of often unfounded personal biases
and outside pressures, many of us have at one time been led to believe

that big company names are the fastest route to highly regarded and risk-free careers.

The prevailing belief was once that big companies—established for many decades—held the most stability. This was especially true in the late 1990s, when the dot.com bubble burst and scores of startups failed. But the Great Recession then brought mass firings of once "safe" big corporate employees. Now the reality is that no company large or small offers jobs with rock-solid stability.

Though all companies can be volatile, opportunities at small companies are vast, and their market share is substantial. The 29.6 million small businesses in the United States account for almost 48 percent of private-sector employees and 41 percent of private-sector payroll. Small businesses accounted for almost 62 percent of all net new jobs from 1993 to 2016.[1]

These small businesses are led by individuals who often have opted out of the restrictive nature of corporate America. With miles of bureaucratic red tape, layers and layers of decision making, and the task of institutionalizing benefits for global employees, large companies tend to hold fast to traditional workforce structures and policies. For decades women have left these corporate giants because opportunities to work in any flexible way were nonexistent or scarce.

Great progress has been made on the flexibility front, but it will likely be years before flexibility is status quo across big corporate America or mandated by government. For now, if you're certain your current employer will never grant flexibility or you're just in the market for a new job, your best bet is to head toward smaller companies. More nimble management teams have the leeway to operate as humans, and they are more likely to bend on how work is done—as long as there is a defined structure, it is done efficiently, competitively, and on time. Small employers (50 to 99 employees) are much more likely than large employers (1,000 or more employees) to offer all or most employees these options:

- Traditional flextime or the ability to periodically change start and end times (36 percent versus 17 percent)

- The ability to change start/end times on a daily basis (12 percent versus 4 percent)
- An option to compress the workweek by working longer hours on fewer days (10 percent versus 4 percent)
- The ability to work some regular paid hours at home occasionally (9 percent versus 1 percent)
- Time off for family or personal needs (51 percent versus 33 percent)

You're also likely to find the most flexibility at professional services organizations and nonprofits, as well as companies that were founded more recently and have more women in their workforces. From an employee benefits perspective, smaller companies offer an advantage, too: they are more likely than large employers to pay all health insurance premiums (20 percent versus 6 percent).[2]

Follow the 1 Million for Work Flexibility Movement

1 Million for Work Flexibility (1MFWF) is the first national initiative creating a collective voice in support of work flexibility. You can follow this organization on Facebook and Twitter and stay on top of all the information their website provides about flexibility trends (workflexbility.org).

1MFWF tracks legislation related to work flexibility, so you can identify and keep track of the proposed and enacted city, state, and federal legislation that affects you. In 2017 the Flexibility for Working Families Act was reintroduced in Congress, giving workers the right to request temporary or permanent changes to the number of hours they're required to work, the times they are required to work or be on notice, and where they're required to work.[3]

The Workflex in the 21st Century Act (known as the Workflex bill) was also introduced in 2017 to help employees strike a better work-life balance. Employers who choose to adopt a workflex plan would be required to offer all employees the option to participate in at least one of six flexible scheduling options, such as telecommuting or predictable scheduling.[4]

While this legislation is pending, the majority of states have work flexibility policies that apply to state workers, and there are broader workplace flexibility laws (including right to request laws) in San Francisco, New Hampshire, and Vermont.[5] Especially if you live in one of these areas, your knowledge of flexibility laws could help you shape a work structure that not only fits your life but is also well within the guidelines of a wide range of small to midsize employers.

Roll Up Your Sleeves: Find Smaller Companies with a True Flexwork Culture

Many very smart women I coach tell me they just want a flexible job—without without creating a game plan. Since every company in your area cannot be a possible target, you'll need at least a preliminary short list of smaller companies that truly interest you within a reasonable commuting distance. A targeted list ensures that you'll make some real traction, and you can keep adding and deleting companies on the list as your networking and job searching evolves.

Let's assume, for example, that you want to work for smaller public relations firms in Ohio. There are many ways to begin and conduct a thorough search.

A great way to start is the internet. A search for "award-winning public relations firms in Ohio" or "award-winning public relations firms in Columbus, Ohio" may list many companies you've never heard of; select the ones that look worthy of further research. Checking out individual websites for agencies in your target locations will give more insights to their size, the type of work they do, their client lists, the backgrounds of their management team, and more. Most importantly, you might see evidence that flexibility and work-life balance are part of their company cultures.

Other ways to search might include "fastest-growing public relations firms in Ohio," which will likely include smaller firms; "best Ohio companies for flexible jobs;" or "best companies to work for in Ohio." The broader searches will lead you to lists of many different types of companies, so then you'll have to sift through and see if any are of interest and find out how much flexibility truly exists.

Once you have your initial company target list, the next step is to rev your networking engine. In virtually every job market—whether our economy is booming or near bust—the best way to find a job is through networking. When it comes to flexible jobs at smaller companies, networking is even more of a game-changer. As a general rule, far more full-time jobs are advertised, and it takes some digging to find less traditional roles. Through networking you're likely to find the best opportunities and vet companies that may not have long track records.

Networking is also a much better resource than online job boards. Pressing the "apply" button on an online job listing may seem like the fastest way to a job, but in reality, it is a rocket ship to a great abyss. Thousands and thousands of desperate job seekers send their resumés to any email address they can find, making it necessary for employers to ignore the mountain of resumés that a single job posting generates. Instead, employers often call a friend to say, "Who do you know who would be good for this job?" The "who do you know" game has been played for decades, and now it is a job-search card played by more than the uber-connected elite.

LinkedIn, for example, has leveled the playing field, offering anyone with a solid profile the opportunity to connect to recruiters and managers who were once impossible to access or reach. With more than 400 million members, LinkedIn is a networking goldmine where you could spend weeks on end doing nothing but finding more and more ways to connect to people who could help you find the flexwork you desire.

Exit Your Comfort Zone and Become a Networking Pro

One of my coaching clients, a 56-year-old woman from California who was navigating her way back to the workforce, realized she needed to network far out of her comfort zone. She emailed me this question:

I have connections at organizations where I'd love to work in a flexible way, but they are either people I'm not close to or people I don't feel comfortable approaching. Call it anxiety or an old-fashioned sense that I'd be "using" them to get a job, but it's an obstacle for me. How do I get over this? Just be pleasant and directly state what I want? That's it, done?

Yes, that's pretty much it. Here's how to do it well.

Establish even a very loose connection. Networking involves a shared connection, not just out-of-the-blue cold calls to strangers. Networking connections do not need to be people you know well: you can establish connections through relatives, school or employer alumni groups, club members, or a friend of a friend of a friend. Figure out how to give your connection the comfort level of knowing that in some way you are connected. It could be as simple as having children in the same soccer league or being connected to the same person on LinkedIn.

Be specific about the help you need. No one wants to hear, "I'd just like to pick your brain about flexible fundraising jobs." That's a conversation that could wander aimlessly with no easy end. Busy people want to slot you in for a quick brain dump of specific information they have at hand. A better approach would be, "I'm trying to get an idea of how most large fundraising departments are allocating part-time responsibilities among functions, and I'd like to see how yours is structured in relation to peer organizations." If you lay this out in an email or LinkedIn message, your connection can think about and summarize a worthwhile, bite-sized response. This very focused networking request would help you gather information about where and how your skills and experience would most likely fit at your connection's organization and many others. When you ask a dozen networking connections the same question, you start gathering valuable anecdotal research.

Limit the amount of time your connection needs to invest. Networking meetings over coffee and lunch should be reserved for people who know you well—and people who *offer* that valuable block of in-person time. When you don't know people well, it's best to say, "I'd like to schedule 15 minutes to talk with you by phone about these two things…" This approach is more likely to get you on busy calendars because there's a specific timeframe and agenda and no need for a harried person to leave the office.

Practice networking quid pro quo. Networking is a two-way street, and you're likely to build fruitful relationships when you offer, as well as request, help. It can be as simple as a polite sentence such as "Please let me know how I can help you as well," but it's better to offer something tangible. One great option is the "you should know" approach. Ideally, this should involve offering an introduction to someone you know whom your new connection might like to know as well. If it's difficult to offer a new business connection, then you could still offer something more personal that comes up in your networking conversation, such as a book you'd recommend, an interesting course that might further an interest, an introduction to a mother who has already navigated the college application process, an article on blending work and family, a tidbit of information you can glean from LinkedIn or a Google search … anything that conveys the message of "I want to be of help to you, too."

Convince yourself that networking among strangers and acquaintances is both socially acceptable and expected. When you do it right, you're not being pushy, you're not bothering anyone, and you're not wasting anyone's time. Everyone joins LinkedIn with the expectation that they'll connect with people whom they've never met. Beyond LinkedIn, you can tap into large networks of alumni who have shared your educational and employment experiences, fellow members of professional/social clubs and religious affiliations, residents of your town, or people who have the same attorney. You're even welcome in networking groups affiliated with schools *your children* attended. It's all fair game in an interconnected world where networking is the way to get informed, get noticed, and get ahead—for wallflowers and social butterflies alike.

As you continue the networking research process, you'll not only get the insider's perspective on many companies, you'll also find out which companies have the most ideal and widespread flexwork cultures and which should truly be on your serious target list.

Pursue general "word-of-mouth" intelligence. Ask friends, acquaintances, and loose connections if they know professionals who left the large corporate world to launch a small business of their own, or if they know about smaller, rising companies that have top-ranked clients. Many entrepreneurs need flexible help as they grow their businesses.

Often suburban towns are the homes of executives who semi-retire and need help running smaller ventures. One great example is a tiny firm in a small town run by a household-name, three-time CEO. As a recruiter, I placed a woman at his office, and she basically supports this ex-CEO's personal investments, real estate holdings, and corporate board activity. It's a flexible and exceedingly interesting opportunity for her to gain insights from a legend in the business world—and through networking you can find these influential small business owners, too.

Target small business owners who trained with leading companies. If you're interested in fashion design, for example, you could zero in on small business owners who once worked for Ralph Lauren or Tory Burch. LinkedIn can lead you to former employees of all big-name companies, and some may have small businesses in your area.

Check Chamber of Commerce websites in your target locations. Many entrepreneurs rely on their local business communities to spread the word about their smaller-scale ventures. You can research companies listed on Chamber of Commerce websites.

Join local chapters of major industry organizations. Smaller companies join industry organizations to get greater exposure. When you join, you have access to the membership directory, which can help you separate the wheat from the chaff. The more professional companies looking to build industry stature are more apt to be involved.

See who belongs to organizations that help entrepreneurs launch and grow businesses. Many fledgling company members cannot afford full-time employees, so they often need people who can work part time or on an intermittent project basis. In addition to checking out organization job boards, it's a good strategy to network with officers who are often listed on their sites.

Get Your Foot in the Door of Family-Friendly Companies

A strategic and ultimately successful search for flexwork is a very proactive activity; you shouldn't wait around for desirable job postings to appear online and then send your resumé into that void. Through networking, you need to find every way possible to get your foot in the door of your target companies.

There are never any guarantees that the people you know best will be able to help you make connections, so you can't limit the focus of your networking to the easy and the obvious. Instead, you should always cast a wide net and recognize that *anyone* has the potential to rustle up many connections to *any* small and interesting organization and help you with your flexwork search targets.

To illustrate a very resourceful and relentless networking process (a process that even many women at the senior levels don't use), let's say you decide to target a small but prominent fictitious nonprofit called the Sheridan Foundation, which has a focus on women and a reputation for family-friendly policies. On the organization's website, you find no open jobs listed that fit your profile, but you still want to try to make connections since you know that all open jobs are not necessarily advertised.

Here's how your networking might play out—these are the three best ways you would network to find people of influence who might be able to help you get inside Sheridan.

1. **You check out who is in charge**. First, you check the staff listing on Sheridan's website. You don't know anyone who is listed, so you look at the board of directors. Here you have better luck. You identify one neighbor, one woman who shares your alma mater, and one whom you think is married to an old friend. All three of these directors go on your priority "to connect" list.

2. **You harvest LinkedIn.** Your next step is to see if you have any LinkedIn connections to the organization's leadership team. Right off the bat, you spot a second-degree connection to the president. She is linked to one of your first-degree connections, which gives you a more compelling reason to send her an invitation to connect. You also have second-degree connections to two people on the president's senior team. You put it on your list to send LinkedIn invitations to all these people—not just using the default "I would like to connect with you" message, but sending a short note about who you know in common, your specific expertise, and your interest in flexwork at Sheridan. Once you're connected, you can message them on LinkedIn or look at their contact information for a direct email address.

   Another way you access insiders is by searching for "Sheridan Foundation," using the same search box at the top of your profile page. You find that you have eight first- and second-degree connections to current and past employees, board members, and volunteers. Starting with your first-degree connections (those you can email directly via LinkedIn), you find a former board member and a former director of programs who are likely to know people managing the organization today. You also find a current program consultant (an independent contractor who has some insider knowledge about working flexibly at Sheridan), and a former volunteer whom you know through a different organization.

Moving on to your second-degree connections, you identify some very good prospects: a vice president, a director, and several managers, all of whom you can invite to connect on LinkedIn and then (if they accept) have direct access to via messaging. For each second-degree connection, you check to see who you know in common in case you can ask one of those people for a more personal introduction as well.

3. **You pursue alumni connections.** Because Sheridan is a very small organization, you doubt that you will find any connections who share your alma mater, but you contact the career services departments of the schools you attended, ask if they have any information about Sheridan, and see if they have an online alumni directory. (Most schools do, although they are not all an equal bounty; these directories rely on the participation and updates of alumni, who can be hard to pin down.) As you suspected, you do not find any fellow alumni at Sheridan aside from the one you identified through LinkedIn, but you know that this third step is always worth a shot.

Now that you've gone down these three research avenues, you have a good list of connections who could possibly give you an "in." Your goal is to get their attention through what I call "networking communications"—LinkedIn invitations and messages and personal emails that ask for very specific information and help as described earlier in this chapter.

Interview Employers While They're Interviewing You (Know Who Is Just "Checking the Flexwork Box")

When you're lucky enough to get a new networking connection on the phone, or when you chat over coffee with a business friend who knows one of your target companies well, you want to get answers to many key questions in a short period of time. Your objective is to find out if a company on your target list is really worth pursuing for a truly flexible job.

Finding out the answers to these eight questions will uncover valuable flexwork research information.

1. **How is the company positioned for growth?** Remember that about one-third of small businesses survive their first year and half close down after five years. You want to be sure to join a smaller company that is visibly growing or has a fighting chance to survive. Read the "About Us" section of their website and their profile on LinkedIn, and then write down questions you want to know about the type of work they do, the longevity of their clients (or the ability of a startup to sign on significant clients), who their competitors are, areas/markets where they're looking to expand, etc. And if the company does not have a website, beware. Today most viable companies have a top-quality, well-crafted internet presence.

2. **What's the size and structure of the company?** This may be something you can find out from a company's "About Us" website page. If not, you have to find out if the "company" is actually just one or two people hiring themselves out as consultants or if there is a larger team that may need flexible help as their business ebbs and flows. Consider if you want to work for a solo entrepreneur or be part of a larger team at a small company.

3. **How is the management team and the company structured?** Find out if the company has clear divisions of labor or if it is a general free-for-all environment where a small group of employees are tripping over themselves to put out fires. Job descriptions at smaller companies tend to be amorphous, often encompassing many titles and functions and causing workweeks to extend far beyond the 40-hour mark. You don't want what you possibly gain in flexibility to be overshadowed by what you have to give up because of intense stress.

4. **What's the company's overall work-life culture?** A company can say they offer flexible work, but the real acid test is if they're promoting a reasonable blend of work and life. Even many smaller companies only hire full-time employees and think

they're making big concessions to let them work from home all or part of the time. When employees are then expected to work endless hours, it diminishes any benefit of cutting out the commute and having more time for family. You can reach burned-out status in any office setting.

5. **Is flexwork a policy or a bunch of one-off deals?** Remember that your ultimate objective is "flexibility with predictability." You will always be at risk for losing a flexible job unless a company has some basic flexibility policies in place. It doesn't have to be a chapter in an employee handbook (many smaller companies do not have handbooks), but there should be a universal understanding that certain kinds of flexwork are possible and blessed by senior management for *all* employees. The reality is that bosses (and their flexibility agreements) come and go.

6. **Are employees who have flexible schedules viewed less favorably?** Though the desire for work and a life is a societal force all employers must now reckon with, even plenty of traditional work stalwarts at smaller companies still look askance at anyone who is not working fervently every hour of every day. If you work a flexible schedule, will you run up against many less-progressive managers, or will you have the same chances to advance in title, responsibility, and compensation as employees who never leave employer desks?

7. **What opportunities are there for project work so you and the employer could have a trial run?** Smaller companies can be dominated by big personalities who may or may not foster a healthy or pleasant work environment. In larger companies, there are more safeguards so that a few tyrants and control freaks can't kidnap a company's entire culture. Consider a trial run, especially if there are very few employees. Ask about the kind of projects that could be within your job function at this company so that you can suggest some ideas.

8. **What is the employee benefits eligibility for less-than-full-time employees?** The US healthcare system will likely be in flux for

the near term, with lots of variation on the benefits employers offer—and at what cost to employees. Be clear about the employee benefits that are possible for part-time employees, which sometimes could be more generous than government mandates. A company that has at least 50 employees may be willing to give you a 30-hour, part-time schedule so that you can qualify for healthcare benefits. (Conversely, though, there are companies that keep part-time employees under the 30-hour limit so that they are not required to provide these benefits.)

Once you have a list of questions, prioritize what is most important for a conversation that might be limited to 15 minutes. You need to make every minute count, so word all questions in a way that will give you more than a simple yes-or-no answer—or quick answers intended to be politically correct. For example, don't ask, "Does this company have a work-life balance culture?" If you're talking to a member of the management team you might receive what they think is the obligatory answer of "yes." Dig deeper and invite more nuanced discussion by asking, "How is the workday structured for most employees?"

Armed with all your research, you can head off in specific directions. Every person you speak with is likely to have recommendations of other people who could be helpful as you search for flexwork at smaller companies in your area. When networking is done well, it's a process that mushrooms and mushrooms, and you'll spend entire productive days networking toward the work that fits your life.

Chapter 10

Work Until You've Funded Your Future (If You Think You're "Too Old," You're Not!)

THERE ARE TWO GROUPS OF women who worry that they may be "too old" to work. The first group is women nearing the traditional retirement age of 65 who may want or need to continue working. The second group is women in their 40s and 50s who have been out of the workforce for many years and fear that they've waited too long and reached an undesirable age when it would be too difficult to get back in. In both cases, age is not an insurmountable issue; in fact, age is becoming more of an asset than a liability in today's workforce.

Be an Ageless Star in the Vibrant Older Job Market

Let's first set the stage for women who are nearing or at the traditional retirement age of 65. To put opportunities for older workers in perspective, you first need to understand that the 85-and-over age demographic is the fastest-growing, and it is expected to more than triple by 2060.[1] With falling unemployment rates and this continual aging of the US population, employers will increasingly face shortages of knowledge and skills. This means workers age 65 and over are attractive not only for their seasoned experience but also because most use the government-supplied Medicare for their primary insurance. For these reasons, most employers are no longer anxious to push their oldest workers out the door.

Now workers can be "flexibly retired"—staying with an organization with a different work arrangement and phasing their retirement over time. It also means that women who leave the workforce and want to return in their 50s or even 60s will be in good company as the ranks of older workers rise. During the next 20 years, adults age 50 and over will likely have greater rates of workforce participation into their sixth and seventh decades.[2]

The majority of employers now expect their employees to stay on past traditional retirement age.

- Seventy-seven percent of employers say many of their employees plan to continue working either full time or part time. Companies that outsource talent, like KellyOCG, see employers experiencing a shortage of workers in the science, technology, engineering, and math fields, and they are actually bringing baby boomers back from retirement to be contingent employees.
- Employers recognize that we need a new definition of work as we live longer and need more income—working flexibly and/or in different capacities.
- Thirty-nine percent of employers offer flexwork schedules to help employees transition to retirement, and 27 percent encourage employees to participate in succession planning, training, and mentoring. While these are somewhat low figures, they represent growing trends.[3]

Recognizing that employers are open to older workers, colleges are extending working years, too, with innovative yearlong programs aimed at late-career professionals. The University of Minnesota's Advanced Careers Initiative, Stanford's Distinguished Careers Institute, and Harvard's Advanced Leadership Initiative all provide the "third stage" of higher education and help the age-50-plus demographic develop dynamic new career directions.

To achieve financial security today and long into the future, embrace the idea that you can work at every age and stage—even through years that were once designated solely to "retirement," and even in industries and job functions where you have not built years and years of expertise. Because employer-mandated retirement dates are rare, and there is no hard stop for work at age 65, job seekers are no longer considered "over the hill" at any age. There are endless opportunities for women who need to fill retirement savings coffers, and this is an especially welcome message for the thousands of women who leave the workforce for many years and at some point think they're too old to return.

In 2017, women over age 55 had much lower unemployment rates than younger women just starting careers in the 20- to 24-year-old age bracket (3 percent versus 6.3 percent). Unemployment rates for midcareer women ages 35 to 44 (3.5 percent) are about the same as for older workers. With unemployment for the total population at 4.1 percent, the idea that older women are unable to find or keep jobs is unfounded.[4] It's also important to note that age discrimination charges are declining—albeit slowly—falling more than 14 percent from 2007 to 2017.[5]

The overriding message for today is that those who want to work can work for as long as their health allows. This work is most likely not the traditional, rigid corporate job; we all have the most freedom to create a long income stream through the flexible part-time, freelance, and entrepreneurial work that is now in greater supply and most preferable to women as they age.

Aim High (The Oldest Workers are the Highest Paid)

From a compensation standpoint, the oldest men and women in the workforce also earn the most:

- Baby boomers (born 1946 to 1964, who represent 29 percent of the workforce) are the oldest and slightly highest earners with average salaries of $1,049 per week (up 21 percent since 1979). Nearly 19 percent of women age 65 and older are still working (increasing steadily since 2008). As the population ages, the number of older workers will continue to rise.

- Gen Xers (born between 1965 and 1980, who represent 34 percent of the workforce) earn an average weekly amount that is almost identical to baby boomers ($1,043). Like baby boomers, their compensation has increased almost 21 percent since 1979.
- Millennials (born between 1981 and 1998, who represent 37 percent of the workforce) earn about half the weekly salaries of baby boomers and Gen Xers (a weekly average of $572), and they are the only age group that has lost earning power (down 4.08 percent) since 1979.[6]

This data contradicts persistent misperceptions that new college graduates and midcareer professionals are favored for the most lucrative jobs. Baby boomers and Gen Xers should not feel that they're too old to be working or that they are not in a position to command competitive salaries.

Know Where Older Workers Are in Big Demand

From both compensation and opportunity standpoints, a wide variety of industries are considered as promising job fields for workers over age 50, including health, sales, information technology, advertising/marketing/public relations, engineering, finance, operations, insurance, and human resources.[7] Specific job titles expected to grow for this demographic in the 2012 to 2022 time period include interpreters (46 percent growth), healthcare social workers (27 percent), dieticians (21 percent), accountants/financial managers (13 percent), and personal financial advisers (27 percent). It's not surprising that this list is heavily weighted with healthcare and financial management—two services critical for the aging baby boomer population. Also on the high-growth list for older workers are independent contractor positions that leverage industry expertise[8] and benefit from long and varied life experience.

A terrific resource for age-50-plus job seekers is Nancy Collamer's website (mylifestylecareer.com). Collamer's site, her book (*Second-Act Careers*), and her newsletter highlight the many options for late career reinvention and ways to extend income beyond traditional retirement age. On her website homepage she has a link to a tremendously useful list of "100 Great Second-Act Career Resources" that belie the stereotype that new, interesting, and lucrative work challenges are the domain only of the young.

Women who want professional work past age 50 should not be discouraged by articles that suggest it's easiest for older workers to find low-voltage jobs such as museum tour guide, messenger, or tailor. First of all, there's nothing stopping a 50-something woman from pursuing jobs that would be considered "hot" by anyone at any age. As Collamer points out in her *Second-Act Careers* newsletter, with training older workers can pursue truly popular and lucrative new career paths, such as computer coding (generally considered a hot job for recent college grads).[9]

The other reality is that only so many companies will be highlighted on any "best jobs" list—not accounting for the thousands of employers who hire older workers as employees, freelancers for specific projects or consultants on a longer-term basis. In the job market for retirees, especially, there are lower-level jobs for people who are just looking to fill long days and higher-level jobs for people who want to keep building impressive resumés and their retirement accounts. Today women can focus less on which industries have the most plentiful jobs for any age group. They can worry less about whether a certain industry caters to the young, because as all companies hire more experts for short-term assignments, women with many years of experience will be considered attractive resources. Employers will have many more jobs across the board for women who know how to position and sell skills and experience for part-time and freelance opportunities in what is becoming a long runway and a wide-open market for lifetime flexible work.

Make Confidence Your Age-Discrimination Foil

Despite encouraging trends toward increased older-worker employment, no one can dispute the fact that ageism does lurk in some workplace shadows. My strong belief, however, is that women are not powerless to overcome any hiring manager's archaic preferences for early career professionals and recent college grads. In my experience, age is most often an issue *if you make it an issue*. It's a combination of your perceived energy level (how you act) and your overall presentation (how "current" your wardrobe appears and how well you sell your seasoned strengths). It's not just a pithy quote that "you're defined by attitude, not age."

Whether you're a current or returning professional, choosing a professional wardrobe is the relatively easy part. What takes more time is cultivating the right attitude—and the right "presence"—that defies your biological age. A wonderful primer is Sylvia Ann Hewlett's book on *Executive Presence*,[10] which she calls the missing link between merit and success. Though this book may be more widely read among current professional women, it is equally useful for women navigating their way back to work. Hewlett describes executive presence as "a dynamic, cohesive mix of appearance, communication, and gravitas." To have true executive presence, she says you must know how to use all elements to your advantage: "Executive presence is an amalgam of qualities that true leaders exude, a presence that telegraphs you're in charge or deserve to be." Though I know few women aiming to be at the very top of the work world, transmitting leadership qualities for any position is key.

I'll use my elderly father as a good example of professional presence and confidence. He's 89, but he carries himself as if he is 20 years younger. Hearty "age be damned" defiance propels my father to the stage. At about age 60, he left a career in office technology behind and followed his passion to sing. He formed a band that includes musicians with highly acclaimed global resumés, and he redirected his marketing skills toward high-profile performances at big corporate events and entertainment venues. Few would disagree that the music business favors the young, but my father just barrels ahead, believing that all potential opportunities are fair game.

My octogenarian Dad doesn't lose valuable time thinking about age discrimination, but it's a phrase that is hinted at or deeply discussed over and over in my coaching practice—and by some of the most unlikely people. A woman in her early 60s who has created a powerful resumé, authored a highly acclaimed book, appeared frequently on TV, and developed a contact list that reaches into every nook and cranny of the corporate world told me she didn't land a desired job because of her age (never considering that her skills were actually not a good fit). Women in their 40s and 50s routinely tell me they can't fathom returning to the workforce because "no one" would hire anyone *their age* (based possibly on only one uncomfortable interview with a young hiring manager in sneakers). Both women and men see a late career layoff as the end of the line, because lots of people still mistakenly believe that no one can find a job after the clock strikes 50-plus.

Despite the fact that "60 is the new 50," "50 is the new 40," and similar proclamations designed to promote feelings of eternal youth, there is still a misplaced belief that employers are most interested in those who wore a cap and gown in the recent past. As a former recruiter, I can tell you with great conviction that this is simply not true. In all my work with women, I have learned one simple truth: the roots of ageism are in a widespread deficiency of *confidence*, the powerful job search tool that propels us forward with our head held high. Too many women let their age strip away confidence as each birthday passes by.

Even those with the most outward bravado have more hushed moments of fear and uncertainty. This was crystal clear to me the day an accomplished and seemingly hyper-confident woman (who never missed an opportunity to brag profusely about her many talents) told me that at her age, she felt too insecure to attend a black-tie dinner alongside younger heads of fashion, industry, and the arts. "What would I possibly have to say to those people?" asked the woman who never seemed at a loss for self-important words.

Then there was the time I met a "career coach to the stars"—a professional who guides both men and women as they wend their way to the executive suite and wield the power to make stocks go up and down. This executive coach told the story of a woman in her 50s who had been the CEO of several companies. The former CEO was looking for her next big post and needed to revise her resumé. The executive coach told her to summarize her key strengths and most recent accomplishments. Six weeks later, the former CEO said she was still struggling with the task. Despite the fact that she ran several companies, she was having trouble identifying and "bragging about" her skills.

Though the lack of confidence among women can be crippling and very widespread, there are plenty of role models who don't let age stop them in their tracks. The spirit and determination I see in my father, I also see in impressive 50-, 60-, and 70-year-old women who continually reinvent themselves in and outside of corporate America. The woman who, at age 80, still worked at a New York City museum, and lectured around the world. Another at 85 who still commutes to New York City from the suburbs three times a week to work at a major nonprofit. The 75-year-old executive coach who still travels to clients nationwide. All of these women shun stereotypes and negativity, and they avoid making assumptions based on very limited—or no—research. Women of this ilk never let age define their job search or think that a certain birthday closes certain doors. They have energy, enthusiasm, ideas, perspective, and the confidence that they can sell their expertise for years to come.

Believe You're Always Young Enough to *Return* to Work, Too

Now let's talk more specifically about the second group of women who think they are too old to work: women who waffle about or are anxious to return to the workforce. Women who have been out of the workforce for more than a couple of years—and have had more than a couple of birthdays past age 40—are the ones who, most of all, fear later-in-life reinvention and firmly believe there's an age limit on work. One Twitter profile I read belongs to a woman who left the workforce; she noted, "I used to be interesting." This is a sad commentary on another kind of confidence plunge that occurs when women leave the workforce. It's obviously not true that only people who work are interesting, but sometimes women are made to feel that way when they don't have tales of compelling recent *professional* work to offer up in casual conversation.

> " As I return to the workforce, my ideal is a full-time, 9:00 a.m. to 5:00 p.m. position that doesn't require significant evening/weekend time. When I left, my industry considered full time to be 50 to 60 hours a week."
>
> —Woman in her 30s, Pennsylvania, master's degree

The fact that employers *do* want the talents of women beyond the age of 40 was very apparent even a decade ago when I held several large-scale "Professional Connections Forums" that brought returning professional women together with corporate and Wall Street giants. I've also seen it more recently at iRelaunch "Return-to-Work" conferences, where there may as well have been a huge welcome sign blinking in neon lights. At one of these events, Edith Cooper, global head of human capital management at Goldman Sachs, called returning professional women "gems of the workforce."[11] It would be hard to find a more resounding affirmation that when you dive back in you can surely find lucrative, professional work.

As iRelaunch cofounder Carol Fishman Cohen explains,[12] returning professional women (presumably those out of their 20s and 30s) have significant life experience, fewer likely work interruptions from maternity leaves or spousal job relocations, and a mature perspective. If you look at your outdated resume and still see a diamond in the rough, I highly encourage you to read some of the 300-plus success stories that can be found at irelaunch.com.

Many of these success stories are the result of internships or "returnships" for older workers sponsored by an array of forward-thinking large companies. These return-to-work opportunities are heavy in the finance world (Barclays, Morgan Stanley, Credit Suisse, Fidelity, Goldman Sachs,

J.P. Morgan, Dow Jones, UBS, Merrill Lynch, and more), but they also have representation in other industries via companies such as Deloitte, Ford, General Motors, Johnson & Johnson, LinkedIn, PayPal, Texas Instruments, Booz Allen Hamilton, GM, IBM, Verizon, PepsiCo, and Facebook. Returnships can be pathways to permanent work or solid recent experience on a back-to-work resumé.[13]

In the advertising world, an increasing number of marketers are pressuring their agencies for more female representation on seasoned account teams. General Mills, Verizon, and Hewlett Packard are a few of the companies that asked their agencies to meet diversity requirements or lose their business. Women who have years of experience or the recent training from returnships can be big assets for these agencies.[14]

Take an Ounce of Prevention to Succeed
in Any Flexwork Reinvention

As you consider a return to the workforce or a move from your current job to one that offers more flexibility, avoid setting off impetuously toward flexible jobs that may have the right hours and the right location, but not the right fit. Career reinvention, recycling, or rebranding requires careful thinking and planning to make sure that the work you choose is both personally fulfilling and financially sound. Here are five preliminary steps I've learned through trial and error, four entrepreneurial ventures, and many career incarnations.

1. **Get a full financial tune-up**. Find out if your flexwork idea makes long-term dollars and sense. Melissa Ciotoli, a certified financial planner and financial counselor at Resnick Advisors, once transitioned to the workforce after a 10-year family hiatus. She now tells clients to thoroughly research how a career break or the compensation for any new job or entrepreneurial venture will impact long-term security. "Very often," Ciotoli notes, "career reinvention requires financial re-engineering. Even a

slight dip in income—or period of no income while building a business—can negatively impact retirement savings."[15]

When I cofounded a recruiting business, for example, startup experts told us we wouldn't be writing ourselves paychecks anytime soon. They said most new businesses don't turn a profit for an average of five years. And they were right on the money—or the lack thereof. As a new entrepreneur, you need to plan for a similar lapse in income. That income lapse is a double whammy because you're not earning money you can spend *and* save. Assume during a five-year startup period you suspend a monthly savings schedule of $500. Ciotoli estimates that the $30,000 you would have saved during that period could have grown (using a conservative 5 percent interest rate) to more than $70,000 in 20 years. Think far ahead and consider if a similar "loss" in an entrepreneurial venture or a new, but perhaps lower-paying, professional pursuit would likely be offset by a period of higher earnings down the road.

2. **Rebalance your life portfolio**. Reinvention gives you the opportunity to find work flexibility and fit a new career more neatly into all aspects of your life. David Corbett, a thought leader on life transitions for professionals, created the concept of a "portfolio life" to illustrate how we all should invest in a diversified set of experiences. His seminal book by the same name, *Portfolio Life: The New Path to Work, Purpose, and Passion after 50*,[16] encourages readers to integrate income-producing activities, family, interests, travel, giving back, new learning, and more for a life that is more balanced and satisfying.

Rebalancing is particularly in order when you're considering an entrepreneurial venture. How much time will be left for your family, exercise, hobbies—the things that keep you happy, less stressed, and fulfilled? Unless you have the ability to hire staff on day one, a business can consume all waking hours of your life. My Type A personality and zeal for building out a business make the "off" button elusive. Without a lot of self-control and reminders of all ways I find life satisfaction, my personal time dwindles down to zero fast.

3. **Take a deep dive into your true motivations**. You could *want* to be an organic farmer or a teacher in an underserved school, but whether you *should* be is another important matter. There's no changing or downsizing your professional DNA: for true happiness, fulfillment, and success you can't ignore your core motivations. Fulfilling flexwork isn't just about the work structure; it's about the work environment. Debra Levine, Executive Vice President of Miami, Florida–based Paul Hertz Group,[17] began her career with a long coveted—but surprisingly miserable—research job at a world-renowned hospital. Years later she created PRINT®—a quick, easy, and affordable assessment questionnaire to help others avoid career missteps.

   I needed a tool like this when I was a newly minted college graduate with an English degree. At the time, I thought I launched a very logical job search: I liked to write, so I thought I would be happy in any environment where people were writing. What I didn't realize then—and what career assessment tools have shown me since—is that to be really, truly motivated, productive, and happy I have to be in a job where creativity is constantly flowing, new ideas are welcome, and there are lots of opportunities to think up new approaches, products, or services. That's not what I found in my first job, in a big accounting firm's training department, where everything was very sterile, controlled, and "by the book."

4. **Develop your right brain**. Whether you're driven by creativity or analysis, Daniel Pink, author of *A Whole New Mind: Why Right-Brainers Will Rule the Future*,[18] says that right-brainers (people who are more intuitive, thoughtful, and subjective) are poised to rule the world. Life coach Susan Bedsow Horgan assigns Pink's book to all new clients seeking career reinvention. Horgan, a woman in her 60s, is now in her fifth career (including a stint as the Emmy Award–winning producer of a

daytime soap). She says the book gives direction and structure to all professional yearnings.[19] Author Pink chronicles the move from the information age to the conceptual age and tells you how to use right-brain survival tactics for any job you pursue.

Horgan recalls one coaching client who was stuck in a Cincinnati cubicle doing marketing drudge work for a manufacturing company. She had an MFA in creative writing but never thought that degree would help her earn a decent living. When she read Pink's book, she felt there was a professional—and lucrative—future for her right-brain talents. Six months later she left the cubicle and returned to her true passions. Now this right-brainer more than meets all her living expenses through flexwork as a professional writer and a paid adviser to artists who learn to make money doing the work they love.

5. **Find your reinvention gurus**. To keep her business moving in positive directions, Boulder, Colorado–based executive consultant Ginny Corsi[20] (who counts teaching, journalism, executive education, and Wall Street marketing among her many professional lives) greatly respects the words of Brené Brown (brenebrown.com), who speaks eloquently on one of her personal values: "beingness, not just doingness." Brown came to fame with her TED talk on vulnerability and articles like "Exhaustion Is Not a Status Symbol." Brown and many other authors, blog writers, TED speakers, and experts of all kinds can be your inspiration to recharge, renew, reinvent, and find the flexibility that fuels your passions and your ability to support yourself and your family.

Don't Be an Age Snob: Be Open to Reverse Mentoring

A big part of career reinvention is the opportunity to venture forth in a new direction with an openness toward learning new skills, business processes, and ways of thinking. When your confidence and attitude lead you to later-in-life flexwork, you also need to be open to working with many people who could be younger than you are—including those who may be the age of your children. But the fact that many coworkers may be in a different generation is more an opportunity than a disappointment. It's a matter of perspective, and with more people working later in life, you're likely to have plenty of more seasoned company. You can think of yourself with chagrin as one of the "old" employees over the age of 40 or feel empowered by the fact that you bring years of knowledge and experience as one of the more seasoned professionals on the team.

If you just can't tolerate working with younger colleagues, you can avoid industries that are known as magnets for the young. Women's magazines, tech startups, and advertising agencies are just a few that quickly come to mind. But in most workplaces, there's a good distribution among various age demographics, and there are valuable opportunities to get insights from people who were born at different times and who view the business world in different ways. As your professional life progresses—or as you look to re-enter the workforce—it's wise to view reverse mentoring as a valuable chance to learn. One of the best reasons to embrace the idea of working with millennials, for example, is to absorb their vast knowledge of social media. To promote any service or product now requires at least a working knowledge of social media, even if your job title is far from the marketing or communications realm.

Enjoy the Long View: A New Flexwork Path Can Span Three Years or 30

When women are worried about the age issue—especially when they're considering a return to the workforce or moving in a new direction—there's often the sense that they don't have enough time left to achieve anything of significance, especially if additional education or training is required for a field of new interest. As a society, we still get hung up on the idea of "careers" that begin when we're young and end after following the same path for many years. The fact is that there is not a prescribed amount of time that constitutes a significant professional investment. Unlike previous generations, we all can pursue multiple work phases of varying lengths—in a zigzag rather than a straight line.

It only takes a short time to build resumé-worthy skills and experience. Ask most stay-at-home mothers if their post-college work (even if it spanned only a few years) was a significant life experience, and I'm pretty sure most would say it was. For this reason, I've always told women in their 40s and 50s (the decades when the idea of returning to work or reinventing fast-track jobs most often emerges) that they have more than enough time for a second or third go at pursuing interests with a paycheck attached.

One of my greatest work role models was an elderly gentleman who was a trade show pioneer. I met him when I was 30 and he was 90, and he hired me as a consultant to create a large-scale Women's Health Forum and many other exhibitor-filled events. Though the trade show theme ran throughout this man's career, there was always a new twist, a new format, a new industry—a new way to reinvent. Well into his 90s he put on a suit and went to the office every day. He was more on the ball and full of ideas than most 30-year-olds I knew. Unlike so many who decide at a self-prescribed age that their professional ship has sailed, he clearly felt, as we all should, that time, age, and the ability to work are always on our side.

❝ *My goal has never been to get to the top of my profession. I aim for my own definition of personal growth and the ability to always earn a good living."*
—Woman in her 50s, South Carolina,
two master's degrees

For the everyday sisterhood, it's time to set aside the dictionary definition of ambition: "an earnest desire for some type of achievement or distinction, as power, honor, fame or wealth, and the willingness to strive for its attainment." We don't need power for the sake of power, jobs that prove that we can make it to the very top, and recognition of achievement by anyone's measure other than our own. We can keep professional work fairly simple, flexible, manageable, and even-keeled, without shortchanging family or finances and always taking pride in a multiphased professional story along the way.

APPENDIX

Get Organized!
Next Steps Toward Flexible Work

When you let go of the narrow, "get to the executive suite" definition of ambition, you open the door to many flexwork options you can pursue on your own terms—alongside caregiving for children and aging parents. You decide how many hours you want to work, where you want to work, if you want to work for yourself or for an employer, and how many more years you'd like to keep working.

With this freedom to choose your own path comes the responsibility to consistently make it happen. As you've learned in this book, there are too many unexpected hurdles and too many financial needs in a long retirement to make it wise for you to relinquish total responsibility for your personal financial security. The smart money is on creative, broad-thinking, confident women who always keep their skills current and find some kind of work that fits their lives at every age and stage.

To lay a strong foundation for work that is flexible, you may need to switch from a "generalist" to a "specialist" mindset. The work you pursued in the past probably had complex job descriptions, including an array of required skills that morphed toward many different roles. Now, women who can powerfully articulate niche "specialist" skills will find an ever-growing supply of paid work that fits very specific opportunities as employer or client needs expand and contract.

In this appendix, you'll find advice and checklists to help you answer the question of "Where do I start?" These lists (two of the five specifically directed to returning professionals) will also help you make sure you lay the right flexwork foundation and have all the tools and strategies ready to sell your strengths. The easily attainable goal is to identify your professional brand and showcase dominant skills you can use in many flexible and lucrative ways to reach your personal summit of ambition, professional fulfillment, financial well-being, and success.

Plan for Flexwork with 20/20 Vision

When current or returning professional women decide to work flexible hours in a full-time job, take on a part-time role, become an occasional freelancer, start an independent consulting practice, or launch a small business of their own, they can get lost in the idea of more freedom— forgetting to analyze a prospective situation from several vantage points:

- ✓ **Professional**. Will your flexwork reinvention hold you back from or propel you toward your professional goals?
- ✓ **Psychological**. Are you sure you don't need that big job title and nice office to feel like a true professional? Are you okay working for a smaller company that is not a household name? Are you ready to reclaim your professional persona if you have been out of the workforce for many years?
- ✓ **Financial**. How will a more flexible job affect your day-to-day household budget? If you give up a big full-time salary to start your own business, can you afford a period of lean earnings? Will you give up valuable corporate benefits if you work part time for a small firm? Can you keep on track with college and retirement savings? Will your part-time job offer the health benefits your family needs?
- ✓ **Family**. If you've been at home since your children were babies, how will they feel about you not being available 24/7? Will your partner be willing to share more household responsibilities? If you're switching from corporate to independent professional, do you have extra time to devote to building a business or a steady stream of freelance projects?

✓ **Logistical**. How will your proposed flexwork structure affect your childcare situation? Will you need to pay for full-time childcare even if you are working part time? Can your family adapt easily to the more unpredictable schedule of freelance or consulting work?

These are just some of the questions that may pertain to your situation. Think carefully about each category and what could pose a problem down the road.

Especially when children are involved, both parents have to be on board with your new career direction, considering all the issues raised in this checklist. If you're running up against a lot of resistance, go back to each issue and see where more palatable changes can be made.

Negotiate Family Buy-In Before You Run Back to Work

We've established that if you've been out of the workforce for many years you're still wanted in the business world, and for women who have felt they wore that disparaging "displaced homemaker"[1] moniker, it's very exciting news. (But here's the rub: you're probably still wanted at home, too.) In my coaching practice I've seen too many women run with that excitement and start a job search before they've worked out the home-front kinks. Nothing thwarts a back-to-work plan faster than family needs and issues that have not been fully addressed.

To avoid disappointment and false starts, negotiate the terms of your new work venture from every possible source of dissent. Make it your goal to reach a place where everyone has a comfort level—but don't let anything other than very serious or life-threatening problems stand in the way of you contributing in some way to your family's long-term financial security.

To begin, identify all of your caregiving roles. Then consider the following questions:

- What is the cost and availability of full-time or part-time elder caregiving for elderly parents, including any additional family resources or senior citizen programs and transportation that may be offered through your community?

- What is the cost and availability of full-time or part-time childcare during the entire year (school year plus summer), as well as family resources, babysitting sharing, or babysitting co-op alternatives?
- Will the childcare patchwork require occasional or regular school or activity pickups/drop-offs by either or both partners?
- Will some after-school programs/activities/camps need to be eliminated for logistical reasons or added to replace childcare?
- How much homework oversight will your children need? Can this be handled by tutors or capable caregivers?
- Do your children have special needs or situations that require your presence (emotional, educational, or risky behavior issues)?
- What are your backup plans for emergency situations, including sick days and snow days?
- How will your annual summer vacation plans need to be altered?
- What is the desirable length of a commute? Is working in your immediate area a necessity?
- Is a job with even occasional overnight travel out of the question?
- What is your ideal work structure: a traditional full-time job, or a more flexible, part-time schedule that blends work in the employer's office with work at home?
- Is work at home truly feasible, given the age of your children and the ability to set up a dedicated office space?
- Who will pick up the slack in the day-to-day running of the household (e.g., more sharing between partners, more involvement from the kids, and/or more outsourcing)?
- Will your involvement with any community or religious organizations important to your family need to be reduced or eliminated?
- What household and family responsibilities can shift to evenings and weekends?
- How much downtime and personal time needs to be preserved for both partners?

Get All Your Professional Ducks Back in a Row

Once you have family buy-in and you have a clear idea how you will handle household logistics, make sure you are ready to present yourself as a solid returning *professional*, not a tentative back-to-work Mom. Your preparation may require a combination of research, networking, skill building, and soul searching. This list is a good place to start.

- **Connect with the experts who have the best back-to-work advice**. iRelaunch has a seminal guide, *Back on the Career Track: A Guide for Stay-at-Home Moms Who Want to Return to Work*;[2] annual conferences for relaunchers; coaching services; training; and a large pathway to "returnships" with major employers. Other companies are making big strides in getting women back to work as well. Check out Après, Bliss Lawyers, Flexible Resources, FlexProfessionals, HireMyMom.com, Inkwell, Inspiring Capital, MomSource Network, OnRamp Fellowship, reacHire, The Mom Project, Werk, Women's Job Search Network, and Work Muse—all members of my Flexwork for Women Alliance (kathrynsollmann.com).
- **Learn the computer lingo**. Quickly ramp up to speed with today's technology through online courses such as those found on lynda.com or continuing education classes right in your hometown.
- **Aim for a clear job search target**. An "I'll do anything" attitude is actually the job seeker's kiss of death. Sometimes returning professionals say this because they just don't know what they want to do and think employers will like a show of versatility, but this actually puts the onus on employers to figure out where your skills best fit. Do a career assessment and see how your skills and interests may have changed. Tap into online resources, hire a career coach, or seek out help from the career center at your alma mater.
- **Rekindle relationships with former colleagues**. Professionals who recall your skills and expertise may jog your own memory about forgotten projects and accomplishments that could give

you ideas for flexwork now. Among familiar faces who respect your professional work, you're more apt to zero in on all the great things you've done in and out of the workforce.

- **Take a side trip back to school before you venture back to work**. Look into programs that will help you brush up on the skills now required in your industry. Many universities have certificate programs, and even as a part-time student you're often eligible to participate in campus career fairs and recruiter visits.

- **Volunteer with passion and professional precision**. In anticipation of your return to work, limit your volunteer roles to those that require business skills. Look beyond just school committees and check out resumé-building opportunities on sites like idealist.org, volunteermatch.org, and catchafire.org. Also look for organizations that make a special effort to help their volunteers hone professional skills, like Save the Children.[3]

- **Socialize on social media**. Participate in compelling conversations and connect with people who can help you get back to work. Today many recruiters won't even interview people who do not have a presence on LinkedIn (largely because that is the first place they search!). Twitter, Facebook, YouTube, and LinkedIn are all great places to research companies and possible flexwork.

- **Get ready for prime time**. Dust off your interviewing skills, and learn tips and techniques for the now more common conversations that happen via phone, FaceTime, and Skype. Some colleges offer mock interviewing programs; see what you can find locally or through your alma mater.

All these tips make you a more informed and well-prepared job seeker at any life age and stage—and after a paid-work hiatus of any length. You may see yourself as an overscheduled mother focused on carpools, homework, and endless meals—but remember you're still the person who got that great degree, held those great jobs, and wowed that long-ago boss with your skills and strengths. As Carol Fishman Cohen from iRelaunch says, "Your professional reputation is frozen in time."[4]

Women who land jobs after many years out of the workforce don't walk into an interview with a chip on their shoulders or any apologies for their hiatus. The fact is that you decided to leave the workforce and that decision, which you truly felt was the right move at the time, is in the past. Now you're just looking forward, buoyed by the wise decision to get back into earning, saving, and investing mode. There's no need for any lengthy explanation about your long-ago decision; simply plan to say, "I've been out of the work-force for 10 years caring for my family." Then follow with the next critical statement: "In my time out of the workforce I've continued to develop my business skills through XYZ." Fill in the blank with whatever significant volunteer work you pursued that can be described in business terms.

Your Flexwork Roadmap: How to Develop a Strategic Plan

For current or returning professionals, a job search doesn't require a degree in rocket science, but it does require a game plan, tenacity, and a strong commitment to keep at it in every possible way. If you don't want to prolong your search unnecessarily, treat it with as much care, focus and professionalism as you would a paid project. Your strategy starts by defining the criteria for your ideal flexible job.

✓ **Location.**

Given all your family responsibilities and how close you need to be to home, write down key locations where you'd be willing to work. Take into account likely travel routes and how long your commute could take during rush hours.

✓ **Number of hours you can devote to work.**

Back into a number noting the earliest time you can leave your home in the morning, the latest time you could leave the office, and the likely commuting time. Even if you're prepared to work a full-time schedule, don't skip this exercise. You still have to determine if you need a very predictable 40-hour-a-week schedule or if you could find the time to work many more hours as long as your schedule is flexible.

✓ **Type of flexwork.**

Knowing how many hours you can devote to work, what's your ideal work structure? A flexible full-time job? A 30-hour part-time job that includes benefits? A part-time job with fewer than 30 hours? Occasional freelance work? An independent consulting practice? A job that includes partial or full work at home?

✓ **Compensation.**

Decide how much money you need to earn each month. Consider these factors:

- Whether you file taxes jointly or separately, how much of your salary will be taxed, and roughly what you will clear
- The cost of commuting
- The cost of childcare or eldercare, if needed (weighed against the long-term cost of staying out of the workforce for any period of time)
- The cost of additional household help, if needed

✓ **Size of company.**

For flexwork, you're usually better off at a company that is not a huge corporation with tons of bureaucratic red tape. Managers at smaller companies often have more leeway to set their own rules. A small company situation might involve working for a "solopreneur," working for a small startup, or working for a company that has up to 100 employees.

✓ **Industry.**

Zero in on a maximum of three industries you'd like to research. During your research and networking phase, you might add and delete industries. Keep your focus fairly narrow to avoid research overload and confusion.

✓ **Job function.**

Think about the job function or title that interests you most. Again, keep it to a maximum of three if you're interested in several industries. If you're interested in only one industry, however, it's not as difficult to research multiple job functions that might have overlapping responsibilities requiring similar experience and skill sets.

Is It the Job Market or Is It You? Take the Flexwork Search Reality Quiz

More than 4,000 women have already taken my *9 Lives for Women* Job Search Reality Quiz, which measures preparedness for the process and likely outcomes. How well the average woman is prepared can be gleaned in the quiz statistics included in the material that follows.

Job seekers tend to blame everyone but themselves for a job search that does not reap results after many months or even years, and many insist that it's impossible to find flexwork. However, it's not so difficult when you go about it in the right way. This quiz will help ensure that you are using the best job-search strategies.

To conduct a flexwork search, women must be able to answer "yes" to each question below.

✓ **I feel confident and positive about my job search.**

Seventy-three percent of respondents say they are not. Confidence sells strengths and lands jobs.

✓ **I know the general compensation I'm seeking, and the minimum I would be comfortable accepting.**

Most women (92 percent) know these numbers.

✓ **I've fully considered the kind of job commitment (full time, part time, freelance, etc.) that will work best for me and my family, and I have buy-in from all constituents.**

Most women say they have family buy-in (87 percent), which aligns with what I heard as a recruiter. There was a very high eleventh-hour dropout rate, however, when women said they could not accept the job for long-existing family reasons. I also heard that many partners said, "I didn't really think you would go through with it." Since women have such large caregiving responsibilities, be sure to work out all the issues before you start your flexwork search.

✓ **I have a very clear and realistic understanding of the type and level of position I'm qualified for at this time.**

Only 23 percent of women say they have this understanding. When you don't know what you're qualified for, there's a lot of unnecessary tail-chasing. Do your homework through lots of networking to see where and how you'll be the best fit.

✓ **Even though I have many skills and talents, I know that telling employers I'm willing to do any type of job is more negative than positive.**

Only about half of women (51 percent) realize this is not a good strategy. Finding a job is filling a specific need for an employer. Do not say, "I'll do anything," which puts the onus on the employer to determine your best fit.

✓ **I know that employers hire candidates who can jump right in and add immediate value—and I can clearly articulate** examples of problems I can solve, challenges I can meet, and initiatives I can lead in my area of expertise.

Most women (68 percent) know this is critical. About three out of 10 women need to get these examples on instant recall.

✓ **I have an "elevator speech" that quickly summarizes for friends, colleagues, networking contacts, and potential employers the most important work I've done in the past, my specific skills and expertise, and the type of flexwork I'm seeking.**

Most women (65 percent) don't have an elevator speech at the ready, which means they're missing opportunities to quickly sell themselves to a wide range of networking contacts and potential employers.

✓ **I know my underlying work motivations and the kind of company and culture that would be the best fit.**

Finding the right flexwork is not just about job fit; it's also largely about cultural fit. Too many women (42 percent) don't spend enough time thinking about the kinds of companies that will give them the chance to grow personally and professionally and blend work and life.

✓ **I've targeted and thoroughly researched (via websites, current media reports, discussions with current or past employees, etc.) companies that appear to be the right fit for my skill set and underlying work motivations.**

Research is the stage most job seekers forget or shortchange. Seventy percent of women surveyed wing it without careful research or a strategic game plan.

✓ **Whether or not I'm technically "unemployed," I know that when I'm in job-search mode I have a full-time *sales job*. I've adopted traits of top sales professionals: tenacity, resourcefulness, and** persistence. I get up every morning and think, "How could I do an even better job of packaging and selling myself?"

Most women surveyed (70 percent) are getting mired in rejection and the drudgery of the job search rather than taking on a strong and resilient sales persona and forging ahead in the spirit of continual improvement.

✓ **I have only one (two-page maximum) version of my resumé (not several versions directed to different types of jobs), and a summary statement at the top that gives employers (in 50 words or less) a quick snapshot of my key skills and experience.**

Forty percent of women surveyed have multiple versions of their resumés, which means they likely have not zeroed in on skills and expertise that can be transferred to any flexible job in any industry.

✓ **On my resumé, each position description details my major responsibilities and gives potential employers a clear picture of the size and scope of the job as well as the metrics to prove I was successful.**

Most women (70 percent) know they shouldn't list responsibilities only—they also zero in on facts and figures that prove they were successful.

✓ **At least three people who have proven writing and editing skills have proofread my resumé for errors that could cost me an interview.**

About half of the women surveyed are playing with fire. Employers frequently refuse to interview qualified candidates because of simple resumé errors.

✓ **I'm totally on board with the fact that my No. 1 job-search** strategy must be networking—and I don't let any discomfort about "approaching strangers" stand in my way.

Fifty-five percent of women surveyed still don't like that *networking* word. That's too many women who don't realize that LinkedIn has taken so much of the awkwardness out of asking strangers for help.

✓ I've exhausted every possible personal networking contact from my past jobs, alumni groups, religious affiliations, other school parents, book groups, tennis groups, clubs, etc.—and I've considered every possible way I know people, who my husband knows, my sister knows, my friends know, and so on.

This is the most critical finding in the survey. A whopping 72 percent of women are not using the No. 1 job search tool, which is especially vital in the search for flexwork. Networking is, and always has been, the way to find a job.

✓ I know the greatest percentage of my job search time should NOT be searching for opportunities on company or mass market job boards.

Not surprisingly, 61 percent of women surveyed are still looking for jobs on the internet—which is rightfully nicknamed the job searcher's "black hole."

✓ When I pursue a job opportunity I always do more than email my resumé to the appropriate contact person. I always include a cover letter that very specifically sells my fit for the job: a point-by-point match-up of my skills and experience with the stated requirements/responsibilities.

Forty-three percent of women surveyed are not writing cover letters, which probably means they search for jobs primarily online, where there often is not the possibility of including a cover letter.

Women need to focus on opportunities that are marketed by real people, not computers.

✓ **When I prepare for an interview, I don't get ready to apologize for any aspect of my past experience or my time out of the workforce.**

It's good news that only 23 percent of women surveyed feel they need to apologize for some aspect of their resumés. Explain any resumé negatives succinctly. Don't sweat career events that were either out of your control or based on personal work and life decisions.

✓ **I've thought about and rehearsed answers to questions I'll likely be asked in a networking conversation or interview—and my answers will exude confidence and competence.**

Thirty-nine percent of women surveyed say they generally are speaking off the cuff during an interview—rather than planning ahead and formulating strong answers to questions they'll likely be asked.

Where are your weak spots? There are plentiful resources to get to more solid ground. Internet searches about how to pinpoint your dominant expertise, develop your resume and LinkedIn profile, prepare for interviews, research competitive compensation, negotiate job offers and more will lead you to articles and websites (including my site, kathrynsollmann.com) that have great information—all at no cost. Your college career services office will likely give you some time, and local networking groups often include professionals who help job seekers gratis or at a small cost. At a more significant investment, career coaches can guide you as well. Whatever route you choose, take the time to become an informed, prepared, and confident "flexwork" seeker.

RECOMMENDED RESOURCES

Now that you have learned that professional flexwork is available and increasingly widespread, here are 31 websites I've mentioned throughout this book that you should make a point of visiting. All of these resources will help you fully understand today's workplace and take the next steps toward finding the flexwork that fits your life.

FairyGodBoss
fairygodboss.com
This unique, crowd-sourced database gives women insider perspectives and ratings on employers who have part-time or telecommuting jobs, compressed workweeks, allowances for some work-from-home days, or flexible workday start and end times.

Flexcel Network
flexcelnetwork.com
Sophie Wade's website, monthly "Work in Progress Report," and book, *Embracing Progress*, provide a great overview of current innovations in the workplace and what to expect as the "future of work" continues to unfold.

FlexJobs
flexjobs.com
A comprehensive national flexwork job board, this site is also a source of useful data on geographic locations, industries, companies, and job functions where lucrative flexwork of all types is trending. There are many reputable freelance sites as well, but FlexJobs stands out in terms of quality and thought leadership.

The Flexwork for Women Alliance
kathrynsollmann.com
Started under my 9 Lives for Women umbrella, the Flexwork for Women Alliance is a group of 21 firms—primarily boutique recruiting firms specifically focused on helping mid- to senior-level current and returning professional women find lucrative short- and long-term assignments (one firm, Work Options, is a great source for flexwork proposal templates). The list has wide coverage across job functions and geographic locations—expanding the work that you can do far beyond your local area, even for companies not based in the United States.

On my homepage there is a link to all alliance members, including a description of their services and their geographic focus. You can also visit their individual websites listed below.

Après Group
apresgroup.com

Bliss Lawyers
blisslawyers.com

Corps Team
corpsteam.com

FairyGodBoss
fairygodboss.com

Flexible Resources
flexibleresources.com

Flex Professionals
flexprofessionalsllc.com

HireMyMom.com
hiremymom.com

Inkwell
inkwellteam.com

Inspiring Capital
inspiringcapital.ly

MomSource Network
momsourcenetwork.com

OnRamp Fellowship
onrampfellowship.com

PowerToFly
powertofly.com

Prokanga
prokanga.com

ReacHire
reachire.com

The Jills of All Trades
thejillsofalltrades.com

The Mom Project
themomproject.com

The Second Shift
thesecondshift.com

Werk
saywerk.com

Women's Job Search Network
womensjobsearchnetwork.com

Work Muse
workmuse.com

Work Options
workoptions.com

The Freelancers Union
freelancersunion.org
This organization promotes the interests of independent workers through advocacy, education, and business-building networking opportunities. One of their most valuable offerings is affordable health, dental, term life, disability, and liability insurance, which can be a huge challenge for anyone who is not eligible for employee benefits.

LinkedIn ProFinder
linkedinprofinder.com
LinkedIn has automated the process of matching independent professionals with the companies and individuals who need their services. At the premium LinkedIn membership level, freelancers can bid on a constant stream of work in their geographic area.

MyLifestyleCareer
mylifestylecareer.com
A terrific "second career" resource, Nancy Collamer's website (and book, *Second Act Careers*) is particularly focused on reinvention and flexwork for the 50+ age demographic. Her emphasis is on creating money-making opportunities out of hobbies and life passions, and

also finding ways to repurpose lifelong skills into interesting new professions that can extend well beyond the "traditional" retirement age
of 65.

1 Million for Work Flexibility (1MFWF)
workflexibility.org
A sister organization to FlexJobs, 1 Million for Work Flexibility tracks
legislation related to flexwork, so you can identify and monitor the proposed and enacted city, state, and federal legislation that affects you.

The National Association of Women Business Owners
nawbo.org
NAWBO is the only dues-based organization representing the interests
of women entrepreneurs across all industries—with chapters throughout
the United States. The organization creates powerful partnerships and
alliances that give members access to business expansion opportunities,
as well as very active networking among members online, at local events,
and at a national conference.

National Federation of Independent Business
nfib.com
The NFIB is the leading advocate for small business owners—keeping
entrepreneurs on top of tax and regulatory changes and offering advice
on operating and growing small businesses. The organization also offers
cost-effective personal and commercial insurance.

Working Mother
workingmother.com
In addition to a magazine and online articles that help women blend
work and life, Working Mother is also known for their annual lists of
"best" companies: "100 Best Companies for Working Mothers" and "50
Best Law Firms for Women." These lists give women a great starting
point for researching companies that offer some form of flexwork.

ENDNOTES

Introduction

1. Michael Madowitz, Alex Rowell, and Katie Hamm, "Calculating the Hidden Cost of Interrupting a Career for Child Care," Center for American Progress, June 21, 2016, accessed October 11, 2017, https://www.americanprogress .org/issues/early-childhood/reports/2016/06/21/139731/calculating-the -hidden-cost-of-interrupting-a-career-for-child-care/.
2. Nicky Wakefield, Anthony Abbatiello, Dimple Agarwal, Karen Pastakia, and Ardie van Berkel, "Leadership Awakened," Deloitte Insights, Global Human Capital Trends 2016 Report, February 29, 2016, accessed October 12, 2017, https://dupress.deloitte.com/dup-us-en/focus/human-capital-trends/2016/ identifying-future-business-leaders-leadership.html.
3. *Ibid.*
4. "Majority of U.S. Employers Support Workplace Flexibility," WorldatWork, October 5, 2015, accessed February 1, 2018, https://www.worldatwork.org/ docs/worldatworkpressreleases/2015/majority-of-us-employers-support .html.
5. Amanda Weinstein, "When More Women Join the Workforce, Wages Rise— Including for Men," *Harvard Business Review,* accessed February 22, 2018, https://hbr.org/2018/01/when-more-women-join-the-workforce-wages -rise-including-for-men.

Chapter 1

1. Jonathan Rauch, "The Real Roots of Midlife Crisis," *The Atlantic,* December 2014, accessed October 12, 2017, https://www.theatlantic.com/magazine/ archive/2014/12/the-real-roots-of-midlife-crisis/382235/.
2. Anne-Marie Slaughter, "Why Women Still Can't Have It All," *The Atlantic,* July/August 2012, accessed October 24, 2017, https://www.theatlantic.com/ magazine/archive/2012/07/why-women-still-cant-have-it-all/309020/.

Chapter 2

1. Robin J. Ely, Pamela Stone, Laurie Shannon, and Colleen Ammerman, "Life & Leadership After HBS," Harvard Business School, May 2015, accessed October 12, 2017, http://www.hbs.edu/women50/docs/L_and_L_Survey_2Findings_12final.pdf.
2. "The Role of Emergency Savings in Family Financial Security: How Do Families Cope With Financial Shocks?" The Pew Charitable Trusts, October 2015, accessed January 9, 2018, http://www.pewtrusts.org/~/media/assets/2015/10/emergency-savings-report-1_artfinal.pdf.
3. *Ibid.*
4. *Ibid.*
5. "Financial Shocks Put Retirement Security at Risk," Issue Brief, The Pew Charitable Trusts, October 25, 2017, http://www.pewtrusts.org/en/research-and-analysis/issue-briefs/2017/10/ financial-shocks-put-retirement-security-at-risk.
6. Lori Price (Owner, Price Financial Group LLC), interview by Kathryn Sollmann, November 2017.
7. Louise McGlynn (Founding Partner, Conlon & McGlynn LLC), interview by Kathryn Sollmann, November 2017.
8. "Employee Tenure Summary," Bureau of Labor Statistics, United States Department of Labor, September 22, 2016, accessed October 12, 2017, https://www.bls.gov/news.release/tenure.nr0.htm.
9. "The Employment Situation," Bureau of Labor Statistics, United States Department of Labor, August 2017, accessed October 12, 2017, https://www.bls.gov/news.release/pdf/empsit.pdf.
10. Amanda Dixon, "More Americans Are Getting Better about Saving. No, Really!" *Bankrate*, June 20, 2017, accessed February 1, 2018, http://www.bankrate.com/banking/savings/financial-security-0617/.
11. Alison Doyle, "What to Expect in a Severance Package," The Balance, August 25, 2017, accessed February 1, 2018, https://www.thebalance.com/what-to-expect-in-a-severance-package-2063385.
12. "Chances of Disability," Council for Disability Awareness, accessed March 6, 2018, http://www.disabilitycanhappen.org/chances_disability/disability_stats.asp.
13. *Ibid.*
14. *Ibid.*
15. *Ibid.*
16. *Ibid.*
17. *Ibid.*

18. "2018 Social Security Changes," Social Security Administration, accessed March 6, 2018, https://www.ssa.gov/news/press/factsheets/colafacts2018.pdf.

19. "U.S. Federal Poverty Guidelines Used to Determine Financial Eligibility for Certain Federal Programs," US Department of Health & Human Services, accessed March 6, 2018, https://aspe.hhs.gov/poverty-guidelines.

20. "Widowhood," Women's Institute For A Secure Retirement (WISER), accessed October 12, 2017, http://www.wiserwomen.org/index.php?id=275&page.

21. "Widows Under Stress: Widows Confront Years of Undue Hardship After the Loss of A Spouse, New Study Reveals," *New York Life*, November 7, 2014, accessed February 19, 2018, https://www.newyorklife.com/newsroom/2014/widows-under-stress/.

22. "Survey of Recent Widows (2013)," Women's Institute For A Secure Retirement (WISER), accessed November 14, 2017, https://www.wiserwomen.org/images/imagefiles/survey-of-recent-widows-2013.pdf.

23. Stan Hinden, "Women and Social Security Benefits," *AARP*, February 2017, accessed October 12, 2017, http://www.aarp.org/work/social-security/info-2014/women-and-social-security-benefits.html.

24. "Fidelity Study Finds: While 70 Percent of Parents Claim to be Very Comfortable Discussing Will and Estate Plans, More Than Half of Adult Children are Still in the Dark About the Details," Fidelity Investments, January 31, 2017, accessed October 24, 2017, https://www.fidelity.com/about-fidelity/individual-investing/fidelity-study-children-in-dark-about-parents-estate-plans.

25. "Financial Support Study: Understanding Financial Obligations Across Generations," TD Ameritrade, 2015, accessed October 12, 2017, https://s1.q4cdn.com/959385532/files/doc_downloads/research/TDA-Financial-Support-Study-2015.pdf.

26. "Women and Caregiving: Facts and Figures," Family Caregiver Alliance, accessed October 12, 2017, https://www.caregiver.org/women-and-caregiving-facts-and-figures.

27. *Ibid.*

28. Anne-Marie Botek, "The State of Caregiving: 2015 Report," AgingCare.com, 2015, accessed November 14, 2017, https://www.agingcare.com/articles/state-of-caregiving-2015-report-177710.htm.

29. Marlo Sollitto, "Cost of Caring for Elderly Parents Could Be Next Financial Crisis," AgingCare.com, accessed November 14, 2017, https://www.agingcare.com/articles/cost-of-caring-for-elderly-parents-could-be-next-financial-crisis-133369.htm.

30. Lynn Feinberg and Rita Choula, "Understanding the Impact of Family Caregiving on Work," Fact Sheet 271, AARP Public Policy Institute, October, 2012, accessed October 12, 2017, http://www.aarp.org/content/dam/aarp/research/public_policy_institute/ltc/2012/understanding-impact -family-caregiving-work-AARP-ppi-ltc.pdf.

31. Joanna Gordon Martin (Founder and Chief Executive Officer, Theia Senior Solutions), interview by Kathryn Sollmann, November 2017.

32. Kim Parker and Eileen Patten, "The Sandwich Generation: Rising Financial Burdens for Middle-Aged Americans," Pew Research Center, January 30, 2013, accessed October 12, 2017, http://www.pewsocialtrends.org/2013/01/30/the-sandwich-generation/.

33. "Caregiver Statistics: Demographics," Family Caregiver Alliance, 2016, accessed October 12, 2017, https://www.caregiver.org/caregiver-statistics -demographics.

34. *Ibid.*

35. Glenn D. Braunstein, M.D., "Caring for Aging Parents is Labor of Love— With a Cost," *HuffPost,* April 15, 2013, accessed October 12, 2017, https:// www.huffingtonpost.com/glenn-d-braunstein-md/caregivers-aging -parents_b_3071979.html.

36. Anek Belbase and Geoffrey T. Sanzenbacher, "Cognitive Aging and the Capacity to Manage Money," *Center for Retirement Research at Boston College,* no. 17-1 (January 2017): 1-7, accessed October 31, 2017, http://crr .bc.edu/wp-content/uploads/2017/01/IB_17-1.pdf.

37. Ginger Nash, N.D., interview by Kathryn Sollmann, November 2017.

38. Elise Gould, "Young Workers Face a Tougher Labor Market Even as the Economy Inches Towards Full Employment," *Working Economics Blog,* Economic Policy Institute, July 19, 2017, accessed October 12, 2017, http:// www.epi.org/blog/young-workers-face-a-tougher-labor-market-even-as -the-economy-inches-towards-full-employment/.

39. Richard Fry, "It's Becoming More Common for Young Adults to Live at Home—And for Longer Stretches," Pew Research Center, May 5, 2017, accessed October 12, 2017, http://www.pewresearch.org/fact-tank/2017/05/05/its-becoming-more-common-for-young-adults-to-live-at-home -and-for-longer-stretches/.

40. Lauren Weber and Melissa Korn, "Where Did All the Entry-Level Jobs Go?" *The Wall Street Journal,* August 6, 2014, accessed October 12, 2017, https://www.wsj.com/articles/want-an-entry-level-job-youll-need-lots -of-experience-1407267498?mg=prod/accounts-wsj.

41. "Fidelity Finds 'Personal Finance' May Be Too 'Personal' To Talk About," Fidelity Investments Money FIT Women Study, Fidelity Investments, 2015, accessed October 24, 2017, https://www.fidelity.com/about-fidelity/ individual-investing/fidelity-finds-personal-finance-too-personal-to-talk -about.

42. "New Allianz Life Study Finds Majority of Women Now Responsible for Household Finances," Allianz Women, Money, and Power Study, Allianz Life, February 8, 2017, accessed October 24, 2017, https://www.allianzlife.com/ about/news-and-events/news-releases/Women-Money-and-Power-Study.

Chapter 3

1. Cindy Hounsell (President, Women's Institute for a Secure Retirement), interview by Kathryn Sollmann, November 2017.

2. "New Allianz Life Study Finds Majority of Women Now Responsible for Household Finances," Allianz Women, Money, and Power Study, Allianz Life, February 8, 2017, accessed October 24, 2017, https://www.allianzlife.com/ about/news-and-events/news-releases/Women-Money-and-Power-Study.

3. Alison Chin-Leong, "Why Women Make Great Investors," Wells Fargo Stories, July 25, 2017, accessed February 14, 2018, https://stories.wf.com/ women-make-great-investors/.

4. "2017 RCS Fact Sheet #5: Gender and Marital Status Comparisons Among Workers," 2017 Retirement Confidence Survey, Employee Benefit Research Institute and Greenwald & Associates, accessed October 24, 2017, https:// www.ebri.org/pdf/surveys/rcs/2017/RCS_17.FS-5_Gender.Final.pdf.

5. "New Allianz Life Study Finds Majority of Women Now Responsible for Household Finances," Allianz Women, Money, and Power Study, Allianz Life, February 8, 2017, accessed October 24, 2017, https://www.allianzlife .com/about/news-and-events/news-releases/Women-Money-and-Power-Study.

6. "2017 RICP Retirement Income Literacy Gender Differences Report," The American College of Financial Services, New York Life Center for Retirement Income, accessed October 12, 2017, http://retirement.theamericancollege.edu/ sites/retirement/files/Gender_Differences_in_Retirement_Income_ Literacy_Report.pdf.

7. "The Pay Gap's Connected to the Retirement Gap," Women's Institute for a Secure Retirement (WISER), accessed October 24, 2017, http://www .wiserwomen.org/index.php%3Fid%3D266%26page%3Dpay-gap -retirement-gap.

8. Stan Hinden, "Women and Social Security Benefits," AARP, February 2017, accessed October 12, 2017, http://www.aarp.org/work/social-security/info-2014/women-and-social-security-benefits.html.

9. "Calculators: Life Expectancy," Social Security Administration, accessed October 12, 2017, https://www.ssa.gov/planners/lifeexpectancy.html.

10. Catherine Collinson, "The Current State of Retirement: Pre-Retiree Expectations and Retiree Realities," Transamerica Center for Retirement Studies, December 2015, accessed October 12, 2017, https://www.transamericacenter.org/docs/default-source/retirees-survey/retirees_survey_2015_report.pdf.

11. "2016 Employer Health Benefits Survey," Henry J. Kaiser Family Foundation, September 14, 2016, accessed October 24, 2017, https://www.kff.org/health-costs/report/2016-employer-health-benefits-survey/.

12. "2017 Retirement Health Care Costs Data Report," HealthView Services, accessed October 24, 2017, https://www.hvsfinancial.com/2017/06/12/2017-retirement-health-care-costs-data-report/.

13. *Ibid.*

14. "Status of the Social Security and Medicare Programs: A Summary of the 2017 Annual Reports," Social Security Administration, accessed October 12, 2017, https://www.ssa.gov/oact/trsum/.

15. "Selected Long-Term Care Statistics," Family Caregiver Alliance, January 31, 2015, accessed October 12, 2017, https://www.caregiver.org/selected-long-term-care-statistics.

16. Thomas Day, "Guide to Long-Term Care Planning: About Nursing Homes," 2004 National Nursing Home Survey, National Care Planning Council, accessed October 12, 2017, http://www.longtermcarelink.net/eldercare/nursing_home.htm.

17. "Compare Long Term Care Costs Across the United States," Genworth Cost of Care Survey (2017), Genworth Financial, Inc., accessed September 25, 2017, https://www.genworth.com/about-us/industry-expertise/cost-of-care.html.

18. Thomas Day, "Guide to Long-Term Care Planning: About Nursing Homes," National Care Planning Council, accessed October 12, 2017, http://www.longtermcarelink.net/eldercare/nursing_home.htm.

19. Kim Parker and Juliana Menasce Horowitz, "Family Support in Graying Societies: How Americans, Germans and Italians Are Coping with an Aging Population," Social and Economic Trends, Pew Research Center, May 21, 2015, accessed October 12, 2017, http://www.pewsocialtrends.org/2015/05/21/family-support-in-graying-societies/.

20. Laura L. Carstensen, Ph.D. (Director, Stanford Center on Longevity), interview by Kathryn Sollmann, October 2017.

21. Mitch Tuchman, "The 25 Best Retirement Websites," *Forbes*, August 18, 2017, accessed February 19, 2018, https://www.forbes.com/forbes/welcome/?toURL=https://www.forbes.com/sites/mitchelltuchman/2017/08/18/24-best-retirement-websites/&refURL=&referrer=#6eb136b9336a.

22. Andrew Lisa, "How Long $1 Million Will Last in Retirement in Every State," GoBankingRates, August 21, 2017, accessed October 12, 2017, https://www.gobankingrates.com/investing/how-long-million-last-retirement-state/.

23. Nari Rhee, Ph.D., "The Retirement Savings Crisis: Is It Worse Than We Think?" National Institute on Retirement Security, June 2013, accessed October 12, 2017, https://www.nirsonline.org/reports/the-retirement-savings-crisis-is-it-worse-than-we-think/.

24. "Fidelity Retirement Savings Analysis: Savings Rates, Account Balances Climb to Record Levels in First Quarter," Business Wire, May 12, 2017, accessed October 12, 2017, http://www.businesswire.com/news/home/20170512005051/en/Fidelity-Retirement-Savings-Analysis-Savings-Rates-Account.

25. Monique Morrissey, "The State of American Retirement: How 401(k)s Have Failed Most American Workers," Retirement Inequality Chartbook, Economic Policy Institute, March 3, 2016, accessed May 18, 2018, http://www.epi.org/publication/retirement-in-america/.

26. "Average Published Undergraduate Charges by Sector and Carnegie Classification, 2017-18," The College Board, accessed February 1, 2018, https://trends.collegeboard.org/college-pricing/figures-tables/average-published-undergraduate-charges-sector-2017-18.

27. "How America Pays for College 2016," Sallie Mae, accessed October 12, 2017, http://news.salliemae.com/files/doc_library/file/HowAmericaPaysforCollege2016FNL.pdf.

28. "Average Published Undergraduate Charges by Sector and Carnegie Classification, 2017-18," The College Board, accessed February 1, 2018, https://trends.collegeboard.org/college-pricing/figures-tables/average-published-undergraduate-charges-sector-2017-18.

29. Maurie Backman, "The Average Social Security Benefit in 2018—And Why You Can't Live Off It," The Motley Fool, January 14, 2018, accessed February 19, 2018, https://www.fool.com/retirement/2018/01/14/the-average-social-security-benefit-in-2018-and-wh.aspx.

30. Alison Doyle, "2018 Federal and State Minimum Wage Rates," The Balance, January 8, 2018, accessed February 19, 2018, https://www.thebalance.com/2017-federal-state-minimum-wage-rates-2061043.

31. Catherine Collinson, "Seventeen Facts About Women's Retirement Outlook: Select Findings from the 17th Annual Transamerica Retirement Survey of American Workers," Transamerica Center for Retirement Studies, March 2017, accessed October 12, 2017, http://www.transamericacenter.org/docs/default-source/women-and-retirement/tcrs2017_sr_women_and_retirement_17_facts.pdf.
32. Lisa Greenwald, Craig Copeland, and Jack VanDerhei, "The 2017 Retirement Confidence Survey: Many Workers Lack Retirement Confidence and Feel Stressed About Retirement Preparations," *Employee Benefit Research Institute,* No. 431 (March 21, 2017), accessed October 12, 2017, https://www.ebri.org/pdf/briefspdf/EBRI_IB_431_RCS.21Mar17.pdf.
33. "Labor Force Projections to 2024: The Labor Force is Growing, But Slowly," Bureau of Labor Statistics, United States Department of Labor, December 2015, accessed October 6, 2017, https://www.bls.gov/opub/mlr/2015/article/labor-force-projections-to-2024.htm.
34. Alicia H. Munnell, Wenliang Hou, and Geoffrey T. Sanzenbacher, "Do Households Have a Good Sense of Their Retirement Preparedness?" *Center for Retirement Research at Boston College,* no. 17-4 (February 2017), accessed October 6, 2017, http://crr.bc.edu/wp-content/uploads/2017/02/IB_17-4.pdf.
35. "Finances in Retirement: New Challenges, New Solutions," Age Wave/Merrill Lynch, 2017, accessed October 6, 2017, https://www.ml.com/articles/age-wave-survey.html.
36. Nancy Altman and Eric Kingson, "America's Retirement Security Crisis Is Huge and Quickly Approaching," *HuffPost,* December 6, 2017, accessed February 2, 2018, http://www.huffingtonpost.com/nancy-altman/americas-retirement-secur_b_6508510.html.
37. "Finances in Retirement: New Challenges, New Solutions," Age Wave/Merrill Lynch, 2017, accessed October 6, 2017, https://www.ml.com/articles/age-wave-survey.html.

Chapter 4

1. Michael Madowitz, Alex Rowell, and Katie Hamm, "Calculating the Hidden Cost of Interrupting a Career for Child Care," Center for American Progress, June 21, 2016, accessed October 11, 2017, https://www.americanprogress.org/issues/early-childhood/reports/2016/06/21/139731/calculating-the-hidden-cost-of-interrupting-a-career-for-child-care/.

2. Dana Anspach, "How Much Are Your Social Security Benefits Worth?" The Balance, January 8, 2018, accessed February 20, 2018, https://www .thebalance.com/how-much-are-your-social-security-benefits-worth -2388926.

3. "How Do I Earn Social Security Credits and How Many Do I Need to Qualify for Benefits?" Social Security Administration, accessed November 16, 2017, https://faq.ssa.gov/link/portal/34011/34019/Article/3829/How-do -I-earn-Social-Security-credits-and-how-many-do-I-need-to-qualify-for -benefits.

4. "Affordable Care Act: Coverage Terms," Society for Human Resource Management, accessed January 9, 2018, https://www.shrm.org/resource sandtools/hr-topics/benefits/pages/aca-coverage-terms.aspx.

5. "Quality of Life: Balancing Work-Life Demands," PwC, accessed October 6, 2017, https://www.pwc.com/us/en/about-us/diversity/pwc-work-life -balance.html.

6. Elizabeth King, "Starbucks Covers IVF Treatments for Full- AND Part-Time Employees—Here's Why," Brit + Co, September 8, 2017, accessed November 12, 2017, https://www.brit.co/starbucks-covers-ivf-treatments-for -full-and-part-time-employees-heres-why/.

7. "Rewards and Benefits," Accenture, accessed October 9, 2017, https://www .accenture.com/us-en/careers/your-future-rewards-benefits.

8. Lucinda Shen, "These 19 Great Employers Offer Paid Sabbaticals," *Fortune,* March 7, 2016, accessed October 6, 2017, http://fortune.com/2016/03/07/ best-companies-to-work-for-sabbaticals/.

9. Samantha Samel, "Unlimited Vacation Helps Companies Attract Female Talent," *Fairygodboss,* accessed October 6, 2017, https://fairygodboss.com/ articles/limited-vacation-helps-companies-attract-female-talent.

10. "Paid Maternity Leave: 180 Companies Who Offer The Most Paid Leave In 2017," *Fairygodboss,* accessed October 6, 2017, https://fairygodboss.com/ articles/paid-maternity-leave-companies-who-offer-the-most-paid-leave.

11. Rachel Feintzeig, "When Your Employer Plans Your Baby Shower," *Wall Street Journal,* April 4, 2017, accessed October 9, 2017, https://www.wsj .com/articles/the-latest-perk-to-keep-mothers-at-work-1491298206.

12. Paul Schrodt, "12 Companies with the Most Luxurious Employee Perks," *Money,* October 9, 2017, accessed October 11, 2017, http://time.com/ money/4972232/12-companies-with-the-most-luxurious-employee-perks/.

13. Carol Fishman Cohen (Chief Executive Officer, iRelaunch), interview by Kathryn Sollmann, October 2017.

14. "The Power of Compounding," Vanguard, accessed January 9, 2018, https://personal.vanguard.com/us/insights/guide/power-of-compounding.

15. Galia Gichon (Founder, Down-to-Earth Finance), interview by Kathryn Sollmann, January 2018.

Chapter 5

1. Reverend Galen Guengerich, "Everywhere to Go," sermon, All Souls Church, New York City, October 2, 2011, accessed May 18, 2018, http://www.allsoulsnyc .org/atf/cf/%7B641C68F5-A0A1-4017-851B-66985A3B0DF3%7D/ everywhere-to-go.pdf.

Chapter 6

1. Sophie Wade, *Embracing Progress: Next Steps for the Future of Work* (South Carolina: Advantage Media Group, 2017).

2. Carol Stubbings and Jon Williams, "Workforce of the Future: The Competing Forces Shaping 2030," PwC, 2017, accessed October 9, 2017, https://www .pwc.com/gx/en/services/people-organisation/workforce-of-the-future/ workforce-of-the-future-the-competing-forces-shaping-2030-pwc.pdf.

3. "New Future Workforce Report Finds Nearly Half of Companies Are Thinking beyond Traditional Employment to Embrace More Flexible Teams," Upwork, February 28, 2017, accessed October 9, 2017, https:// www.upwork.com/press/2017/02/28/future-workforce-report/.

4. Alexandra Levit, *Humanity Works* (London: Kogan Page, 2018).

5. Jennifer Parris, "How Companies Can Prepare for the Future of Work," *FlexJobs* (blog), September 18, 2017, accessed October 9, 2017, https://www .flexjobs.com/employer-blog/companies-can-prepare-future-of-work/.

6. "Alternative Work Arrangements: The New Norm?" The Creative Group, April 18, 2017, accessed October 26, 2017, https://www.prnewswire.com/news-releases/alternative-work-arrangements-the-new-norm-300440423.html.

7. Brie Weiler Reynolds, "What Is a Flexible Job?" *FlexJobs* (blog), June 12, 2017, accessed October 9, 2017, https://www.flexjobs.com/blog/post/what-is-a -flexible-job/.

8. "The 2017 State of Telecommuting in the US Employee Workforce," Flex-Jobs and Global Workforce Analytics, accessed October 9, 2017, https:// www.flexjobs.com/2017-State-of-Telecommuting-US/.

9. Jennifer Parris, "6 Unexpected Employer Benefits of Telecommuting," *1 Million for Work Flexibility* (blog), January 2, 2015, accessed October 9,

2017, https://www.workflexibility.org/6-unexpected-employer-benefits-of
-telecommuting/.

10. "Labor Force Statistics from the Current Population Survey," Bureau of
Labor Statistics, United States Department of Labor, January 19, 2018,
accessed February 1, 2018, https://www.bls.gov/cps/cpsaat08.htm.

11. "Freelancing in America 2016," Upwork and Freelancers Union, accessed
October 9, 2017, https://www.upwork.com/i/freelancing-in-america/2016/.

12. Brian Rashid, "The Rise of the Freelancer Economy," *Forbes*, January 26,
2016, accessed October 9, 2017, https://www.forbes.com/sites/brianrashid/
2016/01/26/the-rise-of-the-freelancer-economy/#3d1ef85b3bdf.

13. Michelle King, "KPMG's Lynn Doughtie on Why Women Are the Future
of Work," *Women@Forbes*, May 23, 2017, accessed October 9, 2017, https://
www.forbes.com/sites/michelleking/2017/05/23/kpmgs-lynne-doughtie
-on-why-women-are-the-future-of-work/#68b6642d114c.

14. Stephen J. Dubner, "After the Glass Ceiling A Glass Cliff," Freakonomics
Radio, podcast audio, February 14, 2018, accessed May 18, 2018, http://
freakonomics.com/podcast/glass-cliff/.

15. "The 2017 Working Mother Best Law Firms for Women," *Working Mother*,
July 25, 2017, accessed February 19, 2018, https://www.workingmother
.com/best-law-firms-for-women-2017.

16. Fortune Editors, "The 50 Best Workplaces for Parents," *Fortune*, accessed
November 28, 2017, http://fortune.com/2017/11/28/best-companies-working
-parents/?utm_source=fortune.com&utm_medium=email&utm_campaign
=broadsheet&utm_content=2017112813pm.

17. Jacquelyn Smith, "50 Companies Hiring for Part-Time Jobs," *FlexJobs*
(blog), April 23, 2017, accessed October 9, 2017, https://www.flexjobs.com/
blog/post/companies-hiring-for-part-time-jobs/.

18. *Ibid.*

19. "Affordable Care Act: Coverage Terms," Society for Human Resource
Management, accessed October 9, 2017, https://www.shrm.org/resource
sandtools/hr-topics/benefits/pages/aca-coverage-terms.aspx.

20. Laura Shin, "Work from Home in 2017: The Top 100 Companies Offering
Remote Jobs," *Forbes*, January 31, 2017, accessed October 9, 2017, https://
www.forbes.com/sites/laurashin/2017/01/31/work-from-home-in-2017
-the-top-100-companies-offering-remote-jobs/#520627f642d8.

21. "Latest Telecommuting Statistics," GlobalWorkplaceAnalytics.com, June
2017, accessed October 9, 2017, http://globalworkplaceanalytics.com/
telecommuting-statistics.

22. Chris Weller, "IBM Was a Pioneer in the Work-From-Home Revolution—Now It's Cracking Down," *Business Insider,* March 27, 2017, accessed October 9, 2017, http://www.businessinsider.com/ibm-slashes-work-from-home-policy-2017-3.

23. Peter Cohan, "4 Reasons Marissa Mayer's No-At-Home-Work Policy Is an Epic Fail," *Forbes,* February 26, 2013, accessed October 9, 2017, https://www.forbes.com/sites/petercohan/2013/02/26/4-reasons-marissa-mayers-no-at-home-work-policy-is-an-epic-fail/#3a670a72246b.

24. Brie Weiler Reynolds, "Top 15 States with the Most Telecommuting Jobs," *FlexJobs* (blog), March 19, 2017, accessed October 9, 2017, https://www.flexjobs.com/blog/post/top-states-with-the-most-telecommuting-jobs-2016/.

25. Jeanne Sahadi, "Dell *Really* Wants You to Work from Home...If You Want," CNN Money, June 9, 2016, accessed October 9, 2017, http://money.cnn.com/2016/06/09/pf/dell-work-from-home/index.html.

26. Brie Weiler Reynolds, "Top 15 States with the Most Telecommuting Jobs," *FlexJobs* (blog), March 19, 2017, accessed October 9, 2017, https://www.flexjobs.com/blog/post/top-states-with-the-most-telecommuting-jobs-2016/.

27. Jessica Howington, "20 Most Common Work-from-Home Job Titles," *FlexJobs* (blog), January 3, 2018, accessed February 1, 2018, https://www.flexjobs.com/blog/post/20-most-common-work-from-home-job-titles/.

28. Rachel Jay, "15 Executive-Level Jobs for Telecommuters," *FlexJobs* (blog), May 14, 2017, accessed October 9, 2017, https://www.flexjobs.com/blog/post/great-executive-level-jobs-for-telecommuters/.

29. "Latest Telecommuting Statistics," GlobalWorkplaceAnalytics.com, June 2017, accessed October 9, 2017, http://globalworkplaceanalytics.com/telecommuting-statistics.

30. Kathleen Elkins, "8 Work-from-Home Jobs that Can Pay Over $100,000," CNBC, February 9, 2017, accessed October 9, 2017, https://www.cnbc.com/2017/02/09/8-work-from-home-jobs-that-can-pay-over-100000.html.

31. "Independent Contractor Defined," Internal Revenue Service, accessed October 9, 2017, https://www.irs.gov/businesses/small-businesses-self-employed/independent-contractor-defined.

32. "Self-Employment Tax (Social Security and Medicare Taxes)," Internal Revenue Service, accessed October 9, 2017, https://www.irs.gov/businesses/small-businesses-self-employed/self-employment-tax-social-security-and-medicare-taxes.

33. Jonathan Dison, "4 Tips to Become a Consultant for Your Second Career," Next Avenue, October 11, 2017, accessed October 25, 2017, http://www.nextavenue.org/become-consultant-second-career/.

34. "2017 Workforce Productivity Report: A Comprehensive Study of Workforce Productivity, Talent Management and Business Transformation in Corporate America," Work Market and KRC Research, accessed November 16, 2017, http://content.workmarket.com/2017-productivity -research/.

35. Jonathan Dison, "4 Tips to Become a Consultant for Your Second Career," Next Avenue, October 11, 2017, accessed October 25, 2017, http://www.nextavenue.org/become-consultant-second-career/?utm _source=sumome&utm_medium=facebook&utm_campaign=sumome _share.

36. Michael S. Solomon, "The Real Cost of Freelancers vs. Full-Time Employees," *HuffPost,* April 13, 2017, accessed October 9, 2017, https://www .huffingtonpost.com/entry/the-real-cost-of-freelancers-vs-full-time -employees_us_58efd87de4b0156697224d86.

37. William Johnson, "4 Gig Economy Trends You Shouldn't Ignore," *Small Business Trends,* November 2, 2017, accessed November 9, 2017, https:// smallbiztrends.com/2017/10/gig-economy-trends.html.

38. "Freelancing in America 2016," Edelman Intelligence, accessed November 15, 2017, https://www.slideshare.net/upwork/freelancing-in-america-2016/1.

39. Shannon Gausepohl, "Want to Join the Gig Economy? 15 Companies Hiring Freelancers," Business News Daily, April 20, 2017, accessed February 19, 2018, https://www.businessnewsdaily.com/5985-best-freelance-jobs.html.

40. William Arruda, "Mastering the Gig Economy: A New Way to Land Fortune 500 Jobs," *Forbes,* May 23, 2017, accessed October 9, 2017, https:// www.forbes.com/sites/williamarruda/2017/05/23/mastering-the-gig -economy-a-new-way-to-land-fortune-500-jobs/#15e898886527.

41. "Freelancing in America 2016," Edelman Intelligence, accessed October 9, 2017, https://www.upwork.com/i/freelancing-in-america/2016/.

42. "The State of Independence in America: Rising Confidence Amid a Maturing Market," MBO Partners, 2017, accessed October 9, 2017, https:// www.mbopartners.com/uploads/files/state-of-independence-reports/ StateofIndependence-2017-Final.pdf.

43. John Rampton, "Employers Are Paying Freelancers Big Bucks for These 25 In-Demand Skills," *Entrepreneur,* May 23, 2017, accessed October 9, 2017, https://www.entrepreneur.com/article/294718.

44. John Nemo, "The 2017 Workforce Trend LinkedIn Users Are Going Crazy For," *Inc.,* December 22, 2016, accessed October 9, 2017, https://www.inc .com/john-nemo/the-2017-workplace-trend-linkedin-users-are-going -crazy-for.html.

45. "Freelancing in America 2016," Edelman Intelligence, accessed October 9, 2017, https://www.upwork.com/i/freelancing-in-america/2016/.

46. "LinkedIn ProFinder Reveals Brand New Findings on Freelance Economy," LinkedIn, September 14, 2017, accessed November 14, 2017, https://www.linkedin.com/profinder/blog/linkedin-profinder-reveals-brand-new-findings-on-freelance-economy.

47. "The 2016 Field Nation Freelancer Study: The Changing Face of the New Blended Workforce," Field Nation, accessed February 1, 2018, https://www.fieldnation.com/wp-content/uploads/2017/03/The_2016_Field_Nation_Freelancer_Study_R1V1__1_-2.pdf.

48. Abdullahi Muhammed, "79 Websites to Get Freelance Jobs Fast," *Forbes*, June 16, 2017, accessed February 19, 2018, https://www.forbes.com/sites/abdullahimuhammed/2017/06/16/79-websites-to-get-freelance-jobs-fast/#60fa44731688.

49. "The 2016 State of Women-Owned Businesses Report: A Summary of Important Trends, 2007-2016," American Express OPEN, April 2016, accessed October 10, 2017, http://www.womenable.com/content/userfiles/2016_State_of_Women-Owned_Businesses_Executive_Report.pdf.

50. 99designs Team, "How Mompreneurs Balance Business and Family," *99designs* (blog), 2017, accessed June 26, 2017, https://99designs.com/blog/business/mom-entrepreneur-infographic/?clickid=wVl0-Q36SzY02b23isXdlSZZUkm3TcR1z1gSUc0&utm_medium=27795&utm_content=99designs%20Logo&utm_campaign=VigLink&utm_source=affiliates&network=ir.

51. Georgia McIntyre, "What Percentage of Small Businesses Fail? (And Other Similar Stats You Need to Know)," *Fundera Ledger,* August 29, 2017, accessed October 10, 2017, https://www.fundera.com/blog/what-percentage-of-small-businesses-fail.

Chapter 7

1. Katie Bugbee, "How Much Does Child Care Cost?" Care.com, 2017, accessed October 10, 2017, https://www.care.com/c/stories/2423/how-much-does-child-care-cost/.

2. "First Step Overview," DC.gov, Office of the State Superintendent of Education, July 12, 2017, accessed October 10, 2017, https://osse.dc.gov/publication/first-step-overview.

3. Sheryl Sandberg, *Lean In: Women, Work, and the Will to Lead* (New York: Knopf, 2013).

4. Claudia Goldin and Joshua Mitchell, "The New Life Cycle of Women's Employment: Disappearing Humps, Sagging Middles, Expanding Tops," *Journal of Economic Perspectives*, Volume 31, Number 1 (Winter 2017), accessed October 10, 2017, http://pubs.aeaweb.org/doi/pdfplus/10.1257/jep.31.1.161.

5. Allison Preiss, "New CAP Calculator Reveals the Hidden, Lifetime Costs of the Child Care Crisis in the U.S.," Center for American Progress, June 21, 2016, accessed October 10, 2017, https://www.americanprogress.org/press/release/2016/06/21/139014/release-new-cap-calculator-reveals-the-hidden-lifetime-costs-of-the-child-care-crisis-in-the-u-s/.

6. Katie Bugbee, "How Much Does Child Care Cost?" Care.com, 2017, accessed October 10, 2017, https://www.care.com/c/stories/2423/how-much-does-child-care-cost/.

7. Brian McKenzie and Melanie Rapino, "Commuting in the United States: 2009," American Community Service Reports, ACS-15, US Census Bureau, September 2011, accessed October 10, 2017, https://www.census.gov/prod/2011pubs/acs-15.pdf.

8. Melanie Pinola, "This Calculator Shows How Much You Should Pay Your Babysitter," LifeHacker, June 16, 2015, accessed February 19, 2018, https://lifehacker.com/this-calculator-shows-how-much-you-should-pay-your-baby-1711689076.

9. "2017 Working Mother 100 Best Companies," *Working Mother*, accessed February 19, 2018, https://www.workingmother.com/working-mother-100-best-companies-2017.

10. Matthew Frankel, "Your Complete Guide to the 2018 Tax Changes," The Motley Fool, December 29, 2017, accessed February 19, 2018, https://www.fool.com/taxes/2017/12/29/your-complete-guide-to-the-2018-tax-changes.aspx.

11. Katie Bugbee, "How Much Does Child Care Cost?" Care.com, 2017, accessed October 10, 2017, https://www.care.com/c/stories/2423/how-much-does-child-care-cost/.

12. Karen Wallace, "Ways to Make Child Care More Affordable," *Morningstar*, March 30, 2017, accessed April 3, 2017, http://news.morningstar.com/articlenet/article.aspx?id=800381.

13. Matthew Frankel, "Your Complete Guide to the 2018 Tax Changes," The Motley Fool, December 29, 2017, accessed February 19, 2018, https://www.fool.com/taxes/2017/12/29/your-complete-guide-to-the-2018-tax-changes.aspx.

14. Julia Beck, "How Some Companies Are Making Child Care Less Stressful for Their Employees," *Harvard Business Review*, April 14, 2017, accessed

October 10, 2017, https://hbr.org/2017/04/how-some-companies-are-making-child-care-less-stressful-for-their-employees.

15. Kathryn Mayer, "Patagonia's Secret to Employee Engagement? Onsite Daycare," *Employee Benefit News,* June 28, 2017, accessed October 10, 2017, https://www.benefitnews.com/news/patagonias-secret-to-employee-engagement-onsite-daycare.

16. Christine Michel Carter, "The Hard Financial Impact of Child Care on Millennial Salaries," *Forbes,* March 28, 2017, accessed October 10, 2017, https://www.forbes.com/sites/christinecarter/2017/03/28/aflac-and-sas-weigh-in-the-hard-impact-of-child-care-on-todays-salary/2/#39044a30106d.

17. Rose Gilbert, "[University] Opens New Daycare Facility to Meet Faculty Childcare Needs," *The Daily Princetonian,* September 19, 2017, accessed October 11, 2017, http://www.dailyprincetonian.com/article/2017/09/new-u-daycare-facility.

18. "The Fortune 100 Companies that Offer On-Site Day Care to Employees," The Outline, May 31, 2017, accessed November 15, 2017, https://theoutline.com/post/1610/the-fortune-100-companies-that-offer-on-site-day-care-to-employees.

19. "The Cisco Family Connection - Cisco IOS Multicast Connects Parents with Their Children," Cisco Systems, Inc., accessed October 10, 2017, https://www.cisco.com/c/dam/en/us/products/collateral/ios-nx-os-software/ip-multicast/prod_case_study0900aecd803108f6.pdf.

20. Herbert Lee, "Planned Expansion in Child Care Services and On-Campus Employee Housing," University of California Santa Cruz, May 31, 2017, accessed October 10, 2017, https://news.ucsc.edu/2017/05/childcare-services-employee-housing.html.

21. Heather R. Huhman, "Are Your Childcare Benefits Outdated? Here's How To Fix Them," *Entrepreneur,* May 18, 2017, accessed October 10, 2017, https://www.entrepreneur.com/article/294430#.

22. Scott Broden, "Murfreesboro City Schools to Offer Childcare for Employees," *USA Today Network – Tennessee,* June 23, 2017, accessed October 10, 2017, http://www.dnj.com/story/news/2017/06/23/murfreesboro-city-schools-offer-childcare-employees/423150001/.

23. "The Children's Campus at Alston & Bird," Bright Horizons, accessed October 10, 2017, https://child-care-preschool.brighthorizons.com/ga/atlanta/abcampus/our-center.

24. Julia Beck, "How Some Companies Are Making Child Care Less Stressful for Their Employees," *Harvard Business Review,* April 14, 2017, accessed

October 10, 2017, https://hbr.org/2017/04/how-some-companies-are-making -child-care-less-stressful-for-their-employees.

25. Ken Yeung, "On-Demand Child Care Startup Trusted Expands to New York," *VentureBeat,* May 18, 2017, accessed October 10, 2017, https:// venturebeat.com/2017/05/18/on-demand-child-care-startup-trusted -expands-to-new-york/.

26. "About PIWI," Parenting in the Workplace Institute, accessed October 27, 2017, https://www.babiesatwork.org/about-piwi.

27. Alison Green, "Is 8-6 the New 9-5?" Ask A Manager, accessed March 7, 2018, http://www.askamanager.org/2015/10/is-8-6-the-new-9-5.html.

28. Michael Chandler, "Non-Traditional: New Co-Working Spaces Offer Women Career and Child-Care Help," *Washington Post,* February 25, 2018, accessed April 8, 2018, http://www.greensboro.com/jobs/non-traditional-new-co-working -spaces-offer-women-career-and/article_b2782662-6e4e-5953-81e2 -7665e0f8df1b.html?utm_medium=social&utm_source=twitter&utm_ campaign=user-share.

29. Kimberley Mok, "Why Aren't More Co-Working Spaces Offering Childcare—And a List that Do," TreeHugger, Narrative Content Group, January 12, 2017, accessed October 10, 2017, https://www.treehugger.com/ culture/co-working-childcare-for-parents-with-children.html.

30. Heather Osbourne, "New Business Office Offers Office Space and Child-care," *Northwest Florida Daily News,* February 5, 2018, accessed February 19, 2018, http://www.nwfdailynews.com/news/20180205/new-business-offers -office-space-and-child-care.

31. Rachel Weaver, "Flexable Helping Match Parents, Child Care Providers," *Trib Total Media,* February 18, 2017, accessed February 20, 2017, http:// triblive.com/lifestyles/morelifestyles/11921147-74/care-child-flexable.

32. Jessica Layton, "Parents Get Creative to Find Good Childcare in Digital Age," *CBS New York,* June 8, 2017, accessed February 20, 2018, http://newy- ork.cbslocal.com/2017/06/08/finding-good-childcare/.

33. Caroline Cakebread, "A San Francisco Startup Wants to Fix Childcare by Helping Educators Start Their Own Schools Out of Their Homes," *Business Insider,* June 20, 2017, accessed June 22, 2017, http://www.businessinsider .com/wonderschool-childcare-teachers-education-2017-6.

34. Susan Edelman, "Pre-K Home-School Provider to Open 150 'Boutique' Programs," *New York Post,* January 27, 2018, accessed January 30, 2018, https://nypost.com/2018/01/27/pre-k-home-school-provider-to-open-150 -boutique-programs/.

Chapter 8

1. Max Nisen, "Ursula Burns: Seeking Perfect Work-Life Balance Is a Fool's Journey," *Business Insider*, March 20, 2013, accessed February 19, 2018, http://www.businessinsider.com/ursula-burns-work-life-balance-2013-3.
2. Stewart D. Friedman, *Total Leadership: Be a Better Leader, Have a Richer Life* (Pennsylvania: Stewart D. Friedman, 2008).
3. Sue Shellenbarger, "The XX Factor: What's Holding Women Back?" *The Wall Street Journal*, May 7, 2012, accessed October 30, 2017, https://www.wsj.com/articles/SB10001424052702304746604577381953238775784.
4. Laura Vanderkam, *I Know How She Does It: How Successful Women Make the Most of Their Time* (New York: Portfolio/Penguin, 2015).
5. Laura Vanderkam (Author), remarks at 9 Lives for Women "Make Work Fit Life" event, Stamford, CT, May 2016.
6. *Ibid.*
7. Brad Harrington (Executive Director, Boston College Center for Work & Family), interview by Kathryn Sollmann, November 2017.
8. Kenneth Matos, Ellen Galinsky, and James T. Bond, "National Study of Employers," Society of Human Resource Management, 2017, accessed October 16, 2017, http://whenworkworks.org/downloads/2016-National-Study-of-Employers.pdf.
9. *Ibid.*
10. Karyn Twaronite (Partner, Ernst & Young), remarks at 9 Lives for Women "Make Work Fit Life" event, Stamford, CT, May 2016.
11. Katie Donovan (Founder, Equal Pay Negotiations, LLC), interview by Kathryn Sollmann, November 2017.

Chapter 9

1. "Frequently Asked Questions about Small Business," US Small Business Administration, Office of Advocacy, August 2017, accessed October 11, 2017, https://www.sba.gov/sites/default/files/advocacy/SB-FAQ-2017-WEB.pdf.
2. Kenneth Matos, Ellen Galinsky, and James T. Bond, "National Study of Employers," Society of Human Resource Management, 2017, accessed October 16, 2017, http://whenworkworks.org/downloads/2016-National-Study-of-Employers.pdf.
3. "Flexibility for Working Families Act," Congress.gov, Summary: S.997—115th Congress (2017-2018), accessed October 11, 2017, https://www.congress.gov/bill/115th-congress/senate-bill/997.

4. "Rep. Mimi Walters Introduces New Workplace Flexibility Legislation," www.walters.house.gov, November 2, 2017, accessed April 8, 2018, https:// walters.house.gov/media-center/press-releases/rep-mimi-walters -introduces-new-workplace-flexibility-legislation.
5. Jennifer Parris, "New Hampshire Becomes Second State with Right To Request Flexibility," *1 Million for Work Flexibility* (blog), June 16, 2016, accessed October 11, 2017, https://www.workflexibility.org/new-hampshire -becomes-second-state-with-right-to-request-flexibility/.

Chapter 10

1. Wendy Fox-Grage, "The Skyrocketing of the Age 85+: AARP Data Explorer Provides Long-Term Services and Supports Data for Policy Solutions," AARP, March 11, 2016, accessed October 11, 2017, http://blog .aarp.org/2016/03/11/the-skyrocketing-of-the-age-85-aarp-data-explorer -provides-long-term-services-and-supports-data-for-policy-solutions/.
2. Richard Eisenberg, "The Future of Work for People 50+ Will Surprise You," Next Avenue, May 22, 2017, accessed October 11, 2017, https://www .forbes.com/sites/nextavenue/2017/05/22/the-future-of-work-for -people-50-will-surprise-you/#55062cc072e7.
3. Catherine Collinson, "All About Retirement: An Employer Survey," 17th Annual Transamerica Retirement Survey, Transamerica Center for Retire- ment Studies, August 2017, accessed October 16, 2017, https://www.trans americacenter.org/docs/default-source/employer-research/tcrs2017_sr _employer_research.pdf.
4. "Labor Force Statistics from the Current Population Survey," Bureau of Labor Statistics, United States Department of Labor, January 5, 2018, accessed February 1, 2018, https://www.bls.gov/web/empsit/cpseea10.htm.
5. "Age Discrimination in Employment Act (Charges Filed with EEOC) FY 1997—FY 2017," US Equal Opportunity Employment Commission, accessed February 1, 2018, https://www.eeoc.gov/eeoc/statistics/enforcement/ adea.cfm.
6. "Compensation and Salary Trends by Generation," Adecco, October 25, 2017, accessed February 1, 2018, https://www.adeccousa.com/employers/ resources/salary-trends-industrial-stem-creative-marketing/.
7. David Frank, "10 Promising Job Fields for Workers Over 50," AARP, October 9, 2017, accessed October 30, 2017, https://www.aarp.org/work/ job-hunting/info-2017/job-fields-workers-in-demand-fd.html?intcmp =WOR-FEED.

8. Kerry Hannon, "Great Jobs for Workers Over 50," *AARP Bulletin*, accessed October 30, 2017, https://www.aarp.org/work/working-after-retirement/info-2015/great-jobs-for-50-plus-photo.html#slide2.

9. Nancy Collamer, "Coding as a Second-Act Career," MyLifestyleCareer.com, accessed October 11, 2017, http://www.mylifestylecareer.com/career-reinvention-2/career-reinvention-strategies/coding-as-a-second-act-career/.

10. Sylvia Ann Hewlett, *Executive Presence: The Missing Link Between Merit and Success* (New York: HarperBusiness, 2014), 1–5.

11. Edith Cooper (Executive Vice President and Global Head of Human Capital Management, Goldman Sachs), remarks at iRelaunch "Return to Work Conference," New York, NY, October 2013.

12. Carol Fishman Cohen (Chief Executive Officer, iRelaunch), interview by Kathryn Sollmann, October 2017.

13. "70+ Paid Corporate Reentry Internship Programs around the World," iRelaunch, accessed February 1, 2018, https://www.irelaunch.com/paidcorporateprograms.

14. Adrianne Pasquarelli, "How 'Returnships' Are Helping Agencies Bridge Diversity Gap," *Ad Age*, February 10, 2017, accessed October 11, 2017, http://adage.com/article/news/returnships-helping-agencies-bridge-diversity-gap/307936/.

15. Melissa Ciotoli (Certified Financial Planner and Financial Counselor, Resnick Advisors), interview by Kathryn Sollmann, October 2017.

16. David Corbett, *Portfolio Life: The New Path to Work, Purpose, and Passion After 50* (California: Jossey-Bass, 2006).

17. Debra Levine (Executive Vice President, Paul Hertz Group), interview by Kathryn Sollmann, October 2017.

18. Daniel H. Pink, *A Whole New Mind: Why Right Brainers Will Rule the Future* (New York: Riverhead Books, 2006).

19. Susan Bedsow Horgan (Life Coach), interview by Kathryn Sollmann, October 2017.

20. Virginia Corsi (President, Corsi Associates), interview by Kathryn Sollmann, October 2017.

Appendix

1. Linda Napikoski, "Displaced Homemaker: Definition, Laws, Programs," ThoughtCo., December 1, 2017, accessed February 19, 2018, https://www.thoughtco.com/displaced-homemaker-3528912.

2. Carol Fishman Cohen and Vivian Steir Rabin, *Back on the Career Track: A Guide for Stay-at-Home Moms Who Want to Return to Work* (New York: Grand Central Publishing, 2008).

3. "Volunteer," Save the Children, accessed February 21, 2018, http://www .savethechildren.org/site/c.8rKLIXMGIpI4E/b.8631379/k.FB66/Volunteer .htm.

4. Carol Fishman Cohen (Chief Executive Officer, iRelaunch), interview by Kathryn Sollmann, November 2017.

INDEX